Way, Learning, and Politics
Essays on the Confucian Intellectual

SUNY Series in Chinese Philosophy and Culture
Edited by David L. Hall and Roger T. Ames

Way, Learning, and Politics
Essays on the Confucian Intellectual

Tu Wei-ming

STATE UNIVERSITY OF NEW YORK PRESS

The Author

Dr Tu Wei-ming is Professor of Chinese History and Philosophy and Chairman of the Department of East Asian Languages and Civilizations at Harvard University. Since he received his Ph.D. in History and East Asian Languages at Harvard in 1968, he has taught philosophies of China, Chinese intellectual history, and Confucian thought at Princeton University (East Asian Studies), University of California at Berkeley (History), Peking University (Philosophy), and Taiwan University (Philosophy and History). Professor Tu is a fellow of the American Academy of Arts and Sciences, a consultant at the Woodrow Wilson Center for Scholars, an advisor at the East-West Center, and a governor of IEAP. His publications include *Centrality and Commonality: An Essay on Chung-yung*, *Neo-Confucian Thought in Action: Wang Yang-ming's Youth*, *Humanity and Self-Cultivation*, *Confucian Ethics Today: The Singapore Challenge*, and *Confucian Thought: Selfhood as Creative Transformation*.

Published by
State University of New York Press, Albany

© 1993 State University of New York

First published by The Institute of East Asian Political Economy

For information, address State University of New York Press,
State University Plaza, Albany, N.Y., 12246

Production by Cathleen Collins
Marketing by Dana Yanulavich

Library of Congress Cataloging in Publication Data

Tu, Wei-ming.
    Way, learning, and politics : essays on the Confucian intellectual
/Tu Wei-ming.
        p.   cm.—(SUNY series in Chinese philosophy and culture.)
    Contents: Includes bibliographical references and index.
    ISBN (invalid) 0-7914-1755-1.—ISBN 0-7914-1776-X (pbk.)
    1. Confucianism. 2. Confucian ethics. 3. China—Intellectual
life. I. Title. II. Series.
BL1852.T8   1993
181'.112—dc20   93-18447
                                                          CIP

10 9 8 7 6 5 4 3 2 1

To my teachers and friends
Dr Wu Teh Yao and Dr Lau Wai Har

Their Christian faith and indefatigable spirit
have helped to launch the arduous task of
the "Confucian Project" in Singapore.

Abbreviations

LTCS	*Liu-tzu ch'üan-shu*	劉子全書
SPPY	*Ssu-pu pei-yao*	四部備要
SPTK	*Ssu-pu ts'ung-k'an*	四部叢刊
SYHA	*Sung Yüan hsüeh-an*	宋元學案
TSCC	*Ts'ung-shu chi-ch'eng*	叢書集成
YS	*Yüan-shih*	元史

Contents

Preface to the North American Edition

This collection of essays, originally published by the Institute of East Asian Philosophies in Singapore in 1989, contains articles written on a variety of occasions from 1982 to 1987. Although it was not entirely clear to me at the time, I was deeply immersed in a painstaking effort to understand the Confucian intellectual, as both a historical examplar and a modern witness of the Confucian Way. Consequently, these essays, divergent as they are, offer historical and comparative cultural perspectives on the Confucian intellectual. The underlying thesis is that to the extent that the Confucian literatus conscientiously repossesses the Way, transmits culture, and rectifies politics, he (or, increasingly in the modern context, she) exemplifies the intellectual spirit. This is predicated on the assumption that the intellectual spirit, as we understand it today, originally emerged in Czarist Russia in the nineteenth century and spread throughout the world via numerous brilliant incarnations in Western Europe and North America.

Notwithstanding the seeming commensurability of the Confucian literatus (or a morally cultivated person) and the modern intellectual as politically engaged and socially concerned scholar, my task has been to explicate the salient features of the Confucian project as a way of measuring the dimensions of exemplary personalities in the Confucian tradition. The purpose is to bring its rich symbolic resources to bear on the rather impoverished modern Chinese idea of the "knowlegeable person." Instead of imposing the Russian and modern Western conception on the Confucian phenomenon, my attempt is to retrieve the profound significance of learning to be a scholar (a literatus or a morally cultivated person) embedded in the cumulative tradition of Confucian humanism.

Hopefully such an inquiry will enable us to empower the modern Chinese idea and perhaps also to enrich the modern Western conception of the meaning of being an intellectual.

The nine essays in this book are grouped in three interrelated parts. The first part (involving four essays) explores the conceptual apparatuses and symbolic resources in the classical period, focusing on the perception of Way, Learning, and Politics with emphasis on the moral metaphysics which chart an overall spiritual direction for the Confucian project. The core values as embodied by Confucius and his disciples, through self-cultivation and personal knowledge, provide a basis for Confucian ethics. The second part contains three intellectual excursions into the Neo-Confucian era, offering concrete descriptions of the shape of Confucian scholarship from significantly different interpretive strategies. The pluralism inherent in the Neo-Confucian appropriations of the classical Confucian heritage broadly defines the Confucian faith in the improvability of the human condition through self-effort as a communal act. Active participation in politics, vigorous reflection on philosophical insights, and earnest pursuit of humanist scholarship are all legitimate Confucian pursuits. Yet, the Confucian way demands that moral rectitude precedes political expediency, that social responsibility underlies contemplative thought, and that a sense of historical consciousness and cultural relevance be fully articulated in scholarly inquiries.

My experience as a Fulbright scholar conducting a course on Confucian philosophy at Peking University in the spring of 1985 evoked powerful memories of personal encounters with the works of Joseph Levenson and Vitaly Rubin. While Levenson lamented the modern fate of Confucian China, Rubin celebrated the emergence of New Confucianism as "an extremely significant phenomenon in Chinese cultural and intellectual life outside Communist China." As an eyewitness to the intellectual effervescence of that time with its profound implications for Confucian studies in the People's Republic of China, I deeply felt the poignant provocative of Levenson and Rubin's contrasting modes of interpretation. However, the two essays in Part Three are more than reponses to the challenges of these two teachers and friends. They were also prompted by a desire to think through the relevance of my work in the Confucian tradition to issues raised in the outpouring of iconoclastic attacks on the feudal order launched by some of the most brilliant minds in Mainland China since 1979.

Indeed, the arduous task of retrieving the meaning of lost traditions or, in Ted de Bary's term, "repossessing the Way," is necessary for genuine creativity in Confucian studies; we need to reanimate the old in order to attain the new. Nevertheless, the intellectual dynamism in cultural China (Mainland, Taiwan, Hong Kong, Singapore, and Chinese communities throughout the world) and in East Asia (including Vietnam for cultural reasons) nowadays has generated so much tension between the core values and their pluralistic manifestations in the Confucian tradition that we (students of Confucian studies) are compelled to entertain the possibility of major ruptures as well. On this view, the essays in this collection are indications of a departure as well as traces of a return. In either case, they are no more than intimations of a complex and intriguing project which can never be fully realized but, as a joint venture, will unfold through persistent collaborative effort.

Tu Wei-ming
Cambridge, Mass.
January 1993

Preface

At the continuous urging of Benjamin Nelson, founder of the Society for Comparative Civilizational Studies, I gathered together twelve of my published essays on Confucian thought in the spring of 1977. As a result, my first collection of essays on Confucianism in English, *Humanity and Self-Cultivation* (1979), came into existence. The idea of a second collection of essays, *Confucian Thought: Selfhood as Creative Transformation* (1985), occurred to me when I visited the State University of New York at Stony Brook in the fall of 1983. The encouragement of Professors Robert Neville, Song-bae Park, David Hall, and Roger Ames was instrumental in transforming a fleeting idea into a reality. The current collection, a series of studies on the Confucian intellectual, was prompted by my desire to actively participate in the on-going conversation at the newly established Institute of East Asian Philosophies in Singapore.

The Confucian intellectual, whose form of life is embodied in the spiritual quest of poets, historians, statesmen, and thinkers in the Axial Age, has been a standard of inspiration for all public-minded youth throughout Chinese civilisation. Indeed, the well-known designation of the typical Confucian as a scholar-official underscores the Confucian aspiration for public service as a vocation. The Confucian "calling", however, addresses a much more profound humanistic vision than political participation alone, no matter how broadly conceived, can accommodate. The symbolic resources that the Confucians tap for their own personal development and for the realisation of their communal idea of humanity is ethico-religious as well as political. In fact, their perception of "politics" not only as managing the world in economic and social terms but also as transforming the world in the educational and cultural sense impels them to root their political leadership in social conscience. Confucian intellectuals may not actively seek official positions to put their ideas into practice, but they are always engaged politically through their poetic sensitivity, social responsibility, historical consciousness, and metaphysical insight.

The essays collected here can hardly do justice to the Confucian intellectual as a historical phenomenon, which in recent years has attracted considerable scholarly attention on both sides of the Taiwan Strait, and as a personality ideal, which, like the Greek philosopher and the Hebrew prophet, continues to stimulate our minds and hearts. I hope that some of the specific lines of thinking suggested in these essays can be further explored and my general interpretive position on the Confucian intellectual further critiqued so that the conversation on such a vitally important subject will be greatly enriched.

I am grateful to a coterie of scholars from Singapore, mainland China, Taiwan, Hong Kong, Korea, Japan, Europe, and North America for making the Institute a truly international centre for Confucian studies. I am also indebted to Director Wu Teh Yao 吳德耀. Since his tenure as President of my alma mater Tunghai University in the 1950s, he has been a constant source of support as my teacher-friend. Under his leadership, the able staff made the demanding editorial work, such as providing the Chinese characters for the text, an easy task, even a delightful diversion. In particular, I owe much to Mr Lee Ching Seng 李金生, the Institute's librarian and Mr Teo Han Wue 張夏悼, the Institute's research associate and editor, who supervised the whole process of production with professionalism and dedication. I feel honoured and privileged that Professor F. W. Mote of Princeton University graced this book with his Foreword. The issues he raises in a sympathetic and yet critical reading of my interpretive stance are rich food for thought and define, for me, the agenda for further reflection on Confucian humanism.

Can Confucian moral rationality be appreciated in terms of spiritual insights drawn from major historical religions, such as Judaism, Christianity, Islam, Hinduism, Jainism, and Buddhism? Can the "core curriculum" of Confucianism be enriched by these great traditions without losing sight of its religionless humanistic quality? In what sense, is the Confucian intellectual's ethical life not only politically and socially significant but also religiously relevant? These are some of the questions that have shaped the direction of my recent thinking on Confucian humanism as an anthropo-cosmic vision.

Although the various papers in this volume have been revised for editorial purposes, in general they have not been updated to incorporate new scholarly and interpretive insights not available at the original composition.

The following are the sources of the articles when they first appeared. I acknowledge, with gratitude, reprint permissions granted by the publishers:

"The Way, Learning, and Politics in Classical Confucian Humanism", Occasional Papers, no. 2 (1985), Institute of East Asian Philosophies, Singapore.

"The Structure and Function of the Confucian Intellectual in Ancient China", in S. N. Eisenstadt, ed., *Origins and Diversity of Axial Age Civilizations* (Albany, N.Y.: State University of New York Press, 1987), pp. 360–373.

"The Confucian Sage: Exemplar of Personal Knowledge", in John S. Hawley, ed., *Saints and Virtues* (Berkeley: University of California Press, 1987), pp. 73–86.

"Pain and Suffering in Confucian Self-Cultivation", *Philosophy East and West*, 34:4 (October 1984), 379–388.

"Towards an Understanding of Liu Yin's Confucian Eremitism", in Hoklam Chan and Wm. T. de Bary, eds., *Yuan Thought: Chinese Thought and Religion under the Mongols* (New York: Columbia University Press, 1982), pp. 233–277.

"Subjectivity in Liu Tsung-chou's Philosophical Anthropology", in Donald Munro, ed., *Individualism and Holism: Studies in Confucian and Taoist Values* (Ann Arbor: Center for Chinese Studies, The University of Michigan, 1985), pp. 215–238.

"Perceptions of Learning in Early Ch'ing Thought", in *Symposium in Commemoration of Professor T'ang Chün-i* (Taipei: Student Book Co., 1983), pp. 27–61.

"Toward the 'Third Epoch' of Confucian Humanism", in Irene Eber, ed., *Confucianism: Dynamics of a Tradition* (New York: Macmillan Company, 1986), pp. 3–21, 188–192.

"Iconoclasm, Holistic Vision, and Patient Watchfulness: A Personal Reflection on the Modern Chinese Intellectual Quest", *Daedalus*, 116: 2 (Spring 1987), 75–94.

Cambridge, Massachusetts   Tu Wei-ming
March 1988

Foreword

As a lecturer and as a writer on Confucianism, Tu Wei-ming 杜維明 has displayed to a remarkable degree the capacity to stir modern minds, to evoke powerful responses to his sense of the Confucian vision, or what he calls the "Confucian project" for mankind. The present volume of his recent essays, some of which took form as lectures delivered before Chinese audiences, conveys to us clearly why that is so. For we find here sound scholarly command of the Confucian tradition in the larger context of Chinese and East Asian civilisation, and we find coupled with that the ability to focus on issues that hold special meaning for late-twentieth-century persons, Chinese and non-Chinese. Primarily these are issues that define our humanity and explore our human capacities for self-realisation. The Confucian vision of course must be understood in relation to the civilisations in which it emerged and has been sustained through more than two millennia of constant social change. Tu Wei-ming is a historian sensitive to that process of Confucian response to the evolving needs of East Asian civilisations. He also asks us to consider Confucianism as a living force whose prospects for continuing importance in the post-modernised world, once pretty well written off by modern scholars, now must be re-evaluated. These essays bring us directly into the arena of such concerns; we cannot read them without being induced to believe that the ideas they offer for our reflection are vitally and intriguingly important. We are shown what has constituted the life-blood of Confucianism throughout its history, and are led to understand how it still lives. We are made to see where it resides in the world today, especially within the consciousness of modern East Asians (whether or not so identified by them) and increasingly, in the awareness of philosophers and historians of thought everywhere.

The enduring relevance of the Confucian vision finds a committed advocate in Tu Wei-ming. But his commitment does not restrict his critical faculties. Over the years he has modified his views even as he has deepened them, has re-examined his positions in the light of further reflection and study, and has remained open to the consideration of differing views. That is quite in keeping with the non-dogmatic nature of the Confucian tradition. One has always been able to engage Tu Wei-ming in debate and discussion with a sense of utter freedom, knowing that he truly welcomes differences of opinion as spurs to his own further development as scholar and thinker. When he asked me to write a "critical introduction" to the present volume I thought I should refuse, but not at all because I doubted the sincerity of his urgings to be "the more critical the better". Rather, it is because any "critical views" that I might hold could not be as deeply learned as his scholarly essays, nor as roundly and deeply considered as his philosophical positions. Nonetheless, his concern with the nature of Chinese civilisation past and present parallels my own, and I find his writings so stimulating that I am emboldened to raise here some of the issues these essays have forced me to reflect upon. In the following remarks I shall raise for discussion a few issues that seem to me to have large significance for our understanding of this volume. If that can be called criticism, then in the guise of a "foreword" this may serve as the "critical introduction" that he asked me to write.

One of the striking features of Tu Wei-ming's developing sense of Confucianism is his increasing stress on its religious dimension. I have never been one who denied the large role of religious thought and attitude in the life of the Chinese people, past or present. Nonetheless, I have been quite satisfied with a perception of a Confucianism that can be a complete system of ideas and values, at the level of a philosophy that does not require one to admit any specifically religious content. It has seemed convincing to me that Hsün Tzu could decisively lay to rest all need for non-rational explanations of even the most mystifying of natural phenomena, and that he could echo Confucius in relegating further inquiries into the nature of Nature (*t'ien*, or heaven) to the realm of the inconsequential.* Discussions of "Was Confucius Agnostic?" have seemed to me (possibly also to Tu Wei-ming) to express the parochial, culture-bound attitudes of Westerners. But I am now prepared to believe that I have taken the Hsüntzian Confucian arguments several steps farther than Tu Wei-ming would take them, by allowing them to signify for me that at both its philosophical and its practical levels of meaning, the Confucian system was complete without admitting into it

---

* See the discussion of *Hsün Tzu, ch.* 17, in K. C. Hsiao 蕭公權, *History of Chinese Political Thought* (i.e. the English translation of his *Chung-kuo cheng-chih ssu-hsiang-shih* 中國政治思想史), Chapter Three, Section Seven, pp. 206–213.

any role for the transcendental. By "transcendental" I mean that elements of what one regards as truth may not be fully comprehensible by purely rational means. Hsün Tzu clearly rejected Mencius' mind set in this regard,** and I have found it particularly satisfying to contemplate that strong re-affirmation of Chou rationalism by the last great Confucian thinker of pre-imperial times.

Although I am not yet prepared to give much ground on this issue, I can see that I am in some measure guilty of anachronism in the way I read relevant passages of Confucius, Mencius, and Hsün Tzu 荀子. The ancients, as also the majority of Confucians well into the present time, probably were less attracted to the narrowly rational mentality than are most twentieth-century intellectuals. I am reminded of a classroom discussion in my student days about Shakespeare's attitudes towards prognostication and destiny: the instructor reminded us that astronomy and astrology were not clearly dis-tinguished in European scientific writing until the eighteenth century, and only much later in common discourse. Our all too easy modern assumption that the thinkers of more than two thousand years ago probably defined "the rational" as we would define it today is no doubt an anachronistic, culturally parochial, unexamined assumption of analogy, however appealing it is to moderns.

Even if that is so, however, the problem remains of how we should correct for that fault. "Religion", as I would define it for purposes of this discourse, no matter how rational-minded it in general may be, must nonetheless in some degree accept certain aspects of its truth on faith; it must admit a de-gree of non-rationality into its system of thought. When a Confucian thinker (e.g. arguably Mencius, more clearly a number of leading Neo-Confucians) does that, are we to see it as the expected norm for all Confucians or as the peculiar characteristic of some individuals? In either case, is it consistent with the shared cosmological ground of early Chinese thought, or does it represent an unresolved inconsistency there?

To proceed one step further, if the acceptance of non-rationally verifiable truth is shown to be consistent with that early Chinese cosmological ground of thought, how shall we then make room for such a concept within the now widely acceptable description of China's organismic world view? Will the non-rational aspects of "truth" (i.e. "truth here meaning what philosophers of the time held to be true), especially those bearing on cosmology and on causality in nature, imply a challenge to our sense of Chinese organicism? I can of course accept some measure of the non-rational in Confucianism as possibly consistent with the organismic cosmology, but if it were to be

** vide K. C. Hsiao, op. cit., pp. 180–181, and note no. 84.

defined in ways that clearly imply a challenge to the concept of the organismic, self-generating cosmos, I should find that difficult to accept.

Morever, I still prefer to regard the Hsüntzian stance as the norm for early Confucianism and the Mencian as the aberration, the latter reflecting in that respect an unresolved, or perhaps unperceived inconsistency between the roles it assigns to transcendental elements and the requirements of that cosmology. I presume that Tu Wei-ming will demur, and I can believe that he could make a very good show of setting me straight. But for the present this must perhaps remain one of those issues in scholarship on which reasonable persons can reasonably disagree.

Tu Wei-ming makes significant contributions to our understanding of the problems that hinge on the place of religious concepts in Chinese thought. Yet many of the terms that must be employed in such discourse can be understood in more than one sense, as can some of their Chinese counterparts. One must, I believe, clarify the overarching context in which such terms are or were used, in particular the cosmological context, to know what meaning we should assign to them. How, for example, should one express notions of "the holy" within the scope of a cosmology that allows for no "holy (or wholly) other"? How should we translate the original intent of Confucian writers who, in English translation, seem to be naming "the divine" or "God" or "the sacred" as parts of their cosmos? All of the preceding terms appear in that way in the present volume. Above all, how can we discuss these issues in modern time for modern minds without becoming culturally incongruous, or seriously anachronistic?

Tu Wei-ming is cautious in exploring the religious dimensions of Confucian thought; he is conscious of and more or less successfully avoids the usual tendency to imply inappropriate parallels with Western thought. Nevertheless, he imputes considerably larger scope and significance to the purely religious dimension of Chinese thought, including pre-Ch'in Confucian thought, than one usually encounters. For the sake of discussion I shall briefly review here some of the pertinent issues.

In the first essay in the present volume, while carefully rejecting a "dichotomy of the sacred and the profane" as alien, he nonetheless states that Confucius by calling himself a mere transmitter of ancient learning, intended thereby to symbolise "his conscious attempt to provide a transcendental anchorage for human civilisations" (page 2). In support of that view, he writes that the Confucian norms for civilisations were not merely the devices of humans but were also sanctioned and sponsored by the Mandate of Heaven. He cites Confucius (*Analects* 9/5) saying that heaven will not allow this culture (*ssu-wen* 斯文) to perish, and writes "heaven" with a small "h" although he quotes W. T. Chan's 陳榮捷 translation in which it is written

"Heaven", as in most other translations of the *Analects*. This suggests that he does not want the reader to read "Heaven" for "God" as a Western reader might. Nonetheless there is an ambiguity here. The other-than-human sanctions for and sponsorship of the civilisation's ethical norms and ritual practices seem to imply the existence of a guiding force somewhere beyond the realm of the self-contained organismic process. And in the passages Tu cites here and elsewhere, *t'ien* 天 or heaven (or "nature") is described as·a "knowing" – even as a "seeing" agency. *T'ien*, it follows, is the source of the human endowment and purposefully aids humans to realise their endowed characteristics. We might, it is true, be able to interpret these ideas as figures of speech intended to convey the concept of rationally comprehensible functions of cosmic (i.e. natural, "within nature") forces, thus compatible with the concept of a self-generating cosmic process. Yet Tu takes us at least to the outer limits of that possibility as repeatedly, throughout this volume, he describes Confucian belief in "ethico-religious" (i.e. non-rational, transcendental) norms for humanity. Yet having gone that far in stressing the religious tenor of Confucian belief, he nonetheless carefully eschews explanations in terms of "revelatory theology or theoretical cosmology" (page 5), saying that the Confucian mode represents "another type of symbolic thinking". What kind of symbolic thinking that is he sets forth in fascinating argument, providing me no grounds for objecting until he suddenly interjects the comment that to characterise Confucius' "attitude toward God as gnostic is misleading" (page 9). For whether we accept the argument about gnosticism is beside the point; the words "attitude toward God" come quite without the reader having been prepared for any discussion of "God". Suddenly faced with the problem of admitting "God" with a capital "G" into this set of concepts, the reader must assume that Confucius *had* an attitude towards God (whether or not his attitude was gnostic). In like manner, Tu states: "The Confucians never established a full-fledged priesthood." The reader must assume that they *did* establish a priesthood (i.e. vicarious sacrificants on behalf of mankind to that God?), whether or not it ever became full-fledged (pages 12–13; 16). Similarly, we find Confucians undertaking a "divine mission" (page 19). And, Confucian sages are seen as persons who could assume "a godlike stature in the pantheon" (page 32), and had a "sacred mission" (page 39).

If that unexpected sequence of ideas seems to lead the Western reader comfortably into agreement with our familiar Western cosmos understood as the handiwork of a God external to it, Tu nonetheless points him away from such a mistaken analogy. For Confucians, he reminds us, benefited from no "divine intervention", even as they, according to Mencius, were "chosen to perform the divine tasks", not by an external summons, to be sure, but by man's "spontaneous manifestations of inner spirituality" (page 48). Such a human, Tu argues, must be seen as a "co-creator of the universe" in conjunction with the "vital forces (or *ch'i* 氣, as energy fields)" of the universe itself (pages 2, 52, etc). That "anthropocosmic outlook" marks the Confucian mind. Ultimately, "The Confucian demand that a man serve society is primarily an ethico-religious one." (page 87) In discussing the late Ming philosopher Liu Tsung-chou 劉宗周, in the profoundly thoughtful Chapter Six of the present volume, Tu finds that "humanity is divine" (page 113) in Liu's philosophical anthropology, for "it is human to be divine".

At the end of the last essay in this volume Tu Wei-ming states that it delights him to think "both philosophically and religiously about perennial human problems from Confucian roots ..." (page 193). As modern philosophy this volume of essays will delight the philosophical or religious minded reader. Yet, "to put it in theological terms" (page 4), as Tu does at many points throughout this volume, despite the circumspect attention to the special characteristics of Chinese civilisation, seems at times to blur the distinctiveness of the Chinese intellectual tradition. Even if that gains for Chinese thought an easier entree into the modern Western world of philosophical and religious discourse, and thereby universalises its contemporary significance, that gain may exact a price in understanding of the past. Tu Wei-ming's own understanding is not in question; that of his non-sinological readers may be. Perhaps the writer of a Foreword to a volume for which he has great admiration may be permitted to raise such a warning.

To look now beyond the issue of Confucian thought's religious dimension, one finds many aspects of Confucian tradition clarified and brilliantly argued here. I must call attention in particular to Chapter Five, "Toward an Understanding of Liu Yin's 劉因 Confucian Eremitism" because in this essay Tu Wei-ming re-investigates a subject on which I wrote an earlier essay thirty years ago, cited in Tu's footnote number 10. My study was focused on the dilemma facing Confucian social activists because of their inescapable sense of responsibility for the world's ills in an age when to participate politically demanded compromises of principle. One might argue that political participation always faced Chinese thinkers with some measure of that dilemma, but conditions in Yüan 元 China, under the abnormal circumstances engendered by Mongol overlordship, greatly intensified the issues. My rather simple purpose was to attempt a definition of a "Confucian eremitism" as exemplified by the great scholar and thinker Liu Yin (1249–93). When I first encountered Tu Wei-ming's much more profound philosophical analysis of Liu Yin's choices, in a talk he gave at Princeton several years ago, I saw how much more meaning can be found in that historical episode. He has traced the symbolism in Liu's autobiographical essay (upon which I had also drawn), and in arguing that Liu Yin made an early commitment to a particular ethico-religious tradition of Neo-Confucian origin, he shows that my one-sidedly political explanation of Liu Yin may tell less than the whole truth. The section on Liu Yin's criticism of Taoist escapism is particularly penetrating, and the analysis of Liu Yin's assessment of the elements of Confucian education provides a model for the handling of this important subject. Tu Wei-ming's essay adds greatly to our understanding of the Yüan period and of the longer range trends in Neo-Confucian development.

For many readers the last two essays in this volume will hold particular interest. They assess the deeply intriguing question of whether we can foresee "a third epoch of Confucian humanism" in the contemporary world (page 152). No subject could hold greater importance for students of modern East Asia, or for its one-and-one-half billion residents, even though only a fraction of the latter would think of this issue in such terms. Among scholars and journalists, however, the subject of what significance should be assigned to the Confucian heritage has aroused a spate of books and articles, and public discussion in symposia and conferences. Those have not always been as learned or as reflective as one would hope. As antidote, Tu Wei-ming's deeply felt and eloquently expressed thoughts on this subject should be carefully pondered by all. Tu is personally engaged, as the title of the final chapter proclaims, and as any reader long since would have realised. The very intensity of that engagement may lie behind what may be primarily his admonition to himself in the final paragraph of this volume where he says that a fruitful path to the re-animation of Confucian humanism in our times, in the phrase quoted from Edward Shils, is: "... a task for patient watchfulness and tact of the utmost delicacy." This volume adds importantly to a quest in which I wish its author well, and for whose contributions to it we must all be grateful.

F. W. Mote
Princeton, 1988

1

The Way, Learning, and Politics in Classical Confucian Humanism

The difficulty in reaching an analytical understanding of Confucian humanism, one of the most complex and influential living traditions in East Asia, lies mainly in the high-level integration of the areas of concern central to Confucius' 孔子 (551–479 B.C.) original insights into the human condition. To appreciate the internal dynamics of this tradition in the classical period (sixth to third century B.C.), I propose that we examine three of its primary and interrelated concepts. Genetic and boundary issues aside, the emergence of the Confucian phenomenon as a response to the decline and fall of the Chou 周 civilisation addresses specific *Problematiken* that later became defining characteristics of Confucian humanism. Three core ideas in the Confucian *Analects* 論語 designate these *Problematiken*: *Tao* 道 (the Way), *hsüeh* 學 (learning), and *cheng* 政 (politics).

Tao, or the Way, addresses the question of the ultimate meaning of human existence. The question is posed at a level of sophistication in symbolic thinking comparable to that of questions raised in fundamental theology or theoretical cosmology, even though the point of reference is anthropological or, more appropriately, anthropocosmic in nature. A great deal of misunderstanding of the Confucian project by modern interpreters, especially by those under the influence of May Fourth (1919) positivism and pragmatism, is due to an insensitivity to or an ignorance of this dimension of Confucian concern. Confucius may have insisted on the importance of focusing our attention on life rather than death and on humans rather than gods, but to argue, accordingly, that Confucius was exclusively concerned with the living person here and now in the manner of secular humanism is a gross mistake. Confucius was not at all preoccupied with the secular world; nor did he simply treat the secular as sacred. In his perception of the Way, as shown in

1

the great tradition of the cultural heroes of his dynasty, exemplified by the Duke of Chou 周公, the paradigmatic living example is not a mere creature but in fact a co-creator of the world in which we live, a guardian of the natural process, and a participant of the creative transformation of heaven and earth.[1] The question of the ultimate meaning of human existence, in light of the agelong belief that "it is man that can make the Way great and not the Way that can make man great,"[2] is thus an anthropocosmic question.

The "transcendental breakthrough", if we dare employ such a loaded expression for comparative purposes, assumes a particular significance in Confucian humanism. It is not the emergence of the sharp dichotomy of the sacred and the profane nor the breaking away from the magic garden of an archaic religion that marks the distinctive feature of a new epoch. Rather, Confucius' insistence that he loved the ancients and that he was a transmitter rather than a maker[3] symbolises his attempt to provide a transcendental anchorage for human civilisation. To Confucius, what had already been created, notably the "ritual and music" of the human community, was not merely of humans, it was also sanctioned and sponsored by the mandate of heaven. Confucius' strong conviction that heaven will not allow "this culture" (*ssu-wen* 斯文) to perish[4] must therefore be taken to mean that his sense of mission, far from being a conservative desire to return to the past, was inspired by his awareness that "Heaven knows me!"[5] This awareness, predicated on a deep-rooted faith in the continuation of human culture not only as an historical fact but also as the unfolding of a transcendent reality, enabled Confucius to cultivate a sense of mission. The idea of "this culture" is thus laden with cosmological significance.

[1] A paradigmatic expression of this idea of man as the co-creator of heaven and earth is found in *Chung-yung* 中庸 (The doctrine of the mean): "Only those who are absolutely sincere can fully develop their nature. If they can fully develop their nature, they can then fully develop the nature of others. If they can fully develop the nature of others, they can then fully develop the nature of things. If they can fully develop the nature of things, they can then assist in the transforming and nourishing process of Heaven and Earth. If they can assist in the transforming and nourishing process of Heaven and Earth, they can thus form a trinity with Heaven and Earth." For this translation, see Wing-tsit Chan 陳榮捷, trans. and comp.; *A Source Book in Chinese Philosophy* (Princeton: Princeton University Press, 1969), 107–8.

[2] *Analects* 15:28; Chan, 44.

[3] *Analects* 7:1.

[4] The complete statement in *Analects* 9:5 reads: When Confucius was in personal danger in K'uang 匡, he said, "Since the death of King Wen 文王, is not the course of culture 文 (*wen*) in my keeping? If it had been the will of Heaven to destroy this culture, it would not have been given to a mortal [like me]. But if it is the will of Heaven that this culture should not perish, what can the people of K'uang do to me?" (Chan, 35).

[5] *Analects* 14:37.

Confucius' concern that the deep meaning of the Chou civilisation – the crystallisation of the collaborative effort to create a humane society based on ritual and music – be retrieved impelled him to search for the Way in the living person here and now.[6] His mode of questioning, conditioned by the cultural heritage he cherished and the historical moment he recognised, did not permit him to find his answers in revelatory religion or in speculative philosophy. Instead, through his experiential encounter with the highest moral excellence, which was thought to have characterised "this culture" in its most brilliant period in history, he found the Way in the inner resources of man anthropocosmically defined.

The focus on the centrality and the fruitfulness of the idea of humanity (*jen* 仁) in the *Analects* was an epoch-making event in the symbolic universe of ancient Chinese thought and clearly indicates that the "breakthrough" is "transcendental" in the sense that humanity, for the first time in Chinese history, came to mean that ultimate value goes beyond life and death: "Confucius said, 'A resolute scholar and a man of humanity will never seek to live at the expense of injuring humanity. He would rather sacrifice his life in order to realise humanity.'"[7]

To realise humanity as the ultimate value of human existence eventually became the spiritual self-definition of a Confucian. Even at the time of Confucius, this was widely accepted among his students. Tseng Tzu 曾子, a Confucian disciple who can be described as a knight of humanity, made the following pronouncement: "A knight (*Shih* 士) must be great and strong. His burden is heavy and his course is long. He has taken humanity to be his own burden – is that not heavy? Only with death does his course stop – is that not long?"[8]

Confucius' faith in the perfectibility of human nature through self-effort, as an answer to the dehumanising tendencies of the historical moment in which he was inalienably circumscribed, directed his energies to the transformation of the world from within. This focus was predicated on a belief that the ultimate value of human existence was near at hand and that the desire for humanity entailed the strength for its realisation.[9]

---

[6] For a discussion of the ethico-religious implications of this Confucian insight, see Tu Wei-ming 杜維明 , "A Confucian Perspective on Learning to Be Human", in Frank Whaling, ed., *The World's Religious Traditions* (Edinburgh: T. and T. Clark, 1984), 55–71.

[7] *Analects* 15:8; Chan, 43.

[8] *Analects* 8:7; Chan, 33. It should be noted that Chan translates *shih* 士 as "officer".

[9] In emphasising the ever-present possibility of realising one's own humanity through self-effort, Confucius asserts: "Is humanity far away? As soon as I want it, there it is right by me." (7:29; Chan, 33).

Mencius' 孟子 (371–289 B.C.) theory of the moral propensities of all human beings as an elaboration of the Confucian thesis that men are born righteous[10] provides a transcendental justification for self-cultivation as an essential way of learning to be human. Even Hsün Tzu 荀子 (fl. 298–238 B.C.), who criticised Mencius' theory of human nature, acknowledged that the cognitive function of the mind is capable of recognizing and thus controlling human desires.[11] Hsün Tzu thus insists that self-cultivation is necessary and desirable and that the highest manifestation of humanity in the form of sagehood can be attained. He thus fully subscribed to the Confucian faith in the perfectibility of human nature through self-effort. In theological terms, the Confucian idea of learning to be human suggests a possibility for human beings to become "divine" through personal endeavour. This must have been Mencius' assumption when he depicted the six stages of human perfection:

> The desirable is called "good".
> To have it in oneself is called "true".
> To possess it fully in oneself is called "beautiful", but to shine forth
>   with this full possession is called "great".
> To be great and be transformed by this greatness is called "sage";
>   to be sage and to transcend the understanding is called "divine".[12]

The reason that Mencius could suggest, as a matter of course, that we can become not only good, true, beautiful, and great but also sage and divine through personal self-cultivation lies in a fundamental anthropocosmic assumption in his moral metaphysics:

> For a man to give full realisation to his heart is for him to understand
> his own nature, and a man who knows his own nature will know
> Heaven. By retaining his heart and nurturing his nature he is
> serving Heaven. Whether he is going to die young or to live to
> a ripe old age makes no difference to his steadfastness of purpose.
> It is through awaiting whatever is to befall him with a perfected
> character that he stands firm on his proper destiny.[13]

---

[10] *Analects* 6:17 states: "Man is born with uprightness. If one loses it he will be lucky if he escapes with his life" (Chan, 29).

[11] For Hsün Tzu's discussion of the cognitive functions of the mind, see the *Hsün Tzu* 荀子, chap. 21. For a convenient edition, see Liang Ch'i-hsiung 梁啓雄, *Hsün Tzu chien-shih* 荀子簡釋 (Peking: Chung-hua 中華 Book Co., 1983), 294–300.

[12] *Mencius* 7B:25. For this translation, see D. C. Lau 劉殷爵 trans., *Mencius* (Middlesex, England: Penguin Classics, 1970). Quotations from the *Mencius* in this essay are all based on D. C. Lau's translation.

[13] *Mencius* 8A:1.

The Confucian "transcendental breakthrough" paradoxically symbolised by the continuity, mutuality, and even organismic unity of humanity and heaven cannot be properly understood in terms of either revelatory theology or theoretical cosmology. Rather it represents yet another type of symbolic thinking of the Axial Age different from either Judaeic religion or Greek philosophy.

If we take the Confucian reflection on the Way as analogous to fundamental theology, Confucian learning (*hsüeh*), the second area of concern mentioned above, addresses issues comparable to those addressed in systemic theology. It is likely that the Confucian sacred texts, known today as the Five Classics 五經, did not assume their definitive shape until as late as the second century B.C., during the former Han 漢 dynasty (206 B.C.–A.D. 8). Several texts reconstructed after the burning of the books of the Ch'in 秦 dynasty (221–206 B.C.) must have undergone significant changes in the hands of the Han editors. However, if we take the classics not only as written texts but also as broadly conceived humanistic visions, they can show us the scope of Confucian learning in the classical period. Learning, as portrayed in that period, involves five interrelated visions: poetic, political, social, historical, and metaphysical. Taken together, they represent the unfolding of a comprehensive project to retrieve the deep meaning of human civilisation in a crisis situation.

The poetic vision, which emphasises the internal resonance of the human community, involves the language of the heart. It speaks to the commonality of human feelings and to the mutuality of human concerns without resorting to the art of argumentation. A society harmonised by poetry possesses a synchronised rhythm. The interaction among people in such a society is like the natural flow of sympathetic responses to familiar musical tunes and dance forms. This kind of "primitive commune" was perhaps idealised in Confucian historiography, in which the poetic vision reigned. It must have become a faint memory by the classical period, but the appeal to the heart remains strong even in the highly sophisticated philosophy of government in the writings of Mencius: "No man is devoid of a heart sensitive to the suffering of others. Such a sensitive heart was possessed by the Former Kings and this manifested itself in compassionate government. With such a sensitive heart behind compassionate government, it was as easy to rule the Empire as rolling it in your own palm."[14]

The idea of benevolent government underlies the Confucian political

---

[14] Ibid. 2A:6.

vision.[15] The strong belief in the inseparability of morality and politics and in the correlation between the self-cultivation of the ruler and the governability of the people makes it difficult to conceive of politics as a mechanism of control independent of personal ethics. Indeed, the etymology of the word *cheng* 政 (politics) is "rectification" (*cheng* 正), with a distinctive moral overtone. However, the presumption that the moral persuasion of the elite can easily prevail over the people is based on a considered opinion that a significant role and function of the government is ethical teaching and not on a naive assumption that the masses are simple-minded and thus pliant.[16] The significance of the concept of virtue (*te* 德), which features prominently in Confucian political thought, is that since "Heaven sees as the people see and Heaven hears as the people hear",[17] the real guarantee for the well-being of the rulership lies in its acceptable performance rather than in its pre-conceived mandate. The right of the people to rebel against a tyrannical dynasty, the right of the aristocracy to remove an unjust imperial house-hold, the right of the imperial clansmen to replace an unsuitable king, and the right of the bureaucrats to remonstrate with a negligent ruler are all sanctioned by a deep-rooted conviction that political leadership essentially manifests itself in moral persuasion and that the transformative power of a dynasty depends mainly on the ethical quality of those who govern.

The social vision is never of an adversary system but of a fiduciary community. Like-minded people, motivated by a sense of participation and bound by a sense of duty, become part of an "organic solidarity" in and through which they realise themselves as fully matured human beings. The rituals that have provided the proper context for self-expression and communication in society are not rules and regulations superimposed by an external authority. Rather, they are vehicles by which people learn to stand, to sit, to walk, to eat, to speak, and to greet in a way desirable to themselves and pleasing to others. The Confucian six arts 六藝 — ritual, music, archery, charioteering, calligraphy, and arithmetic — broadly speaking, are all "rituals" designed to discipline people's bodies and minds so that they can act suitably in all human situations. Learning to be human, in this sense, can be understood as a process of ritualisation, which involves submitting to routine exercises, deferring to experienced elders, emulating well-established models, and discovering the most appropriate way of interacting with other

---

[15] *Analects* 12:19; 13:3; 14:45; and 15:5 are a few examples of how "benevolent government" is considered the best course of action in politics.

[16] *Analects* 12:29.

[17] *Mencius* 5A:5.

human beings. Confucius' ability to assume different demeanours in accord with the various occasions that he encountered, as vividly depicted in the tenth chapter of the *Analects*, is a case in point.[18]

The specificity of the depiction of Confucius' attire, facial expressions, gestures, and mannerisms is telling; it unequivocally conveys the humanness of the Master. There is little "magic" in the way Confucius walked, spoke, ate, and taught. He was, as he himself described, an untiring learner and teacher. Nor is there anything mysterious about his personality. However, to his students and to those who followed his teachings in later centuries, the plainness of Confucius' style of life was awe-inspiring. To them, his great strength as an exemplary teacher lay in his everydayness. His conscious choice not to resort to the extraordinary, the powerful, the superhuman, or the transmundane to impress the people was greatly respected as a sign of inner strength.

The emphasis of the Confucian social vision on the ritual of human interaction addresses the way we naturally and inevitably act with each other in conversation. Language, as social property, is familiar to all participating members of a community. The Master inspires us not because he uses a different language from ours but because his mastery of the one that we are all supposed to know is so perfect that he often surprises us with delightfully nuanced utterances. We are in awe of him for he enables us to broaden and deepen our own sense of language and what we say on a daily basis.

The Confucian historical vision, in the same manner, brings new dimensions to the world in which we live here and now. It tells us, often in graphic detail, how the remote past remains relevant to the lived experience near at hand. Collective memory does not impose a radically different perception of reality upon us but suggests a more comprehensive way of perceiving what we take to be uniquely ours. History, so conceived, is a judicious judgment of why things did not turn out to be what they could have been and not a chronological record of what happened. This "moralised history", however, is not simply an arbitrary application of preconceived standards of praise and blame. Rather, history's function is that of wise counsel about the future as well as the present, which is offered as a communal verdict written by an informed observer and not as a private opinion.

The historian so conceived is the conscience of the collective memory we all share. His responsibility is not only to show what has already been done but also to suggest, whenever appropriate, what other possibilities may have existed and why the failure to realise them has led to disastrous

---

[18] See particularly *Analects* 10:3, 4, 13, 16 and 17.

consequences. To write history is therefore a political act committed in the name of the human community as a whole. The sense of dread with which Confucius undertook the task of working on the *Spring and Autumn Annals* 春秋, as noted in the *Book of Mencius* 孟子, indicates that the very act of doing history presumes an air of prophecy and the dignified posture of setting up standards for future generations.[19] In a tradition where communal participation is highly valued, the judgmental act of writing history is not taken lightly and is always considered to be tragic. As Mencius pointed out, only when the age of poetry disappeared did the age of history emerge.[20]

A systemic inquiry into the Confucian perception of the human condition cannot be complete without reference to the metaphysical vision. It is commonly assumed that Confucius was neither theistic nor atheistic, but to characterise his attitude towards God as gnostic is misleading. Confucius never claimed any positive knowledge of spiritual matters and yet he implied that he had acquired a tacit understanding with heaven. It was a two-way relationship: he reported that he knew the mandate of heaven 天命 when he became fifty years of age[21] and he lamented, in extreme adversity, that only heaven knew him.[22] Although the idea of heaven is not clearly articulated in the *Analects*, the sense of mutuality between man and heaven underlay much of the tradition that Confucius inherited. The Confucian metaphysical vision reached fruition in the *Mencius* 孟子, the *Doctrine of the Mean* 中庸, and the *Great Commentary of the Book of Change* 易大傳. The idea of forming a trinity with heaven and earth and taking part in the transformative processes of the cosmos through personal knowledge and self-cultivation later became a defining characteristic of Confucian moral metaphysics. Learning to be human, in this particular connection, not only entails the possibility of going beyond the anthropological realm but demands continuous effort to transcend anthropocentrism. It is in this sense that true humanity must be sought in the anthropocosmic vision of the unity of man and heaven.

In our synoptic description of the Confucian project, we have noted the five visions that inform the Confucian perception of the human condition. A person, in this perspective, is a poetic being, a political being, a social being, a historical being, and a metaphysical being. This highly condensed and complex view makes it difficult to understand Confucian ideology as

---

[19] *Mencius* 3B:9.

[20] Ibid. 4B:21.

[21] *Analects* 2:4.

[22] Ibid. 14:37.

praxis. The Confucian counterpart to practical theology is often misunderstood as "adjustment to the world". Recent reflections on Max Weber's interpretation of Chinese religion have certainly provided a corrective to the outmoded thesis that a typical Confucian is no more than a well-adjusted man: "A well-adjusted man, rationalising his conduct only to the degree requisite for adjustment, does not constitute a systemic unity but rather a complex of useful and particular traits."[23] However, it is not enough simply to note that there is a functional equivalent of an inner-directed personality in the Confucian tradition. To confront the Weberian mode of questioning, we must analyse, both historically and philosophically, what the Confucian project is. Thus far, in our preliminary attempt, we have outlined the fundamental thrust of the Confucian Way and the areas of concern that are constitutive of the Confucian perception of the human condition. This provides the necessary background for us to understand Confucian thought in action.

Confucius' existential decision to retrieve the deep meaning of human civilisation as a way of rethinking the human project made it impossible for the Confucians to detach themselves totally from the world. They had to work through the world because their faith in the perfectibility of human nature through self-effort demanded that they do so. Had they been offered a choice of rendering to Caesar what is Caesar's and to God what is God's, in which the kings minded political business and the Confucians were allowed to devote themselves wholly to spiritual matters, they would have had to reject it. The separation of the sacred and the profane would have seemed to them arbitrary and superficial. However, even though they were in the world, they could not identify themselves with the status quo. To be sure, they did not appeal exclusively to a transcendent referent as a source for symbolic action. Nor did they develop a realm of values totally independent of the political culture of which they were a part. Nevertheless, they had a rich reservoir of symbolic resources at their disposal in which the transcendent referent featured significantly.

The Confucians differed in two essential ways from their counterparts who tapped the symbolic resources of either a revelatory religion or a speculative philosophy. Since they considered themselves guardians of human civilisation, they could not in principle sever their relationships with politics, society, and history. As a result, they assigned themselves the task of appealing to the common sense, good reason, and genuine feeling of the people, especially of those in power, to re-establish the order of the world. The first difference, then, is the Confucian faith in the ultimate transformability and

---

[23] Max Weber, *The Religion of China*, trans. and ed. Hans H. Gerth (New York: The Free Press, 1968), 235.

intrinsic goodness of the human community. The second is that having failed to change the course of history and bring about universal peace in the world, the Confucians created within the "system" a realm of values intersecting the social and political structures, structures that were basically alien to the Confucian perception of the moral order. Thus, even though they were in the world, they were definitely not of the world. However, unlike the Taoists who chose to become hermits, the Confucians who were alienated from the centre of power gained much influence by their sophisticated manipulation of the symbolic universe in which political power was defined, legitimised, and exercised. Specifically, they became teachers, advisers, censors, ministers, and bureaucrats.

The Confucians never established a full-fledged priesthood. Whether by choice or by default, the separation of church and state was never made in Confucian culture. This style of politics, developed by Confucians for their intellectual and spiritual self-definition, turned out to be a mixed blessing. We witness, on the one hand, the impressive historical record of the ability of the Confucians to moralise politics and to transform a legalist or military society into a moral community. Yet we must also recognise that Confucian moral values have often been politicised to serve an oppressive authoritarian regime. At the same time that the Confucian moralisation of politics has become a distinctive feature of Chinese political culture, the politicisation of Confucian symbols in the form of an authoritarian ideology of control has been a dominant tradition in Chinese political history.

The full participation of the Confucians in the political life of the state, as exemplified by Confucius' spirit of engagement in the politics of the Spring and Autumn 春秋 period (722–481 B.C.), made it impossible for them to become either priests or philosophers. However, they could neither adjust themselves to the status quo nor permit themselves to accept the rules of the game defined in narrowly conceived power relationships since their concerted effort to change the world was dictated by a comprehensive vision of the human project. Their concern for rituals, for the rules of conduct, for the maintenance of a common creed, and for the grounding of human worth on a transcendental base led them to perform functions in society comparable to those performed by the priests. Their quest for knowledge, for wisdom, for the dignity of being human, for social norms, and for the good life impelled them to assume the roles of philosophers.

The priestly function and philosophical role in both the public image and the self-definition of the Confucian scholar compel us to characterise him not only as a literatus but also as an intellectual. The Confucian intellectual was an activist. His practical reasoning urged him to confront the world of *realpolitik* and to transform it from within. His faith in the perfectibility of human nature through self-effort, the intrinsic goodness of the human community, and the possibility of the unity of man and heaven enabled him to maintain a critical posture toward those who were powerful and influential. Mencius' idea of the "great man" 大人 is a case in point. Having characterised the most powerful ministers of the time as docile concubines, he gave an account of the Confucian form of life:

> A man lives in the spacious dwelling, occupies the proper position, and goes along the highway of the Empire. When he achieves his ambition he shares these with the people; when he fails to do so he practices the Way alone. He cannot be led into excesses when wealthy and honoured or deflected from his purpose when poor and obscure, nor can he be made to bow before superior force. This is what I would call a great man.[24]

It should be noted that since Mencius clearly defines humanity as man's peaceful abode and righteousness as his proper path,[25] "the spacious dwelling", "the proper position", and "the highway" refer to the symbolic resources that the Confucian intellectual could tap in formulating his own distinctive form of life.

Indeed, a significant part of the *Book of Mencius* can be read as a "special pleading" for the worth of the Confucian intellectual who, despite his lack of contribution in productive labour, is an indispensable member of the moral community: "A gentleman transforms where he passes, and works wonders where abides. He is in the same stream as Heaven above and Earth below. Can he be said to bring but small benefit?"[26] This awareness of the ethico-religious role and function of the Confucian intellectual is particularly pronounced in Mencius' argument against the physiocratic claim that all values are derived from the cultivation of the land. Mencius first presents an analysis of the functional necessity of the division of labour in any complex society. He then elaborates on the mutual dependency of those who labour with their muscles and those who labour with their minds. He concludes with the observation that the management of the state is so demanding and requires so much tender care that it fully occupies the time and mental energies of the rulers: "It is not true that Yao 堯 and Shun 舜 did not have to use their minds to rule the Empire. Only they did not use their minds

---

[24] *Mencius* 3:2.

[25] Ibid. 4A:10.

[26] Ibid. 7A:13.

to plough the fields."[27] By implication, the intellectuals as members of what may be called the "service sectors"[28] of the society also have their own urgent business to attend to, such as cultivating themselves, teaching others to be good, "looking for friends in history",[29] emulating the sages, setting up the cultural norms, interpreting the mandate of heaven, transmitting the Way, and transforming the world into a moral community.

In short, the Confucian intellectual endeavours to realise the full meaning of humanity not as an isolated individual but as a communal act and a dialogical response to the transcendent.

---

[27] Ibid. 3A:4.

[28] The modern expression "service sector", as contrasted with the "production sector", remarkably resembles the Mencian division of labour between those who labour with their minds and those who labour with their muscles. See *Mencius* 3A:4.

[29] *Mencius* 5B:8.

2

The Structure and Function of the Confucian Intellectual in Ancient China

The emergence of classical Confucian humanism in the sixth century B.C., as an expression of the Axial Age, significantly shaped the ethico-religious direction of Chinese culture.[1] Although the mode of thought fashioned by Confucius 孔子 (551–479 B.C.) and by two of his many followers, Mencius 孟子 (371–289 B.C.) and Hsün Tzu 荀子 (fl. 298–238 B.C.), was only one of several prevalent intellectual currents prior to the unification of China by the Ch'in 秦 dynasty in 221 B.C., it was the dominant spiritual force that eventually defined the otherwise nebulous concept of "Chinese culture" (中國文化).

Fung Yu-lan 馮友蘭, who was associated with the anti-Confucian movement during the Cultural Revolution in the People's Republic of China, has recently attempted to formulate his interpretation of Confucianism. He observed that Confucianism helped inspire the self-conciousness of the Chinese people as a distinct cultural entity.[2] Fung's observation is not particularly innovative; it simply affirms what Ch'ien Mu 錢穆, T'ang Chün-i 唐君毅, Hsü Fu-kuan 徐復觀, Mou Tsung-san 牟宗三, and other New Confucian Humanists have taken for granted for decades.[3] However, his

---

[1] For the idea of the "Axial Age", see K. Jaspers, *Vom Ursprung und Ziel der Geschichte* (Zurich: Teil Weltgeschichte, 1949), pp. 15–16. For a discussion of the Chinese case in the perspective of the "transcendental breakthrough", see Benjamin I. Schwartz, "Transcendence in Ancient China", *Daedalus* (Spring 1975): 57–69.

[2] For an indication of his current thinking on the matter, see his Response at the Columbia University Convocation in his honour on September 10, 1982, in the *Proceedings of the Heyman Center*.

[3] For a general discussion of the shared assumptions of the New Confucian Humanists, see Chang Hao 張灝 "New Confucianism and the Intellectual Crisis of Contemporary China", in Charlotte Furth, ed., *The Limits of Change: Essays on Conservative Alternatives in Republican China* (Cambridge, Mass.: Harvard University Press, 1976).

willingness to reopen the Confucian question as *historically* significant in the Levensonian sense is unusual because it opens the door for Marxist historians to explore the roots of Chinese culture in Confucian terms without directly confronting the issue of valuating the role of Confucianism in modern China. Whether this line of questioning will inevitably lead to a complete rethinking of Confucian China and its modern transformation is unknown, but scholars in mainland China have already undertaken major research projects on the Confucian phenomenon as a necessary step toward a more sophisticated understanding of the formation of Chinese culture.[4]

Within this recent renaissance of Confucian studies, Fung Yu-lan's work is part of a collective enterprise to probe the defining characteristics of ancient Chinese thought and society. This enterprise, led by some of the most brilliant minds on the Chinese intellectual scene, may well lead to a fundamental reinterpretation of the inner logic of Confucianism, the role of Confucian humanism in traditional China, and the relevance of Confucian ethics to contemporary China, if not to a complete rethinking of Confucian China and its modern transformation.[5]

The upsurge of interest in the relationship between Confucian ethics and the entrepreneurial spirit in industrial East Asia has raised challenging questions about the Weberian thesis, not only in terms of its specific applicability to China but also in terms of its general validity as an explanatory model for the modernising process. A Confucian response to the Weberian interpretation of modernity, as a way of addressing the complexity of the pluralistic worldview of the twentieth century, may lead to the development of a new conceptual framework for comparative civilisational studies.[6]

My purpose in presenting this brief analysis of the structure and function of the Confucian intellectual in ancient China is twofold: to offer a phenomenological description of an important historical event in the Axial Age, namely, the institutionalisation of Confucian cultural values, and to suggest a method for assessing the far-reaching implications of this event in order to understand Chinese political culture in general. I am aware that this is

---

[4] See "Chung-kuo che-hsüeh nien-chien" 中國哲學年鑑, in The Philosophy Institute, Academy of Social Sciences, ed., *Zhongguo zhexue nianjian* 中國哲學年鑑 (Beijing: The Chinese Encyclopedia, 1982), 104–14.

[5] Especially noteworthy in this regard are works by Li Tze-hou 李澤厚 (Li Zehou), P'ang P'u 龐樸 (Pang Pu) and T'ang I-chieh 湯一介 (Tang Yijie). See Li's article on the reevaluation of Confucius in the second issue of the *Chinese Social Sciences* 中國社會科學 (1980).

[6] For a panoramic view on this issue, see S. N. Eisenstadt, "This Worldly Transcendentalism and the Structure of the World – Weber's 'Religion of China' and the Format of Chinese History and Civilisation". The German version of this essay is included in W. Schluchter, ed., *Max Webers Studie über Konfuzianismus und Taoismus* (Frankfurt: Suhrkamp, 1983), 363–411.

a formidable task and that my research so far allows me to deal with these issues only in a preliminary way. However, my exposure to the most recent literature on Confucian studies in the East and the West has reaffirmed my belief that it is through a reanimation of the old that we can attain the new.[7] By "attaining the new", I am not referring to the future of Confucianism but to a more appropriate methodology, or as I have already suggested, a new conceptual apparatus.

In Chapter 1, I made the following claim:

> The priestly function and philosophical role in both the public image and the self-definition of the Confucian scholar compels us to characterise him not only as a literatus but also as an intellectual. The Confucian intellectual was an activist. His practical reasoning urged him to confront the world of *realpolitik* and to transform it from within. His faith in the perfectibility of human nature through self-effort, the intrinsic goodness of the human community, and the possibility of the unity of man and Heaven enabled him to maintain a critical posture toward those who were powerful and influential.[8]

The Confucian intellectual, so conceived, was relatively weak vis-à-vis the power structure of his time. His moral idealism further undermined his effectiveness as a player in the power game. Lord Shang's 商君 initial failure to gain access to the king of the Ch'in state and to persuade him to follow the path of humanity and righteousness is not an isolated incident.[9] Confucius' sense of homelessness and Mencius' inability to maintain a lasting relationship with those in power clearly show that the Confucian intellectual and, by implication, the Confucian method, was not efficacious in the political arena. Hu Shih's 胡適 effort to define etymologically the term *ju* 儒 (Confucian or scholar) as "weakling" 柔 is, in this connection, most suggestive.[10]

It is quite understandable that the Confucians did not exert much political influence in the period when classical Confucian humanism emerged as a major force in ancient Chinese thought. The politics of the Eastern Chou 東周 (eighth to fifth century B.C.) characterised by the disintegration of the feudal system (*feng-chien* 封建) was uncongenial to the Confucian project

---

[7] Tu Wei-ming 杜維明, *Humanity and Self-Cultivation: Essays in Confucian Thought* (Berkeley: Asian Humanities Press, 1979), xxii.

[8] See above, pp. 10–11.

[9] Ssu-ma Ch'ien 司馬遷, *Shih-chi* 史記 (The historical records; Beijing: Chung-hua 中華, 1959) 8:2228.

[10] Hu Shih 胡適, "Shuo *Ju*" 說儒 (On the character *ju*), in *Hu Shih wen-ts'un* 胡適文存 (Collected literary works of Hu Shih; Taipei: Yüan-tung t'u-shu 遠東圖書, 1953) 4:1–103.

of moralising all forms of human relationship, including that between ruler and minister. As the Middle Kingdom 中國, for a variety of economic and social reasons, gradually but definitely moved away from the elaborate ritual order that had defined the *modus operandi* of the ruling elite, the new power structure, commonly known as the *pa* 霸 (hegemony), subscribed to different rules, those of *realpolitik*. The shapers of the new structure, as a result, were wandering scholars who knew how to flow with the tide.[11] The aforementioned Lord Shang eventually found a sympathetic ear in the king when he discussed concrete ways of enriching and strengthening the state.[12] Mencius, on the other hand, refused to offer advice that would "benefit" (*li* 利) the state of Ch'i 齊.[13] Since the language of power was in the ascendant, the Confucian intellectuals were, at least on the surface, weaklings.

However, the frequent interpretation that the Confucians failed politically whereas Legalists such as Lord Shang succeeded in their power struggle to influence politics is predicated on a narrow conception of how politics actually worked in ancient China. If the political arena is defined in terms of access to the decision-making body of the ruling minority, the Confucians failed miserably; and we might add that they deliberately chose to fail. Mencius' condemnation of the powerful ministers as "weaklings" is a case in point:

> Ching Ch'un 景春 said, "Were not Kung-sun Yen 公孫衍 and Chang Yi 張儀 great men? As soon as they showed their wrath the feudal lords trembled with fear, and when they were still the Empire was spared the conflagration of war." "How can they be thought great men?" said Mencius. "Have you never studied the rites? When a man comes of age his father gives him advice. When a girl marries, her mother gives her advice, and accompanies her to the door with these cautionary words, 'When you go to your new home, you must be respectful and circumspect. Do not disobey your husband.' It is the way of a wife or concubine to consider obedience and docility the norm."[14]

One way of interpreting this statement is to suggest that Mencius was unrealistic and arrogant in reference to power. After all, unlike either a

---

[11] Cho-yün Hsu 許倬雲, *Ancient China in Transition: An Analysis of Social Mobility, 722–222 B.C.* (Stanford: Stanford University Press, 1965), 140–74.

[12] Ssu-ma Ch'ien, 7:2228.

[13] *Mencius* 1A:1.

[14] Ibid 3B:2. For this translation, see D. C. Lau, trans., *Mencius* (Middlesex, England: Penguin Classics, 1970), 107.

priest or a philosopher, Mencius was actively interested in putting his insights into the political machinery of his time. His inability to communicate with those in power seems to have undermined the very basis on which his moral enterprise was to be built. Mencius' inability to wield enough power to establish a distinctively Confucian political institution seems to indicate that in regard to power politics, he was a loser. His characterisation of the powerful ministers as docile and obedient weaklings may seem to have reflected his own sour grapes mentality.

Even though the Confucians never gained access to the decision-making body of the ruling minority during the Warring States 戰國 (403–221 B.C.) period, they did become a notable social force exerting powerful control over the cultural system. This was accomplished mainly through education. The Confucian monopoly on education may have been the single most important factor for the reemergence of Confucian intellectuals in the Han 漢 dynasty (206 B.C.–A.D. 220) as the meaning givers in society and the authority legitimisers in polity.[15] This is not to say that the Confucians alone provided the symbolic resources for China to transform itself from feudal states to imperial dynasties. Far from it; the Legalists, the Yin-Yang 陰陽 cosmologists, the Taoists of both the Chuang Tzu 莊子 and the Huang-Lao 黃老 variety, and the Moists all seem to have played significant roles in this transitional period. The Confucians, with their particular interest in rituals, represented only one of the many approaches, and a relatively colourless one at that.

Yet, the Confucians were unique in transmitting what they took to be "this culture" (ssu-wen 斯文), the cumulative wisdom of the ancients.[16] They made education the vehicle by which they spread their influence as messengers of the Way. Confucius himself played a pivotal role in making education, which had been confined to sons of the nobility, available to commoners. This democratisation of the educational process released a great deal of energy from the lower echelons of society. The channel of upward social mobility, once opened to the literati, significantly changed its character. No longer did brute force determine the strength of a contender for power, for no matter how strong a king was militarily, he relied heavily on the literati to run his bureaucracy: to help him register the people, collect taxes, settle litigation, negotiate with foreign powers, establish the proper

[15] Yü Ying-shih 余英時, "Ku-tai chih-shih chieh-ts'eng ti hsing-ch'i yü fa-chan" 古代知識階層的興起與發展 (The rise of the ancient intellectual class and its development), in his Chung-kuo chih-shih chieh-ts'eng shih-lun – ku-tai p'ien 中國知識階層史論—古代篇 (A historical discussion of the Chinese intellectual class – ancient chapter; Taipei: Lien-ching 聯經, 1980), 1–108.

[16] Analects 論語 9:5.

rituals; in short, to bring law and order to his regime and to enhance his presence in "international" politics.[17] To be sure, the king consolidated his position as a centre of power by military conquest, but, in order to maintain his control, he had to use the civil bureaucracy to extend his influence. It seems anachronistic that the Confucian Lu Chia 陸賈 had to advise the founding father of the Han dynasty that although the empire was conquered on horseback, it could hardly be governed in the same manner.[18] For, prior to the imperial age, the civil bureaucracy had governed China for centuries.

The Confucians were not the first bureaucrats in Chinese history. The diviners, the historians, and the astronomers of the Shang 商 and early Chou 周 (eighteenth to eighth century B.C.) performed bureaucratic functions in ancient China. Nor did the Confucians staff the feudal bureaucracies of the Warring States. Furthermore, their commitment to a holistic education to transmit the cultural norms of Confucian humanism was not primarily oriented toward government service. Yet the Confucians were undeniably the true inheritors of the ancient texts and thus the spirit of the scribe. Unlike the Taoists, who tried to transcend the written word, or the Legalists, who tried to confine it to the letters of the law, or the Moists, who tried to use it as an ideological weapon, or the Yin-Yang cosmologists, who tried to manipulate it as a magic code, the Confucians embraced the entire literature and took it upon themselves, as a divine mission, to breathe vitality into it through the art of interpretation. Their hermeneutic efforts created one of the most comprehensive literary traditions in human history. As a result, the symbolic resources available to the Chinese civil bureaucracy for future developments greatly expanded, and the institutional continuity between the feudal states and the imperial dynasties was greatly enhanced. The Confucian contribution to the identity and adaptation of the Chinese bureaucracy cannot be exaggerated.

In a broader sense, however, the most significant impact of Confucian education on Chinese political culture lies not in civil bureaucracy but in its definition of the intellectual's role in politics. This brings us back to Mencius' contempt for the powerful minister mentioned earlier. The minister was not a "great man", in part because he did not have a "home" of his own.

---

[17] Yü Ying-shih, "Tao-t'ung yü cheng-t'ung chih chien – Chung-kuo chih-shih fen-tzu ti yüan-shih hsing-t'ai" 道統與政統之間—中國知識份子的原始形態 (Between the tradition of the Way and the tradition of politics – an original mode of the Chinese intellectual) in his *Shih-hsüeh yü ch'uan-t'ung* 史學與傳統 (Historical scholarship and tradition; Taipei: China Times, 1982), 30–70.

[18] Hsü Fu-kuan 徐復觀, "Han-ch'u ti ch'i-meng ssu-hsiang chia – Lu Chia" 漢初的啓蒙思想家—陸賈 (Lu Chia – the enlightenment thinker in early Han) in his *Liang-Han ssu-hsiang shih* 兩漢思想史 (History of thought of the Han; Taipei, Hsüeh-sheng 學生, 1976, 2:85–108.

Unlike the true great man who "lives in the spacious dwelling, occupies the proper position, and goes along the highway of the Empire",[19] the powerful minister leaves his own abode and serves in an alien house. His respectfulness and circumspection are clear indications that he is not his own master. The analogy of a girl marrying into a new home is apt here because the minister, by accommodating himself to the demands of the king, has lost his sense of personal dignity, autonomy, and independence. The Confucian intellectual, by contrast, never leaves home to take up residence elsewhere. In other words, he defines what politics is from the centre of his moral being. Since he never reverses the order of priority (morality precedes politics), he cannot be defined by politics. Even in the exercise of "expediency" (*ch'üan* 權), the Confucian counterpart of the Buddhist *upaya* (skilful means), the primacy of moral rectitude is still a precondition for any circumstantial adjustment.[20] The Confucian ideal of "inner sageliness and outer kingliness"[21] 內聖外王 , viewed in this perspective, means that sageliness takes precedence over kingliness and that only a sage is qualified to be a king.

As I noted in Chapter 1, since Mencius defines humanity as man's peaceful abode and righteousness as his proper path, "the spacious dwelling", "the proper position", and "the highway of the Empire" all refer to "the symbolic resources that the Confucian intellectual could tap in formulating his own distinctive form of life".[22] Concretely, the home that the Confucian intellectual constructs for himself is richly endowed with poetic, political, social, historical, and metaphysical visions. He has ready access to sagely texts, ancestral instructions, exemplary teachers, worthy friends, and the rites and music of the ancients.

Moreover, since he has established an internal resonance with the basic feelings of the people, he is also in tune with the rhythm of his own community. Indeed, he is a spokesman for his fellow human beings. As such, he bears witness to the mandate of heaven because, as the ancient proverb states, "Heaven sees as the people see and heaven hears as the people hear!"[23]

---

[19] *Mencius* 3B:2; Lau, *Mencius*, 107.

[20] *Analects* 9:30; *Mencius* 4A:18, 7A:26. For an interpretive essay on the concept of *ch'üan* 權 , see Chao Chi-pin 趙紀彬, "Shih ch'üan" 釋權 (On expediency), in *Chung-kuo che-hsüeh* 中國哲學 (Chinese philosophy; Beijing: San-lien 三聯, 1983): 9:18–29.

[21] This expression is found in the "T'ien-hsia" 天下篇 chapter of *Chuang Tzu* 莊子. See *Chuang Tzu Yin-te* 莊子引得 (Index to Chuang Tzu; Cambridge, Mass.: Harvard-Yenching Institute, 1947), 91/33/15.

[22] See above, p. 11.

[23] *Mencius* 5A:5. For a historical note on this saying, see Lau, *Mencius*, 144.

The transcendent reference has enabled the Confucian intellectual to extend his horizons beyond the social system so that his participation in the political arena is not confined to the social context. The common impression that the Confucian bureaucrat could only voice his discontent from within and that he was incapable of radical protest outside his social role fails to account for the Confucian ability to mobilise massive psychic energy by a direct appeal to transcendental principle, be it the mandate of heaven or the dictates of one's moral will. The convergence of the most generalisable social relevance (the sentiments of the people) and the most universalisable, ethico-religious sanction (the mandate of heaven) has allowed the Confucian to perceive politics in terms of the ultimate meaning of life and as a basic fact of ordinary human existence.

Thus, through education, the Confucians contributed not only to the development of civil bureaucracy but also to the definition of politics in ancient China. In contrast to the powerful Legalist ministers, however, they did not play an active role in the ruling minority in the transition from feudal states to imperial dynasties. From the viewpoint of *realpolitik*, they can be considered relatively weak, but they consciously resisted the temptation to play the game of power politics. Dictated by their core values, they initiated their project through education, from the periphery of the cultural system. Their great efforts to democratise education eventually led to a major transformation of ancient Chinese polity. Paradoxically, the weaklings who repeatedly failed to gain access to the centre of power succeeded in providing the conceptual framework in which politics assumed its significance.

To characterise this transformation of ancient Chinese polity as the Confucianisation of bureaucracy, however, would be one-sided. For one thing, as Confucian intellectuals became actively involved in Han bureaucracy, the values they cherished were also visibly politicised. The politicisation of Confucian values as a way of enhancing the idealogical control of the Han state and the moralisation of politics by the Confucian intellectuals who entered the government service for idealist reasons represent two conflicting currents of thought in Han political culture. The aforementioned Lu Chia, the outspoken scholar-official Yüan Ku-sheng 轅固生, the famous synthesiser Tung Chung-shu 董仲舒, and the literary philosopher Yang Hsiung 揚雄 are ou ·anding examples of Confucian intellectuals who wanted to bring their Way io bear upon the political process. They were concerned with the well-being of sagely learning in the actual functioning of the Han government. Their intention to moralise politics often met with frustration, but their persistence in delivering the Confucian message greatly contributed to a climate conducive to the eventual establishment of Confucianism as the official ideology of the Han dynasty. More important in a broad cultural perspective was their great contribution to the development of a political language or more precisely, a grammar of action for all players in the political arena, including the members of the ruling minority. Remarkably, they managed to accomplish this without gaining direct access to the centre of power.[24]

Needless to say, the process by which highly sophisticated philosophical ideas were translated into operational principles for governing political behaviour was long and complex. The decision of the founding fathers of the Han dynasty to depart from the Legalist model of Ch'in bureaucracy, the legal and political background of those who actually designed the Han system, the necessity of a large governing machinery to run the daily routines of the empire, and other prerequisites of law and order all contributed to the emergence of Confucianism as an official ideology. The Confucian intellectuals, especially those who were innovative and persuasive enough to make Confucian ideas the shared assumptions of the newly emerging political order, were involved in bringing this about. It was neither idle scholarly speculation nor the demand of the objective conditions that helped Confucianism become the predominant intellectual current in Han China. To be sure, the Confucians could not have been fully aware of the political implications of their scholarly work, and the circumstantial forces – the predilection of the emperor, the interests of the chief ministers, and the concerns of the bureaucrats – must have contributed to the so-called triumph of Confucianism over other trends of thought, such as Legalism and Taoism. But the concerted effort of the Confucian intellectuals to present their teaching systematically and pragmatically as the best possible ideological line for the Han empire was the key factor in making this a political reality.

It is commonly assumed that the influential politician Kung-sun Hung 公孫弘 (died 121 B.C.) and the eminent scholar Tung Chung-shu were the principal figures in making Confucianism the predominant philosophy during the reign of Wu Ti 武帝 (141–87 B.C.). Their extraordinary feat is said to have been accomplished by converting Wu Ti, who was as blatantly ambitious and as thoroughly Legalistic as the first emperor of the Ch'in dynasty, into a Confucian monarch. Especially noteworthy, some historians further claim, was the manner in which this monumental phenomenon occurred: no bloodshed, no military coup d'état, no visible power struggle, but a peaceful transition. Although there is a measure of truth in this widely accepted account, the "triumph" of Confucianism was actually the result of a long and strenuous process, stretching over the entire period of the Han dynasty. In the perspective of intellectual history, the Confucianism that

---

[24] Yü Ying-shih, "Tao-t'ung yü cheng-t'ung chih chien", 64–70.

eventually emerged as the predominant court philosophy was no longer the teachings of Confucius and Mencius. Rather, it was an amalgamation of Hsün Tzu's ritualism with Legalist concepts, Yin-Yang cosmological categories, Taoist ideas, and a host of other contemporary beliefs.

The matter is further complicated by the fact that Kung-sun Hung's promotion of Confucian ideology and Tung Chung-shu's construction of Confucian cosmology belong to two significantly different Confucian modes. Wu Ti's adoption of Confucianism as the court philosophy signified the triumph of those Confucians who rose to prominence in his reign. They were the true heirs of the spirit of Shu-sun T'ung 叔孫通, who, in order to find a niche in the Han bureaucracy for himself and his followers, demeaned his role as a Confucian intellectual by designing a court ritual to enhance the prestige of the emperorship.[25] Shu-sun T'ung's success in making a profession out of his expertise in ritual practices suggested a way of accommodating Confucian values to political needs.

Confucian intellectuals such as Lu Chia, Yüan Ku-sheng, Tung Chung-shu, and Yang Hsiung, subscribed to a radically different perception of the Confucian Way. To them, the only niche worth occupying in the government was one from which they could exert moral influence to transform politics into a human order, a world immersed in rites and music. They might serve as ministers or teachers; their primary concern was not the stability of the ruling minority but the well-being of the people. They took part in the governing process not as servants of the emperor but as messengers of their moral ideals. Since their moral ideals were thought to have been commissioned by the mandate of heaven, they appealed to both the transcendent and the people for support. Although their relationship to the power-holders was not adversarial, they could maintain an independent posture toward the king as a teacher, adviser, critic, or friend, but never as an obedient servant.

Contrary to the widely held interpretive position, Tung Chung-shu's cosmology was not an ideological justification for the divinity of the emperor. His famous phrase, "the mutual responsiveness of heaven and man", was not intended to assign transcendent importance to the throne. Rather, he wanted to make the emperor accountable for his actions to heaven above as well as to the people below. In establishing the supremacy of heaven as the final arbiter of human worth, Tung perceived the power of the emperor as a relativised authority. Without the legitimising functions of the cosmic

---

[25] For a general historical account of this transformation from a "materialist" viewpoint, see Hou Wai-lu 侯外盧 et al., eds., *Chung-kuo ssu-hsiang t'ung-shih* 中國思想通史 (*A general history of Chinese thought*; Beijing: Jen-min 人民, 1957–), 2:40–63.

process, the emperor's leadership remained questionable. In Tung's interpretation of omens and portents, which features prominently in his philosophical treatise, the *Luxuriant Gems of the Spring and Autumn Annals* 春秋繁露, he was engaged in the subtle art of political criticism. The whole practice was predicated on the assumption that if the empire was well governed, not only would the human world be in order but the cosmos would also be in harmony. If the cosmic process did not proceed smoothly, the emperor was personally responsible for its failure. To correct this anomaly, the emperor had to become more cautious in his leadership.[26] The very fact that Tung and other Han Confucians were totally committed to this view as self-evidently true rendered it particularly efficacious as a principle of governance. Understandably, Grand Historian Ssu-ma Ch'ien 司馬遷 (died c. 85 B.C.), while condemning Kung-sun Hung as subverting Confucian learning in order to please the world, praised Master Tung as a true follower of Confucius.[27]

With the establishment of the Five Erudites of the Five Classics 五經博士 at court in 136 B.C., the politicisation of Confucian learning entered a new phase. The assignment of fifty official studies to these Erudites in 124 B.C. spurred the development of an imperial university. The number of students at the university is said to have grown to a few thousand in half a century. Toward the end of the dynasty, the students constituted a major force in the political arena.[28] The implementation of examination systems and recommendations based on Confucian ethical and literary criteria further enhanced the power of the Confucian persuasion. By A.D. 1 a hundred successful candidates joined government service annually after passing examinations administered by Confucian scholars, and the number increased substantially in subsequent years. A civil bureaucracy staffed by literati trained in Confucian classics emerged as a natural outcome. From Wu Ti's time on, Confucian learning was a major vehicle for training Chinese bureaucrats.[29] More significant was the establishment of government schools as centres of education throughout the empire. Since the Confucian classics were adopted as the core curriculum and Confucius was honoured as the "patron saint" of the schools, Confucian ethics became the social norm for recruiting the political

---

[26] For a suggestive study of Tung Chung-shu, see Hsü Fu-kuan, "Hsien-Ch'in Ju-chia ssu-hsiang ti chuan-che chi t'ien ti che-hsüeh ti wan-ch'eng" 先秦儒家思想的轉折及天的哲學的完成(The transformation of pre-Ch'in Confucian thought and the completion of the philosophy of Heaven), in his *Liang-Han ssu-hsiang shih*, 2:295–438.

[27] Ssu-ma Ch'ien, 10:3128.

[28] Hou Wai-lu et al., 2:331–63.

[29] Ibid., 364–414.

elite.[30] Pan Ku 班固 (died A.D. 92), the author of *Han-shu* 漢書, commented that the path of profit contributed to the ascendancy of Confucian studies.[31]

The Confucian subversion of the Legalist bureaucracy, or, more appropriately perhaps, the incorporation of Confucian ideas into Legalist practices, resulted in a highly integrated organic system. Beyond doubt, the politicised Confucians greatly influenced the character of the government. For example, the Confucianisation of law, a topic that has attracted much attention in Western sinology, began in the Han and eventually became a permanent fixture in the Chinese art of government.[32] The mixing of the kingly way with that of the hegemon, which one Han emperor frankly admitted was the "family method" of the dynasty,[33] produced a pattern of power relationships that was to become an enduring feature of Chinese politics. The idea that the prime minister, as the executive officer of the bureaucracy, should be treated as a respected guest of the imperial clan was partially realised in Han political history, and the right of the worthies to remain detached from politics was acknowledged by the power elite. Throughout Chinese history, the government strove to elicit either the active support or the tacit acceptance of the hermits. The reenactment of this venerable ritual in the Han set standards for later dynasties. Although the Confucian injunction that the ruler should be courteous toward the worthy and humble toward the scholar was never fully observed, it continued to inspire people of all walks of life to show respect for the educated. It may not be far-fetched to suggest that in the Han dynasty, the idea of the literatus had already assumed particular significance in the Chinese mind.[34]

Nevertheless, even though politicised Confucian ethics represented the predominant intellectual trend in the Han after the reign of Wu Ti and served the Confucianised Legalist state, this is only part of the Confucian story. The rise of Confucian classicism and the spread of Confucian morality in society could not be subsumed under the general rubric of Confucianism

[30] Ibid., 50–55.

[31] See Pan Ku's comment on Emperor Wu's establishment of the Five Erudites, cited in Hou Wai-lu et al., 2:48.

[32] Ch'ü T'ung-tsu 瞿同祖, *Law and Society in Traditional China* (Paris: Mouton, 1961), an English version of the author's earlier work in Chinese.

[33] Ssu-ma Kuang 司馬光, *Tzu-chih t'ung-chien* 資治通鑑 (Comprehensive mirror for aid in governance; Beijing: Chung-hua, 1971) 1:880–81.

[34] Yü Ying-shih, "Han-Chin chih chi shih chih hsin tzu-chüeh yü hsin ssu-ch'ao" 漢晉之際士之新自覺與新思潮 (New currents of thought and new self-awareness of the literatus during the transition from Han to Chin), in his *Chung-kuo chih-shih chieh-ts'eng shih-lun*, 205–30.

as a political ideology. They were closely connected with the attempt of the central government to maintain law and order by ideological persuasion as well as by legal coercion. But they were neither epiphenomena nor dependent variables of political factors. Their course of development was dictated by impulses of a nonpolitical nature, which could and often did become politically significant. The role of the Confucian intellectuals in those areas deserves our special attention.

Confucian learning, in its inception, took the cultivation of the self as its point of departure. The Confucian faith in the perfectibility of human nature through self-effort provided the impetus for cultivating one's own growth as a project of learning. One did not study the classics simply to acquire empirical knowledge but also to deepen self-awareness. Tung Chung-shu's self-imposed rigorous programme of intellectual pursuit for three years so that he could be totally devoted to his scholarly work was a spiritual quest as well as an intellectual pursuit.[35] His dictum "To rectify one's rightness without scheming for profit; to enlighten one's Way without reckoning achievements"[36] meant to suggest that his rigorous effort to interpret the *Spring and Autumn Annals* 春秋 was impelled by a sense of duty to know the sagely truth rather than by a desire to be useful. To Tung, the choice of rightness and profit was a clear one, for the true Confucian commitment to personal dignity, autonomy, and independence was incompatible with the adulterated Confucian interest in wealth and power under the pretext of public service. Learning for the sake of the self demanded that self-cultivation be recognised as a precondition for regulating the family, governing the state, or bringing peace to the world. This sense of priority was irreversible. The insistence that self-cultivation is the root (*pen* 本) and regulating the family, governing the state, and bringing peace to the world are branches (*mo* 末) make it explicit that political service should be a natural outgrowth of personal morality.[37] By implication, those in leadership position must observe strict rules of conduct to make them worthy of their lofty status. The idea of *noblesse oblige* is relevant here except that high birth alone did not guarantee a ready access to power and influence. One needed literary competence, social approval, and moral rectitude to climb the ladder of success. The text of the *Great Learning* 大學 captures this spirit in one of its

---

[35] Ssu-ma Ch'ien 10:3127.

[36] See Tung Chung-shu's memorial to the King of Chiao-hsi 膠西王, quoted in his biography in the *Han-shu*. See Pan Ku, *Han-shu* (Peking: Chung-hua, 1959).

[37] *Ta-hsüeh* 大學 (The great learning), in Wing-tsit Chan 陳榮捷, trans. and comp., *A Source Book in Chinese Philosophy* (Princeton: Princeton University Press, 1969), 87.

concluding remarks: "From the Son of Heaven down to the common people, all must regard cultivation of the personal life as the root or foundation."[38]

In the realm of political culture, this universalist claim that all must regard self-cultivation as the root led to the obvious conclusion that politics was inseparable from morality and that morality must take precedence over politics. Undeniably, however, the Confucian ideal of "inner sageliness and outer kingliness" was impractical and the demand that only sages are qualified to be kings was unrealistic. Actually no emperor in the Han dynasty, or for that matter throughout Chinese history, was sagely. After all, Wu Ti, who is said to have been converted into a Confucian monarch, remained blatantly ambitious, thoroughly Legalistic, and worst of all, ridiculously superstitious. In reality, Confucian ethics rarely touched the inner lives of the rulers. Often it was abused to serve as an ideological weapon for social control. The son of heaven may not have been personally committed to self-cultivation, but he could appreciate the political benefit of ensuring that his ministers were. Although the scholar-officials in power might not put Confucian ethics into practice themselves, they could surely see that their task of maintaining stability in society would be made relatively easy if the common people did so.

What actually happened in the Han was far more complex than this cynical view might suggest. There is, however, clear evidence that the scholar-officials in the court were aware of the desirability of setting standards of behaviour for the society at large. The Erudites' concerted effort to reach an agreement on the governing values of proper human relationships, as reflected in the formulation of the "three bonds" 三綱 and "five constancies" 五常, is a case in point. The fact that well-orchestrated court discussions were organised to ensure that the authority of the ruler over the minister, the father over the son, and the husband over the wife were firmly established, as in the "three bonds", and that the supreme importance of the five basic human relationships 五倫 (father/son, ruler/minister, husband/wife, older brother/younger brother, and friend/friend) was recognised, as in the "five constancies", strongly indicates that the imperial court believed that it was the business of the government to implant ethical norms in the minds of the people.[39]

To use Confucianism as a mechanism for social control turned out to be a double-edged sword for the Han regime. The establishment of the authority

[38] Ibid.

[39] See Hou Wai-lu et al., eds. pp. 232–47. For an English version of the famous discussions in the White Tiger Hall, see Tjan Tjoe Som (Tseng Tsu-sen 曾祖森). *Po hu t'ung* 白虎通, *The Comprehensive Discussions in the White Tiger Hall* (Leiden: Brill, 1949–52).

of the ruler, the father, and the husband may have been an effective way to ensure the stability of the society under the domination of autocracy and patriarchy. Yet the Confucian ideology, with its emphasis on exemplary teaching and mutual responsibility, also required that the ruler live up to the ideal of kingship, that the father live up to the ideal of fatherhood, and that the husband live up to the ideal of householder. The Confucian intellectuals and, to a certain extent, the scholar-officials in general assumed the role of watchdog, not only for the imperial household, but also for the common people. They could help the ruling minority maintain law and order in society and had some coercive power to bring deviants in line. Normally they would exercise their influence through moral persuasion as teachers. At the same time, they could represent the people in addressing their grievances to the higher authority. They could serve as critics and censors when they believed that the sins of the dynasty were still redeemable. They could also advocate the creation of a new dynasty if they felt that the course of degeneration of the present one could not be reversed.

The Confucians certainly did not see their emperors as sage-kings. They also noticed that, historically, sages did not necessarily become kings. Perhaps they were impelled by the sage-king ideal when they honoured Confucius as the "uncrowned king" (*su-wang* 素王).[40] The logic of this is not difficult to see. If only sages are qualified to be kings, it is highly desirable to make sages kings. Confucius was a sage because he embodied the virtues of humanity, rightness, propriety, wisdom, and truthfulness through moral self-cultivation. The reason that he never became king had nothing to do with his personal quality. This was a serious anomaly. If the time had been right, he would have been king. The most appropriate way to honour him, then, was to respect him as though he had been king. The implication of honouring Confucius as the "uncrowned king" is obvious. Emperors who failed to demonstrate sagely qualities were, at most, probationary kings. This Han Confucian perception is a far cry from the unquestioned loyalty toward one's ruler-father found in late imperial China. It is noteworthy that once the emperor began to wonder whether he ought to be sagely, a more tender-minded approach to political matters became inevitable. Understandably, the Confucians focused their attention on the selection and education of the heir apparent.

Unfortunately, although Confucian intellectuals may have substantially reshaped the Legalist state, they never questioned the fundamental principles

---

[40] For a Han use of the term, see the "Kuei-te" 貴德 chapter of Liu Hsiang's 劉向 *Shuo Yüan* 説苑. For the precise reference, see *Index to Shuo Yüan*, Harvard-Yenching Institute Sinological Index Series, no. 1 (reprint; Taipei: Chinese Materials and Research Aids Service Center, 1966), 5/2a.

of the monarchical system. They may have taken an active part in ritualising and humanising the *modus operandi* of the Legalist bureaucracy, but they were unable to restructure it according to the political insights of Confucius and Mencius. The Confucian literati in the *Discourse on Salt and Iron* 鹽鐵論 did raise challenging issues about the nature of polity and society. They opted for a fiduciary community based on mutual respect, the division of labour, pluralism, natural hierarchy, and peaceful coexistence. Yet their idealism was undermined by the Legalist impulse for wealth and power. The arguments of national defence against the threat of the steppe peoples and necessary government expenditures to ensure law and order were overwhelming. As a result, the Confucian literati could only cherish their thoughts in a nostalgic, historical mode.[41] As the idea of the sage-king degenerated into the practice of king-sage, the king who failed to demonstrate any sagely quality demanded moral and ideological authority in addition to his political power. The king-sage may not have been as destructive as the warrior-despot, but his all-encompassing presence was extremely detrimental to the development of the Mencian "great man".

Confucians had longed for the reappearance of the "great unity" under a a universal kingship ever since the disintegration of the feudal order of the Chou dynasty. The Han Empire provided a great opportunity for Confucian ideas to become institutionalised. This was, however, a mixed blessing. The institutionalised Confucian ideology may have ritualised law and moralised bureaucracy, but it never transformed the Legalist state into a fiduciary community. Far from it: the politicisation of Confucian moral symbols for the primary purpose of ideological control, rather than the Confucian intellectual's intention to humanise politics, became the Han legacy to Chinese political culture. It was the practice of the king-sage, not the idea of the sage-king, that became an enduring political reality in Chinese civilisation.

---

[41] Hsü Fu-kuan, "Yen-t'ieh lun chung te cheng-chih she-hui wen-hua wen-t'i" 鹽鐵論中的政治社會文化問題 (The political, social and cultural issues in the *Discourse on Salt and Iron*), in his *Liang-Han ssu-hsiang shih* 3:117–216. For an English translation of chapters 1–19 of the *Discourse*, see Huan K'uan 桓寬, *Discourse on Salt and Iron: a Debate on State Control of Commerce and Industry in Ancient China*, trans. E. Gale (Leiden: Brill, 1957).

3
The Confucian Sage:
Exemplar of
Personal Knowledge

The Confucian conviction that virtue can be learned and that the highest exemplification of virtue, sagehood, is attainable has been a source of inspiration for both the educated elite and the general populace in China. Indeed, a defining characteristic of Chinese culture is its faith in the human capacity for creative self-transformation. The belief that a humble person can become the exemplar of humanity and thus assume a godlike stature in the pantheon of the virtuous is widely held among modern as well as traditional Chinese. To them, sagehood is a manifestation of humanity, and Confucius is the paradigmatic sage.

For centuries Confucius has been a model of humanity. He exemplifies an ideal that is accessible to all, yet curiously elusive because learning to be fully human is continually and intensely personal. That is, what Confucius himself actually attained can never be repeated. As we strive to become fully human, we have no blueprint to follow. We can neither imitate Confucius nor learn to realise ourselves through him. Since we remember that his life was shaped by his awareness that sagehood was ever just beyond his grasp, he inspires us and provides a standard for us in our search for ultimate personal knowledge.

The paradigmatic sage, then, is not only a teacher but also a learner, and the learning that he exemplifies has a definite shape. In this essay I will attempt to convey a sense of how the historical Confucius, who emphatically denied that he ever attained sagehood,[1] emerged in Chinese history as the preeminent sage. My main purpose, however, is not to give a narrative

---

[1] *Analects* 論語 7:34. See D. C. Lau 劉殷爵, trans., *Confucius: The Analects* (Harmondsworth, England: Penguin Books, 1979), 90.

account of how this is thought to have happened but to suggest a way of understanding the Confucian conviction that any person who takes the cultivation of his or her personal knowledge seriously can become the exemplar for the human community as a whole.

When Confucius identified himself as a lover of the ancients and a transmitter of tradition rather than an innovator,[2] he had in mind the age-old wisdom that human beings must learn to be fully human through their own efforts; for that reason the mastery of culture, over and above instinct, is an essential human activity. Animals have little choice in what they are destined to be, but humans, individually and collectively, enjoy an immense range of possibilities. A salient feature of humanity is its malleability, thus its perfectibility.[3]

It is difficult for us to do what Confucius believed that we, as ordinary human beings, should do. His knowledge of himself is instructive in this regard:

> There are four things in the Way 道 of the profound person, none of which I have been able to do. To serve my father as I would expect my son to serve me: that I have not been able to do. To serve my ruler as I would expect my ministers to serve me: that I have not been able to do. To serve my elder brother as I would expect my younger brother to serve me: that I have not been able to do. To be the first to treat friends as I would expect them to treat me: that I have not been able to do.[4]

Because of the "five cardinal relationships" 五倫 in the Confucian tradition, we might also add for the present-day Confucian husband that "to serve my wife as I would expect her to serve me: that I have not been able to do." We may take these statements to mean that Confucius humbly admitted that he fell short of his own ideal of a son, a minister, a younger brother, a friend, and, to complete the full Confucian list, a spouse. Yet the underlying reason for Confucius' self-criticism is more subtle. It relates to his perception of what personal knowledge really entails.

A deceptively simple statement in the *Analects* is pertinent here. Confucius once insisted that the right kind of learning — the sort handed down by the ancient sages — was not learning to please others but "learning for

---

[2] *Analects* 7:1; Lau, *Confucius*, 86.

[3] For a general discussion of this issue, see Donald J. Munro, *The Concept of Man in Early China* (Stanford: Stanford University Press, 1969).

[4] *Chung-yung* 中庸 (*Doctrine of the Mean*), chap. 13, sec. 4. See Wing-tsit Chan 陳榮捷, trans. and comp., *A Source Book in Chinese Philosophy* (Princeton: Princeton University Press, 1969), 101.

the sake of one's self".[5] This message is not an individualistic, romantic assertion about one's existential right to be unique. The rights-consciousness prevalent in modern Western culture is alien to the Confucian tradition. By advocating learning for one's own sake, Confucius did not suppose that the human self is an isolated or isolable "individuality". Nor did he even consider that the self is an autonomous entity distinct from and often in conflict with society. Indeed no one in his world and time entertained such an idea. The "individualists" in ancient China were apolitical but not anti-social. Like Confucius, they understood the self as a connecting point for relationships, an inseparable part of a network of human interaction.

In the Confucian perspective the self can never be reduced to a single dimension, for it acts as the focus for a number of relationships; it can never be considered purely a function of one or more forms of human relatedness.[6] Paradoxically, our uniqueness as persons is made possible by the ever-changing landscape of our social interactions. We may not be fully aware of the complexity of the network in which we are socialised to function in daily life, but as long as we continue to broaden our knowledge of ourselves in the context of our social intercourse, we do not lose "the un-wobbling pivot"[7] (*chung-yung* 中庸) that acts as our personal centre. Learning for the sake of oneself is intended to preserve and strengthen that centre.

Confucius' effort to take things at hand – ordinary daily affairs – as the basis for his ethical teaching makes Confucian learning an intrinsically moral activity at whose core is the task of developing a refined knowledge of oneself. As the exemplar Confucius taught by who he was. And he learned in substantially the same way; hence the style of education with which his name is associated is at heart a realisation of personal know-ledge. I will explore the traditional division of this personal learning into its "elementary" and "great" components and then consider the way in which the sage manages both to teach and to exemplify the process.

---

[5] *Analects* 14:25. D. C. Lau translates this statement as follows: "Men of antiquity studied to improve themselves; men today study to impress others." See Lau, *Confucius*, 128. In Lau's translation, this statement is identified as 14:24. For a thought-provoking discussion of this aspect of Confucian education, see Wm. Theodore de Bary, *The Liberal Tradition in China* (Hong Kong: The Chinese University Press; and New York: Columbia University Press, 1983), 21-24.

[6] See Tu Wei-ming 杜維明, "Selfhood and Otherness: Father-Son Relationship in Confucian Thought", in his *Confucian Thought: Selfhood as Creative Transformation* (Albany: State University of New York Press, 1984), 113-30.

[7] Ezra Pound, *Confucius: The Great Digest and the Unwobbling Pivot* (London: Peter Owen, 1952), 97. "The unwobbling pivot" is Pound's translation of the title of the Confucian classic, *Chung-yung*, which is commonly rendered as *The Doctrine of the Mean*.

Education in the classical Confucian sense is learning to be human. It involves an integrated sequence according to which "elementary learning" 小學 is followed by "great learning". "Elementary learning" primarily involves the ritualisation of the body, and "great learning" 大學 entails the sort of self-cultivation that aims at the "embodiment" of all levels of human sensitivity.[8] Both forms of learning focus on developing an increasingly refined self-awareness.

Personal knowledge in this sense can be understood as a strenuous learning process by which we become acquainted with our bodies and minds so that eventually we become true masters of the "house" we inhabit. Confucius' autobiographical observation on this matter is suggestive: "There are presumably men who innovate without possessing knowledge, but this is not a fault I have. I use my ears widely and follow what is good in what I have heard; I use my eyes widely and retain what I have seen in my mind. This constitutes a lower level knowledge."[9] By stressing empirical knowledge as the means by which he learned to be human, Confucius made it explicit that, unlike the legendary sages Yao 堯 and Shun 舜, he was not "born with knowledge".[10] Rather, he struggled hard to acquire the knowledge that eventually made him free and wise: "I followed my heart's desire without overstepping the line."[11] His spontaneity, far from being the result of a sudden enlightenment, was the crowning success of his lifelong attempt at "accumulating righteous acts" (*chi-i* 集義).[12] The message is clear: no one can afford to bypass "elementary learning" if true humanity is to be realised.

Elementary Learning

Confucians have always been aware that the process of learning to be human begins in infancy. For the baby, personal knowledge may simply mean standing steadily for a few moments or walking a few steps without falling down. To learn the art of centring oneself in its more advanced aspects, however, requires repeated practice and often entails the same experience of trial and error that infants must endure. The question in the beginning of

---

[8] See Tu Wei-ming, "Li as Process of Humanization", in his *Humanity and Self-Cultivation: Essays in Confucian Thought* (Berkeley: Asian Humanities Press, 1979), 17–34.

[9] *Analects* 7:28; Lau, *Confucius*, 89.

[10] *Analects* 7:20.

[11] *Analects* 2:4; Lau, *Confucius*, 63.

[12] A technical concept used by Mencius to designate the gradual process of learning to be fully human. See *Mencius* 2A:2.

the *Analects* – "Is it not a pleasure, having learned something, to try it out at due intervals?"[13] – draws attention to this common experience. Humans, like animals, learn many of the basic skills of life this way. In fact, the ideogram representing the Chinese term *hsi* 習 , which was just rendered as "try it out at due intervals", depicts a young bird learning to fly by flapping its wings. The pleasure that one enjoys in perfecting a skill by repeated practice can be seen as much in the radiant smile of an infant who has just negotiated his or her first steps as in the joy of a virtuoso lute player who has mastered a difficult score. The happiness evident in both cases has to do with the sense that what has been learned is not merely something external, something apart from the learner, but a feature of the learner's expanded vocabulary of self-expression. What has been learned is an aspect of the learner's personhood.

The focus of "elementary learning", education for the very young, is to create a healthy environment in which infants can discover their sensitive and responsive bodies. For the very young, every simple act is a significant accomplishment in self-expression and communication. Gentle persuasion and proper encouragement are integral parts of this collaborative enterprise between the infant and the adults around him or her. Such encouragement helps a new member of the human community develop the first inklings of personal knowledge. At the age of six or seven, after a child has learned to speak and seems to be well adjusted in the loving environment of the immediate family, adults may offer some structured guidance, intended to foster a sense of communal participation. In traditional China the child was first asked to perform easy tasks such as answering short questions and sprinkling water on the floor for cleaning. A more elaborate programme of education then followed: instructions in the "six arts" 六藝 of ritual, music, archery, charioteering, calligraphy, and arithmetic. All this was traditionally subsumed under the heading of "elementary learning".

I have noted elsewhere that the "six arts" can be understood as ways of cultivating the body.[14] This training is not merely physical: it includes mental and spiritual disciplines as well. Yet the focus on ritualising bodily behaviour remains. The training represents a concerted effort to transform the body into a fitting expression of the mental and spiritual resources within. The individual aims not only to establish a social identity but also to cultivate a proper disposition. The art of archery, for example, is intended at once

---

[13] *Analects* 1:1; Lau, *Confucius*, 59.

[14] Tu Wei-ming, "The Idea of the Human in Mencian Thought: An Approach to Chinese Aesthetics", in *Theories of the Arts in China*, Susan Bush and Christian Murck, eds. (Princeton: Princeton University Press, 1984), 57–73.

to improve one's skill as an archer and to discipline one's mind so that it is constantly tranquil. Furthermore, archery requires self-examination: the archer who fails to hit the mark must first search for the fault within.[15] The archer tries to produce a finely tuned disposition that informs every gesture of the body. Thus one becomes thoroughly familiar with one's mental states while learning to do the kinds of things archers do. Yet for all this mental discipline, the bodily form remains the basis of the enterprise and is acknowledged as such in traditional Confucian education. The body so conceived is no purely physical entity; it is inseparable from the mind and spirit.

The ritualisation of the body is, therefore, appropriately more in the nature of invitation than command. The young child, far from being the unsuspecting target of a series of rules imposed from without, is bidden to play ritual games that lead to adulthood by enticement rather than by coercion. If the child is not yet ready to play, he or she should not be forced to join in, and since premature ritualisation is detrimental to the moral growth of the child, voluntary participation in the initial stage is both necessary and desirable. In fact, it is best if initially the child enters the ritual situation with a spirit of playfulness. The solemnity of ritual acts is not compromised so long as the child plays at them conscientiously. For example, in the traditional Confucian family, the oldest grandson (often a young boy) was commonly seated in the most exalted place, the one symbolising the deceased ancestors. He would thus receive bows and prostrations from his father, uncles, and even grandfather in the performance of the ancestral cult and would gain some sense of what it is to be the recipient of filial piety. The whole affair constituted an artfully designed, institutionalised effort to bridge the generation gap.

Seemingly minute daily routines are particularly important for training the child to appreciate the intimate involvement of ritual action in the proper behaviour of a maturing person. Tzu-hsia 子夏 critical comment on Tzu-yu's 子游 obvious misunderstanding of the teaching of their master, Confucius, makes this point:

> Tzu-yu said, "The disciples and younger followers of Tzu-hsia can certainly cope with sweeping and cleaning, with responding to calls and replying to questions put to them, and with coming forward and withdrawing, but these are only details. On what is basic they are ignorant. What is one to do with them?"
>
> When Tzu-hsia heard this, he said, "Oh! how Yen Yu 言游 (Tzu-yu's other name) is mistaken! In the way of the profound person, what

---

[15] *Chung-yung*, chap. 14.

is to be taught first and what is to be put last as being less urgent? The former is as clearly distinguishable from the latter as grasses are from trees. It is futile to try to give such a false picture of the way of the profound person. It is, perhaps, the sage alone who, having started something, will always see it through to the end."[16]

Tzu-hsia captures the Confucian spirit well when he reminds his fellow student that simple ritual acts, such as helping one's parents sweep the floor, responding to simple questions, and greeting elders properly, are essential to the process of learning to be human. Strictly speaking, the various aspects of elementary learning are not branches of self-cultivation but its roots. Tzu-hsia's conception of the teacher as one who "having started something, will always see it through to the end" – or, in an alternate translation, as one "who can unite in one the beginning and the consummation of *learning*"[17] – apparently refers to elementary learning in the first instance and to great learning in the second. But more may be involved. Confucius described himself as an untiring teacher and indefatigable student.[18] The Confucian sage may thus be characterised as someone who brings elementary learning to full fruition.

The significance of elementary learning goes beyond the harmonisation of relationships within the family. To Confucius, it serves as the foundation of good government as well. Actually, living the good life in the confines of one's domestic arena is in itself a profoundly meaningful political statement:

> Someone said to Confucius, "Why do you not take part in government?"
> The Master said, "The *Book of History* 書 says, 'Oh! Simply by being a good son and friendly to his brothers a man can exert an influence upon government.' In so doing a man is, in fact, taking part in government. How can there be any question of having actively to 'take part in government'?"[19]

Implicit in elementary learning, then, is the realisation, through practice, of the cherished Confucian affirmation that the ultimate meaning in life can be attained in ordinary human existence. Confucius as an exemplar never performed miracles to impress his followers; in fact, he chose not to speak of such topics as "prodigies, force, disorder and gods".[20] The real magic

---

[16] *Analects* 19:12; Lau, *Confucius*, 154.

[17] James Legge, trans., *Chinese Classics* (Oxford: Clarendon Press, 1883) 1:137.

[18] *Analects* 7:34.

[19] *Analects* 2:21; Lau, *Confucius*, 66.

[20] *Analects* 7:21; Lau, *Confucius*, 88.

is elsewhere: in an unassuming approach to living. Confucius' magnetic power radiated from his deep personal sense of what he really was:

> The Governor of She 葉 asked Tzu-lu 子路 about Confucius. Tzu-lu did not answer.
>
> The Master said, "Why did you not simply say something to this effect: he is the sort of man who is so immersed in his study that he forgets his meals, who is so full of joy that he forgets his worries and who does not notice the onset of old age?"[21]

Understandably, Confucius taught more by deed than by word. The *Analects* in this sense are as much a record of what the Master did as an account of what he said. Confucian personal knowledge is a form of self-understanding acquired through practice.

Great Learning

Once the body has been properly ritualised to serve as an instrument of self-expression and communication, a person is well on the way to becoming a full participant in society. In the Confucian perspective a young person involved in the process of socialisation is not passively trying to adapt himself or herself to the adult world without being aware of the rules of the game. Children do not socialise themselves, and they do not know the mechanism that shapes every dimension of their lives. But they do participate actively in their own socialisation by responding creatively to their elders' invitations. For they know with increasing sophistication that they are vital to the well-being of the community and that the elders share with them a deep concern for their healthy growth. As they learn that they can better enjoy themselves by taking part in an interactive venture with other members of their community, they become aware that being in the company of their elders enables them to discover their own humanity or "co-humanity", in Peter Boodberg's preferred translation of the Confucian term *jen* 仁.[22] As their comprehension grows and they begin to see that what they have been taught and encouraged to do is not merely a game but the sacred mission of personal growth, they may even take an active role in helping adults to realise themselves further. At this time the "great learning" begins, for it presupposes the emergence of a communal self-awareness in the mind of the young adult.

---

[21] *Analects* 7:19; Lau, *Confucius*, 88.

[22] Peter Boodberg, "The Semasiology of Some Primary Confucian Concepts", *Philosophy East and West* 2, no. 4(1953): 317–32.

Confucius' recollection that "at fifteen I set my heart on learning"[23] has been widely cited by later Confucians as a clear sign that the Master was by then ready to embark on his own journey toward becoming a fully realised human being. The transformation from elementary learning to great learning occurs at the point when a young adult assumes responsibility for his or her own education, and in the Confucian tradition rituals marked that passage. Yet no qualitative break separates a child from a young adult who is mature enough to leave childish preoccupations behind. Confucian great learning builds on elementary learning and often harks back to the simple ritual acts that enable a child to earn a niche in society.

Through elementary learning we acquire the personal knowledge necessary for preserving our individual centres as we enter into an ever-enlarging network of human relationships. But it is not enough to do the right thing at the right moment so that we can earn the approval of our elders as we assume responsible roles in society. More than self-preservation is at stake: the more demanding task is to strengthen the centre in such a way that it can respond creatively to continuous change and generate virtuous transformation itself. Thus the purpose of great learning, as specified in the seminal Confucian text called *The Great Learning* 大學 (originally a chapter in the *Book of Rites* 禮記), is threefold: (1) "to enlighten the enlightening virtue" (*ming ming-te* 明明德) – to cultivate our personal knowledge; (2) "to care for the people" (*ch'in-min* 親民) – to help others to realise themselves; and (3) "to dwell in the highest good" (*chih yü chih-shan* 止於至善) – to strive toward moral excellence.[24]

We cannot rely on external factors, whether the support of our elders or the encouragement of society at large, to attain these lofty goals. We need to nourish our internal resources and develop a sense of personal direction. This path involves disciplined, daily practice. In Mencian terms we need to go through the strenuous effort of "accumulating righteous acts"[25] 集義 so that our vital force can be substantially enhanced. Tseng Tzu 曾子 set a well-known example in this regard: "Every day I examine myself on three counts. In what I have undertaken on another's behalf, have I failed to do my best? In my dealings with my friends have I failed to be trustworthy in what I say? Have I passed on to others anything that I have not tried out myself?"[26] Although Tseng Tzu's method of self-examination has been

---

[23] *Analects* 2:4; Lau, *Confucius*, 63.

[24] *Great Learning*, chap. 1. Cf. Chan, *Source Book*, 86.

[25] *Mencius* 2A:2.

[26] *Analects* 1:4; Lau, *Confucius*, 59.

applauded in the Confucian tradition, his regimen was never intended to suit everyone's situation. Instead each person is expected to take an active role in designing his or her own course of self-improvement. One aspect of the process, however, is held to be of universal importance: the deepening and broadening of communal self-awareness. Confucians wholeheartedly subscribe to the dictum that the unreflective life is not worth living.

There is nothing solipsistic or egoistic about such an inquiry. Since the Confucian self is at the centre of a nexus of relationships, not an isolated monad, it inevitably encounters other selves in the course of pursuing its own growth. Confucian self-cultivation does not take the form of searching for one's own inner spirituality in a lonely quest. Rather, it enriches the self by enabling it to participate in a confluence of many life streams. The idea of an isolated individual who hopes to become the recipient of divine inspiration without any reference to the human community is quite alien to the Confucian perception of the self. Hence it is not accidental that Tseng Tzu's queries to himself all strike an interpersonal note. Each reinforces a social conception of personhood.

Nevertheless, Confucians advocate more than what we normally understand to be social ethics. The first goal of the great learning, "to enlighten the enlightening virtue", draws attention not to the social milieu that makes learning fruitful but to the moral equipment that makes it possible. The phrase "to enlighten the enlightening virtue", which Ezra Pound elaborately renders as "clarifying the way wherein the intelligence increases through the process of looking straight into one's own heart and acting on the result"[27] and Wing-tsit Chan translates more straightforwardly as "manifesting the clear character",[28] presupposes that all human beings are endowed with the "enlightening virtue". As personal knowledge develops, it is understood to be a manifestation of this virtue; as such, it does not come from without but is inherent in one's original nature. The personal knowledge that we attain by rigorous practice is but the exposition and elaboration of the "enlightening virtue" that defines who we truly are from the start.

It may seem that we have an inconsistency here: if we are all endowed with "enlightening virtue" to begin with, what do we need to learn to become moral persons? Confucians do not see this as a problem. They believe that the inborn "enlightening virtue" is a precondition for self-cultivation but not the full expression of humanity. In other words, ontologically we are all sages because the "enlightening virtue" inherent in our human nature

---

[27] Pound, *Confucius*, 27.

[28] Chan, *Source Book*, 86.

defines who we truly are, but existentially we must strive to learn what we ought to be by striving to realise fully the potential that has been within us from the beginning. Learning enables us to clarify and manifest this virtue, transforming it from a latent potentiality into an actualised, daily presence. Each person has the possibility of becoming sagelike, but it takes lifelong work to know experientially that this is indeed the case.

That we are always in a position of having to preserve, clarify, manifest, and realise who we are is not in conflict with the Confucian faith in the goodness of human nature. The creative tension between the ontological reality that we are intrinsically sages and the existential fact that we can never become sages defines the human condition in a most vivid way: we are not what we ought to be, as dictated by our moral sense of rightness, but we learn to become what we ought to be by taking as our point of departure what we are here and now. This is possible because we have innate spiritual resources to tap.

Confucius provides, accordingly, both a realistic appraisal of human limitation and an awe-inspiring demonstration of human excellence. There is an intrinsic safeguard against deification in the historicity of Confucius' personality. Mencius' apt characterisation of the Master as the "timely sage"[29] prevents us from extracting Confucius from the moment in which he learned and taught. To be sure, Confucius has been venerated as a god − a god of culture, to be specific − for more than two millennia in China. But in the folk tradition he is honoured more as a moral force than as a mysterious power. The popular image of Confucius as a bearded wise old man who is the foremost teacher of how to live the life of a civilised person is not far off the mark. It suggests a man who has lived through the entire process of human growth, beginning as a humble student and becoming an exemplar of personal knowledge.

The tradition of "great learning" outlines eight steps as belonging to this process. The first five are concerned with the mobilisation of our inner resources for enhancing personal knowledge, and the remainder refer to an outer dimension − concrete appropriations of our self-awareness in the

---

[29] *Mencius* 5B:1. In characterising Confucius as the sage "whose actions were timely", Mencius further remarked: "Confucius was the one who gathered together all that was good. To do this is to open with bells and conclude with jade tubes. [This refers to music.] To open with bells is to begin in an orderly fashion; to conclude with jade tubes is to end in an orderly fashion. To begin in an orderly fashion is the concern of the wise while to end in an orderly fashion is the concern of a sage. Wisdom is like skill, shall I say, while sageness is like strength. It is like shooting from beyond a hundred paces. It is due to your strength that the arrow reaches the target, but it is not due to your strength that it hits the mark." It seems obvious that, to Mencius, Confucius' timeliness symbolizes the confluence of many temporal features that cannot be imitated as a static model. See D. C. Lau, trans., *Mencius* (Harmondsworth, England: Penguin Books, 1970), 150-51.

service of society. The eight-part sequence is as follows: (1) investigation of things (*ke-wu* 格物), (2) extension of knowledge (*chih-chih* 致知), (3) authentication of the will (*ch'eng-i* 誠意), (4) rectification of the mind (*cheng-hsin* 正心), (5) cultivation of the personal life (*hsiu-shen* 修身), (6) regulation of family (*ch'i-chia* 齊家), (7) governance of the state (*chih-kuo* 治國), and (8) peace making throughout the world (*p'ing t'ien-hsia* 平天下).[30] As the *Great Learning* shows, the whole structure pivots on the fifth step, the cultivation of the personal life: "From the Son of Heaven down to the common people, all must regard cultivation of the personal life as the root. There is never a case when the root is in disorder and yet the branches are in order."[31]

The centrality of self-cultivation, however, is predicated on the conception of the self as an open system, forever learning from the external world by extending its sensitivity to an ever-enlarging network of interconnections. The "investigation of things" in this sense should not be construed as a disinterested study of external facts by an outside observer. Rather, it signifies a form of knowing in which the knower is not only informed but also transformed by the known. To "investigate things" is to inquire into natural phenomena and human affairs for the sake of understanding both the world around us and ourselves.

When we inquire into natural phenomena and human affairs as inside participants as well as outside observers, we "embody" in our sensitivity those aspects of nature and the world that have touched our hearts and minds. But even the cultivation of "enlightening virtue" involves, as Mencius insisted, a mutual nourishment between the internal and the external.[32] The investigation of things in nature and the world adds to our information about the external, but it is the purification of the internal — the authentication of the will and the rectification of the mind — that enables us to be transformed by what we have come to know. Here, Confucius stands as the great exemplar.

Exemplary Teaching

In the "personalist" interpretation of the Confucian approach to education that I have advanced so far, I have stressed the centrality of acquiring personal knowledge as a motive force for moral growth. I have also emphasised

---

[30] *Great Learning*, chap. 1; Chan, *Source Book*, 86–87.

[31] Chan, *Source Book*, 87.

[32] *Mencius* 2A:2.

that self-cultivation is not a private matter. Given the Confucian perception of the self as a focal point for multiple relationships, the quest for one's own personal knowledge must be understood as an act of service to the community as well: "A humane person, wishing to establish his [or her] character, also establishes the characters of others and wishing to enlarge himself [or herself], also helps others to enlarge themselves. To be able to take the analogy near at hand [for understanding others] may be called the method of realising humanity."[33] By the same token the Confucian view of the self necessarily casts the task of self-cultivation in social terms. Learning is a collaborative enterprise and is all-encompassing. We learn not only from our tutors and other elders but from our friends, colleagues, students, children, and acquaintances, and from people on the street. The famous statement about teachers in the *Analects* is relevant here: "The Master said, 'Even when walking in the company of two others, I am bound to be able to learn from them. The good points of the one I copy; the bad points of the other I correct in myself.'"[34]

Since we learn from both positive and negative examples, every human being is potentially our teacher. But how does such teaching transpire? Since the Confucian tradition regards teaching, like learning, as an embodying act, the teaching will have to be undertaken by the whole person; all levels of the self — body, mind, soul, and spirit — will be involved. Personal exemplification is the most authentic and therefore the most effective pedagogy. The Way must be lived — and lived well — to be truly efficacious, and good teachers embody the form of life they advocate. Confucian thinkers have always known that although logical rigour and rhetorical ingenuity may dazzle the mind, only teaching that has the force of personal example can touch the heart, purify the soul, and elevate the spirit. Every aspect of the ritualisation of the body is the result of exemplary teaching. We learn to stand up, sit down, walk, and speak by emulating models around us. And self-cultivation at the higher levels requires the presence of examples in no less measure.

When it comes to the highest learning of all, the learning of virtue per se, the best teacher to model ourselves after is one who perceives himself or herself not strictly as a teacher but also as a learner. This makes it possible for a pupil not only to bear the teacher's stamp, in a relationship of complementarity, but ultimately also to establish a sympathetic resonance with the teacher's whole being — from within, as it were. Again Confucius

---

[33] *Analects* 6:30.

[34] *Analects* 7:22; Lau, *Confucius*, 88.

himself serves as the best model in this regard. His estimate of what he was about has come to be a classic statement of the mentality all teachers should cultivate: "How dare I claim to be a sage or a man of humanity? It might be said of me, that I learn without flagging and teach without growing weary."[35]

As expected, Confucius' disciples responded to the Master's sober humility not with relief at the sense that their own shortcomings could thereby be excused but with a heightened apprehension of how much they had to learn and how difficult it was to do so. Yen Hui 顏回, Confucius' best student, may serve as an example:

> Yen Yuan 顏淵 [Yen Hui], heaving a sigh, said "The more I look up
> at it the higher it appears. The more I bore into it the harder it becomes.
> I see it before me. Suddenly it is behind me. The Master is good
> at leading one on step by step. He broadens me with culture and
> brings me back to essentials by means of the rites. I cannot give up
> if I wanted to, but, having done all I can, it [the way of Confucius]
> seems to rise sheer above me and I have no way of going after it,
> however much I may want to."[36]

Equally telling is the response of another student of Confucius. On hearing the Master's humble words that he did not dare to claim sagehood and that he defined himself as an unflagging learner and a tireless teacher, Kung-hsi Hua 公西華 said, "This is precisely where we disciples are unable to learn from you."[37] Confucius compelled his students to draw the conclusion that learning could not ultimately be a matter of imitation. Acts of virtue might be imitated, but the spirit that made such acts truly virtuous required a personal commitment beyond imitation. It had to be directed not only without but within. Yet the inimitability of the Master could never be an excuse for laziness in the cultivation of virtue:

> Jan Ch'iu 冉求 said, "It is not that I am not pleased with your way,
> but rather that my strength gives out." The Master said, "A man
> whose strength gives out collapses along the course. In your case
> you set the limits beforehand."[38]

Confucius certainly did not "set the limits beforehand", but he fully acknowledged his inability to attain sagehood. In this peculiar way he was

---

[35] *Analects* 7:34; Lau, *Confucius*, 90.

[36] *Analects* 9:11; Lau, *Confucius*, 97.

[37] *Analects* 7:34; Lau, *Confucius*, 90–91.

[38] *Analects* 6:12; Lau, *Confucius*, 82–83.

a sage to his followers but not to himself, and for that reason he became the exemplar of sagehood. As a sage he was, said Mencius, "the first to possess what is common in our minds",[39] for the sage is the one among us who has fully realised the same "enlightening virtue" that is inherent in the nature of each of us. Mencius further observed: "Our body and complexion are given to us by Heaven. Only a sage can give his body complete fulfillment."[40]

Yet by his own admission the paradigmatic sage, Confucius, fell short of this ideal. He perceived himself as a person who was still on the way to "giv[ing] his body complete fulfillment". Thus Confucius, the sage, serves as an exemplary teacher of humanity, not only because of the extraordinary accomplishments that establish a distance between him and the rest of us but because of the aspects of his humanity that bring him near us and make him accessible. The sage, like us, practises the ordinary virtues. When he eats, he observes the same basic etiquette that the rest of us do. Yet there is a difference. While we eat to gratify our need for food or to satisfy our culinary desires, the sage knows the "taste" of eating in a fuller sense: he is able to appreciate the moral and aesthetic force inherent in the simple rituals that regulate the taking of food in a human setting.[41] The sage lives more sensibly, more intensely, more self-consciously than the rest of us; he lives with more feeling. His "allotment" (*fen* 分) or "fate" (*ming* 命) is something that defines him. It makes him, like us, a circumscribed historical being. It is impossible for us to imitate him, yet the personal knowledge that he displays can serve as a source of inspiration for all. Each of us can strive to adapt it to our own situation and thus come close to what sagehood would mean for us.

The Confucian sage attains the highest moral excellence without losing sight of the humanity that unites him with all other members of society. His greatness lies in his effort to transform himself from an ordinary mortal into something awesome: a good, true, beautiful, great, sagely, even spiritual (divine) being.[42] But he is enabled to do this not by abrogating the roles incumbent upon him as a person in the presence of others but by fulfilling his obligations and responsibilities as a member of the human community.

---

[39] *Mencius* 6A:7.

[40] *Mencius* 7A:38; Lau, *Mencius*, 191.

[41] See Tu Wei-ming, *Centrality and Commonality: An Essay on Chung-yung* (Honolulu: University Press of Hawaii, 1976), 30–34.

[42] *Mencius* 7B:25. See Tu Wei-ming, "On the Mencian Perception of Moral Self-Development", in his *Humanity and Self-Cultivation*, 57–68.

Similarly, he earns the respect of his fellow human beings as the "foremost teacher" because he never ceases to be a dedicated student. He devotes himself to elementary learning and great learning in order to practice the art of living and never tires of cultivating the virtue that ultimately makes human beings human.

4

Pain and Suffering in Confucian Self-cultivation

The Confucian belief in the perfectibility of human nature is predicated on the assumption that learning to be human involves a lifelong commitment to and a continuous process of self-education. Self-realisation does not refer to an idealised state of being perfect but to the result of concrete steps by which one is repeatedly renewed and invigorated. To realise the primacy of the self as a conscious, reflective, and ceaselessly transformative being is a precondition for understanding the Confucian idea of human perfectibility. The common impression that the Confucians, dictated by a kind of Pelagian assertion that human nature is good, are naively optimistic about the possibility of moral self-transcendence only scratches the surface of the Confucian project. To be sure, the Confucians are intensely interested in what human beings are existentially. A distinctive feature of Confucian humanism is its adoption as the point of departure in any moral reasoning of what we are here and now in our everyday existence. But the Confucian belief in the perfectibility of human nature is basically a hope for what we can really become and a faith in what we originally are – in our prelapsarian state, as it were.

Mencius' theory of the goodness of human nature is not at all intended to convey a sense of human complacency vis-à-vis other members in the animal kingdom. The main purpose of his argument, as I have tried to demonstrate elsewhere, is to provide an ontological basis for self-cultivation.[1] In the Mencian perspective, the uniqueness of being human is as much a responsibility as a privilege. His argument for the goodness of human

---

[1] Tu Wei-ming 杜維明, "On the Mencian Perception of Moral Self-Development", *The Monist* 61, no. 1 (January 1978): 72–81.

nature is thus a corollary of his insistence on autonomous morality. He insists that all human beings are endowed with the possibility of developing themselves as moral persons through the cognitive and affective functions of the mind. He never suggests that the moral propensity inherent in our nature is all that is needed for us, as moral agents, to realise our goodness fully. The message that Mencius delivers is not naive moral optimism but the necessity and urgency of performing, with absolute seriousness, the task of learning to be human. He observes that pain and suffering are often constitutive elements in the existential conditions for human greatness. Having mentioned several notable historical cases where men of awe-inspiring stature rose from extremely difficult circumstances, Mencius comments, "That is why Heaven 天, when it is about to place a great burden on a man, always first tests his resolution, exhausts his frame and makes him suffer starvation and hardship, frustrates his efforts so as to shake him from his mental lassitude, toughens his nature and makes good his deficiencies."[2]

That a selected few have become cultural heroes as a result of their triumph over extraordinary trials and ordeals is certainly not peculiar to the Confucian tradition. It is noteworthy, however, that the Mencian idea of the heavenly burden, presumably the counterpart of God's calling, is basically a manifestation of human self-consciousness, even though a transcendent reference is implied. To put it simply, those who have succeeded in overcoming extreme odds have done so not because of divine intervention but because of their strong moral fabric. They learned the art of self-transcendence through physical and mental discipline, for their heightened self-awareness has enabled them to bear the heavenly burden as a categorical imperative. It was a sense of duty to their human nature rather than a submission to an external will that impelled them to endure the pain and suffering that they obviously did not deserve.

Mencius perceives an underlying pattern among seemingly unconnected historical events: Shun 舜 rose from the fields; Fu Yüeh 傅說 was raised to office from among the builders; Chiao Ke 膠鬲 amid the fish and salt; Kuan Chung 管仲 from the hands of the prison officer; Sun Shu-ao 孫叔敖 from the sea; and Po-li Hsi 百里奚 from the market.[3] What do these stories tell us: that an Eastern barbarian rose from the wilderness to become a sage-king;[4] a construction worker was eventually appointed prime minister;

---

[2] *Mencius* 6B:15. For this translation, see D. C. Lau 劉殿爵, trans., *Mencius* (Middlesex, England: Penguin Classics, 1970), 181.

[3] Ibid.

[4] *Mencius* 4B:1.

an ex-convict earned the respect of Confucius as a protector of Chinese culture,[5] and so forth? On the surface, Mencius seems to suggest that the reason that heaven placed a great burden on each of them is that they had already been chosen to perform the divine tasks. This interpretation, however, is quite foreign to the Mencian intention. For one thing, the idea of a wilful heaven deliberately choosing its own messengers to do things according to a preconceived design does not feature at all prominently in the Confucian tradition. The lesson that Mencius draws from these anecdotes is straightforward: "As a rule, a man can mend his ways only after he has made mistakes. It is only when a man is frustrated in mind and in his deliberations that he is able to innovate. It is only when his intentions become visible on his countenance and audible in his tone of voice that others can understand him."[6] Thus, Mencius concludes, "Only then do we learn the lesson that we survive in adversity and perish in ease and comfort."[7]

Yet the underlying pattern that Mencius perceives suggests a far more complex lesson than simply moralising about the value of endurance. What is the relevance of the great burden that heaven is supposed to have placed on Shun, Fu Yüeh, Chiao Ke, and others to us as ordinary human beings? If they were not chosen by heaven to perform divine tasks, how did they become so extraordinary that they appear to us mortals as superhumans? Before we attempt to answer these questions, Tseng Tzu's 曾子 characterisation of the true Confucian scholar, or, if you will, the knight of the Way, can provide a background understanding for Mencius' idea of the great burden. In the *Analects*, Tseng Tzu is said to have remarked that a true Confucian scholar "must be strong and resolute, for his burden is heavy and the road is long."[8] The reason for this, one may surmise, is that the knight of the Way has been summoned by heaven to perform a divine task on earth. However, we have already noted that the Confucian sense of mission is not predicated on a wilful heaven and that the idea of the chosen is alien to the Confucian mode of thought. Strictly speaking, the burden is not an external command but an internally motivated sense of duty. Tseng Tzu makes this rather explicit: "He takes humanity as his burden. Is that not heavy? Only with death does the road come to an end. Is that not long?"[9]

---

[5] *Analects* 14:17.

[6] *Mencius* 6B:15.

[7] Ibid.

[8] *Analects* 8:7.

[9] Ibid.

What Tseng Tzu envisions is the long and strenuous process of realising one's own humanity. Since humanity, in the Confucian perspective, can never be the private possession of a single individual, self-realisation entails the task of bearing witness to the dimension of humanity that is communal and, in the ultimate sense, transcendent. The burden for the true Confucian scholar, then, is to learn to be fully human in such profundity and breadth that the Way itself can, as a result, be enlarged.[10]

Accordingly, the burden that heaven is supposed to have placed on the great cultural heroes is the same burden that those of us who aspire to be knights of the Way must shoulder. The reason that they appear to us to be superhumans is not because of divine intervention but because they, as witnesses of the highest excellence of humanity, have borne the burden for us all with the utmost of their strength. This partly explains why Mencius' insistence on the possibility of understanding heaven through a deep knowledge of human nature and the full realisation of the human mind[11] does not lead to the romantic assertion that human perfection involves only the spontaneous manifestation of inner spirituality, with no suffering and no pain.

Mencius unequivocally maintains that "all things are already complete in oneself. There is no greater joy than to realise that one is sincere upon self-examination",[12] but this bliss is an attainment rather than a state of nature. Actually, it requires "vigorous exercise" to bring it into being.[13] Mencius perceives the human condition, then, as a paradox: ontologically we are irreducibly human, and existentially we must struggle to remain human. What Mencius diagnoses as the predicament of his time seems to have become a perennial phenomenon: "Humanity subdues inhumanity as water subdues fire. Nowadays those who practise humanity do so as if with one cup of water they could save a whole wagonload of fuel on fire. When the flames were not extinguished, they would say that water cannot subdue fire. This is as bad as those who are inhumane. At the end they will surely lose [what little humanity they have]."[14]

So long as we fail to enlarge our humanity until it can overcome the dehumanising tendencies in our society, our once-powerful humanness becomes

[10] Ibid., 15:29.

[11] *Mencius* 7A:1.

[12] Ibid. 7A:4.

[13] Ibid.

[14] Ibid. 6A:18. For this translation, see Wing-tsit Chan 陳榮捷, trans. and comp., *A Source Book in Chinese Philosophy* (Princeton, N.J.: Princeton University Press, 1969), 60.

inoperative as a deterrent against "evil". We may, in our desperation, conclude that there is something basically wrong with our heaven-endowed nature or that our inner strength is essentially deficient to meet the challenge of inhumanity. But, as Mencius maintains, this is a misconception, for intrinsically there is nothing wrong with the premise that we are originally good and that we can become good through self-effort. It is beyond question that humanity subdues inhumanity, just as water conquers fire. Yet given the miserable state we are in, a great deal of humanity is needed individually and communally to turn the situation around. We cannot assume that our inherent capacity to realise our human nature automatically puts us on the right track. If we really want to save a whole wagonload of burning fuel (or our whole world from being incinerated), we have no other long-term recourse but to educate ourselves to increase our supply of humanity.

I have elsewhere discussed the issue of *akrasia*, or weakness of the will, in Mencian thought.[15] In terms of *akrasia*, the main concern is to overcome limitation and inertia so that one's moral development will not be constrained by the desire for short-term gratification, false consciousness, or undesirable habitual forms. The problem we are confronted with here is more fundamental. Mencius condemns those who would say that water cannot subdue fire because it did not extinguish the flames in front of them. Indeed, how can we expect anyone to believe that humanity will prevail when we know that it is often latent and sometimes totally lost? Even though it can be proved empirically that water puts out fire, if there is a constant short supply of water, the danger of being engulfed by fire becomes a reality.

Aware of this human predicament, Mencius proposes that we locate the source of our self-transcendence in sensitivity and feeling. Specifically, he proposes that we underscore our inability to bear the sight of human misery.[16] Mencius considers a sympathetic heart a defining characteristic of humanity. A corollary of this humane response to the suffering of others is the willingness to sacrifice oneself − the root of altruism. Very few of us are capable of living up to the high altruistic standards that our martyrs, saints, and heroes have set up. We may even feel that the burdens laid on the shoulders of poor humanity have already reached a level that is unbearable. But Mencius does not recommend martyrdom, sainthood, or heroism. He simply suggests that we take our sympathetic heart seriously and work gradually and unhurriedly to develop it. This may not get us very far, but it signifies a

---

[15] Tu Wei-ming, *"Akrasia* and Mencius' Philosophy of Self-Cultivation" (paper presented in the Section on Oriental Philosophy, Seventeenth World Congress of Philosophy; Montreal, Canada, August 1983).

[16] *Mencius* 2A:6.

beginning, a turning point. Mencius' advice to King Hsüan 宣 of Ch'i 齊 is pertinent here. The king's experience as reported to Mencius by his minister Hu He 胡亥 is as follows:

> The King was sitting in the upper part of the hall and someone led an ox through the lower part. The King noticed this and said, "Where is the ox going?" "The blood of the ox is to be used for consecrating a new bell." "Spare it. I cannot bear to see it shrinking with fear, like an innocent man going to the place of execution." "In that case, should the ceremony be abandoned?" "That is out of the question. Use a lamb instead."[17]

After a series of dialogues with the king on this, Mencius remarks:

> In other words, all you have to do is take this very heart here and apply it to what is over there. Hence one who extends his bounty can bring peace to the Four Seas; one who does not cannot bring peace even to his own family. There is just one thing in which the ancients greatly surpassed others, and that is the way they extended what they did. Why is it then that your bounty is sufficient to reach animals yet the benefits of your government fail to reach the people?[18]

The analogical method implicit in Mencius' advice to the king involves a twofold procedure: to deepen the source of supply of "this heart here" and to broaden the scope of its application to what is "over there". We may never reach the depth and breadth of sage-kings who suffered so intensely at the sight of human misery that they would assume personal responsibility for any sign of starvation or calamity.[19] They became guardians of humanity because they had extended to the utmost the heart that cannot bear to see the suffering of others. Essentially, their actions provided an expression of human sensitivity. In defining the sage as "simply the man first to discover this common element in my heart", Mencius points to "reason and rightness" (*i-li* 義理) as the common element.[20] But his theory of the "four germs" (*ssu-tuan* 四端) clearly shows that human sensitivity in the form of sympathy is even more fundamental to his perception of human nature:

---

[17] Ibid. 1A:7; Lau, *Mencius*, 54–55.

[18] *Mencius* 1A:7; Lau, *Mencius*, 57.

[19] In *Mencius* 4B:29, we find the following statement: "Yü 禹 looked upon himself as responsible for anyone in the Empire who drowned; Chi 稷 looked upon himself as responsible for anyone in the Empire who starved." (Lau, *Mencius*, 134–35).

[20] *Mencius* 6A:7.

"No man is devoid of a heart sensitive to the suffering of others."[21] What the sage-kings fully realised is commonly available to us all because we are all members of the human community: "For every man there are things he cannot bear. To extend this to what he can bear is humanity. For every man there are things he is not willing to do. To extend this to what he is willing to do is rightness. If a man can extend to the full his natural aversion to harming others, then there will be an overabundance of humanity."[22]

If, however, we are insensitised to the extent that we learn to bear the things that we normally cannot bear, there will be an overabundance of inhumanity. The category of inhumanity, in this connection, is derived from that of humanity. Although inhumanity, like evil, does not have an ontological status, it can be pervasive in our lives so long as we fail to realise the humanity in us or to realise our humanity fully.

The Confucian thinkers of the Sung–Ming 宋明 periods (eleventh to seventeenth centuries) took for granted Mencius' classical formulation of the human condition as a paradox. Although they enthusiastically believed in the perfectibility of human nature, they were aware of the inertia and limitation that every conscientious person encounters in moral self-development. The philosophical anthropology that the Neo-Confucian thinkers envisaged is not what Max Weber characterises in his *Religion of China* as "adjustment to the world".[23] The Weberian interpretation of the typical Confucian literatus as "a well adjusted man, rationalising his conduct only to the degree requisite for adjustment" is a striking example of what Confucius condemned as the "enemy of virtue", the *hsiang-yüan* 鄉原 (the hyper-honest villager) who perfunctorily follows the mores of his time and superficially pleases those apt to maintain the status quo.[24] The Confucian idea of *chün-tzu* 君子 (the profound person) is just the opposite.

Ch'eng I 程頤 (1033–1107) set forth the Confucian *Problematik*, an existential choice between life as a continuous quest for ultimate self-transformation and life as an unreflective and seemingly painless adjustment to the world of desires, in his treatise "What Yen Tzu 顏子 Loved to Learn":

> From the essence of life accumulated in Heaven and Earth, man receives the Five Agents ... in their highest excellence. His original nature

[21] Ibid. 2A:6.

[22] Ibid.

[23] Max Weber, *The Religion of China: Confucianism and Taoism*, trans. Hans H. Gerth (Glencoe, Ill.: Free Press, 1951), 235.

[24] *Analects* 17:11.

is pure and tranquil. Before it is aroused, the five moral principles of his nature, called humanity, righteousness, propriety, wisdom, and faithfulness, are complete. As his physical form appears, it comes into contact with external things and is aroused from within. As it is aroused from within, the seven feelings, called pleasure, anger, sorrow, joy, love, hate, and desire, ensue. As feelings become strong and increasingly reckless, his nature becomes damaged. For this reason the enlightened person controls his feelings so that they will be in accord with the Mean. He rectifies his mind and nourishes his nature. This is therefore called turning the feelings into the [original] nature. The stupid person does not know how to control them. He lets them loose until they are depraved, fetter his nature, and destroy it. This is therefore called turning one's nature into feelings.[25]

The *hsiang-yüan* experiences no pain or suffering; nor is he capable of any real praxis. He is not only in the world but of the world. He is part of the given; there is virtually no transformative potential in his *modus operandi*. A distinctive feature of the *hsiang-yüan* is his deliberate attempt to follow the course of least resistance for the sake of adjustment: "Being in this world, one must behave in a manner pleasing to this world. So long as one is good, it is all right."[26] There is something basically spurious in his cringing attempts to please the world. Mencius explains why Confucius considered such a man an enemy of virtue: "If you want to censure him, you cannot find anything; if you want to find fault with him, you cannot find anything either. He shares with others the practices of the day and is in harmony with the sordid world. He pursues such a policy and appears to be conscientious and faithful, and to show integrity in his conduct. He is liked by the multitude and is self-righteous. It is impossible to embark on the way of Yao 堯 and Shun 舜 with such a man."[27]

The *chün-tzu*, on the other hand, has inner strength for character building. He is dedicated to learning for the sake of himself, the self not as an isolated individual but as a witness of the highest aspirations of the human community. His purpose in life is to become a "knight of the Way", the person who has "taken humanity to be his burden" and has resolved that "only with death does his course [of realising fully the human potential for altruism] end". As the "knight of the Way", the *chün-tzu* intends to reshape the world, to fashion it according to a holistic vision. His learning for the sake of himself is not only contemplation but also action.

[25] Chan, *Source Book*, 547–48.

[26] *Mencius* 7B:37; Lau, *Mencius*, 203.

[27] Ibid.

The action of the *chün-tzu* is not an unintended consequence of a spiritual project oriented toward the transcendent. Rather, it grows inevitably from the deepening and broadening process of ultimate self-transformation as a communal act. Mencius takes it as a matter of fact that "whenever the *chün-tzu* passes through, transforming influence follows; whenever he abides, spiritual influence remains".[28] The social and political efficaciousness of the *chün-tzu* lies in moral persuasion. And since moral persuasion, unlike coercion, depends on voluntary participation, there is no guarantee that it will work quickly to bring order and harmony. In the Confucian perception, however, the real power of the *chün-tzu* comes from a much more profound source of authority than that of the socially accepted ethical norms. According to Mencius, the reason that the presence of the *chün-tzu* is "no small help" to the human community is that his influence "forms the same current above and below with that of heaven and earth".[29] Although the exemplary teaching of the *chün-tzu* is directed to the experienced world around us, its ultimate justification has a transcendent dimension. The *chün-tzu*'s ability to transform the world creatively through personal realisation is predicated not only on his moral rectitude but also on his spiritual resonance with the cosmic transformation of heaven and earth. The moral community that the *chün-tzu* creates in the world is therefore a microcosm of the dynamic universe.

The action of the *chün-tzu*, so conceived, expresses the idea of the human as a co-creator of the universe. As a co-creator, the paradigmatic human is an initiator, a participant, and a guardian of the universe. Since the universe consists of vital forces (or *ch'i* 氣 as energy fields) rather than static matter, it never ceases to be transformative. To model ourselves on the dynamism of heaven and earth, as the *Book of Change* 易經 instructs, we humans ought to engage in "self-strengthening without interruption" (*tzu ch'iang pu-hsi* 自強不息).[30] Implicit in this anthropocosmic outlook is the ability of the human mind-and-heart (*hsin* 心) to relate empathetically to all modalities of being in the universe. Self-cultivation, in this connection, involves a conscientious attempt to open oneself up to the universe as a whole by extending one's horizon of feeling as well as knowing. The more one knows, in the sense of being enlightened about external things, the more one is sensitised to relate meaningfully to the world outside. The idea of regarding

---

[28] *Mencius* 7A:13.

[29] Ibid. 7A:13.

[30] *A Concordance to Yi Ching* 易經, Harvard-Yenching Institute Sinological Index Series, Supplement no. 10 (reprint; Taipei: Chinese Materials and Research Aids Service Center, 1966), 1/1.

heaven and earth and the myriad things as one body is thus a realisable universal experience rather than an abstract concept. To Wang Yang-ming 王陽明 (1472–1529), the purpose of the *Great Learning* 大學 is to underscore the humanity that is inherent in our minds and hearts and forms one body with all beings.[31]

Yang-ming articulates his thesis by stressing the human ability to respond sympathetically to the pains and sufferings of others. We become sensitive and responsible participants of the human community because of our feeling of commiseration. By analogy, we become fellow members of the animal kingdom because of our "inability to bear the pitiful cries and frightened appearance of birds and animals about to be slaughtered";[32] we become part of the living world because of a feeling of pity for the destruction of forest and vegetation; and we become organismically harmonised with the whole ecological system because of a feeling of regret when we see "tiles and stones shattered and crushed".[33]

The embodiment of heaven and earth and the myriad things in one's sensitivity as a defining characteristic of human nature is a shared assumption of the Neo-Confucian thinkers. The person who can heartlessly bear the pain and suffering of those around him is seriously deficient not only in sensitivity but in basic humanity. Ch'eng Hao 程顥 (1032–85) uses the medical description of paralysis of the four limbs as "absence of humanity" (*pu-jen* 不仁) to illustrate this point: "The man of *jen* [humanity] regards Heaven and Earth and all things as one body. To him there is nothing that is not himself. Since he has recognised all things as himself, can there be any limit to his humanity? If things are not parts of the self, naturally they have nothing to do with it. As in the case of paralysis of the four limbs, the vital force no longer penetrates them, and therefore they are no longer parts of the self."[34]

The inability of the paralysed limbs to feel pain clearly shows that, in terms of sensitivity, they are no longer part of the body. By analogy, the inability of the mind-and-heart to feel the suffering of others indicates that its capacity to embody others in its sensitivity has been paralysed. Inhumanity, in this particular sense, means that one has lost the ability to feel pain. Since human beings are defined as the most sentient of all beings, "the mind

---

[31] Wing-tsit Chan, trans. *Instructions for Practical Living and Other Neo-Confucian Writings by Wang Yang-ming* (New York: Columbia University Press, 1963), 269–80.

[32] Ibid., 272.

[33] Ibid.

[34] Chan, *Source Book*, 530.

which cannot bear to see the suffering of others" is universally human. Strictly speaking, commiseration is not something we are supposed to have; it characterises what we are. The experience of pain and suffering not only heightens our sensitivity but also reminds us of our humanness.

To the Neo-Confucians, pain is not "sterilised or disinfected evil";[35] nor is it God's shouting.[36] Rather, it is inherent in the psychophysiological stuff that makes humans the sentient beings par excellence. It is human to feel pain and the experience of pain authenticates our humanity. Through pain and suffering, we form one body with our fellow human beings, with other animals, with trees and plants, and with stones and tiles. The person who has lost the sensation of pain or itch is no longer human, as a Chinese proverb observes. Pain and suffering are necessary for us to know experientially that we are alive and well.

Self-cultivation begins with an awareness that learning to be fully human involves pain and suffering. The vigorous exercise that is required for realising the great joy of inner peace ("knowing that one is sincere upon self-examination") is strenuous. The four words that Chu Hsi 朱熹 (1130–1200) employed to encourage his students shortly before he died, *chien-k'u kung-fu* 堅苦功夫 (the hard and painful effort), capture well the spirit of a lifelong commitment to and a continuous process of self-education.[37]

Wang Yang-ming knew how painful it was to follow the dictates of his conscience in order to lead the life of an upright scholar-official. His belief in the unity of all things was neither a romantic assertion nor a utopian idea. On the contrary, it was a hard-earned resolution: by "a hundred deaths and a thousand hardships",[38] he came to the realisation that the Mencian idea that "all the ten thousand things are there in me" is an experienced universal reality rather than a subjectivistic conjecture. What he advocated was no armchair philosophy. His "enlightenment" occurred after he had been flogged and banished by a despot for a political protest. He suffered

---

[35] C. S. Lewis, *The Problem of Pain* (London: Centenary Press, 1941), 104–5.

[36] C. S. Lewis's complete statement reads: "God whispers to us in our pleasures, speaks in our conscience, but shouts in our pains" (ibid., 81). See also Tu Wei-ming, "A Religiophilosophical Perspective on Pain", in H. W. Kosterlitz and L. Y. Terenius, eds. *Pain and Society* (Weinheim: Verlag Chemie, 1980), 63–78.

[37] Wang Mao-hung 王懋竑, *Chu Tzu nien-p'u* 朱子年譜 (Chronological biography of Master Chu; reprint; Taipei: Commercial Press, 1979); *Ssu-k'u ch'üan-shu chen-pen* 四庫全書珍本 (The rare edition of the Complete works of the Four Treasures) 4:51b.

[38] *Yang-ming ch'üan-shu* 陽明全書 (Complete works of Yang-ming), *Ssu-pu pei-yao* 四部備要 edition (reprint; Taipei: Chung-hua 中華 Book Company, 1970) 33:17b.

great mental and physical pain.[39] His agony could have toughened his soul, but he did not become hard-hearted. Like other Neo-Confucian thinkers, Yang-ming experienced pain and suffering firsthand. His resolution was tested time and again; his body was often exhausted, and he was made to suffer starvation and hardship. As a result, his nature was strengthened and his deficiencies overcome so that he could bear witness to his faith in human perfectibility through self-effort. He philosophised about the import of pain and suffering for forming one body with heaven and earth and the myriad things because he had embodied it in his quest for ultimate self-transformation.

[39] Tu Wei-ming, *Neo-Confucian Thought in Action: Wang Yang-ming's Youth (1472-1509)* (Berkeley and Los Angeles: University of California Press, 1976), 95–118.

5

Towards an Understanding of Liu Yin's Confucian Eremitism

I n a paraphrase of a delightful image in Plato's *Republic*, Thomas More explains in the *Utopia* "why a sensible person is right to steer clear of politics": "He sees everyone else rushing into the street and getting soaked in the pouring rain. He can't persuade them to go indoors and keep dry. He knows if he went out too, he'd merely get equally wet. So he just stays indoors himself, and, as he can't do anything about other people's stupidity, comforts himself with the thought: 'Well, I'm all right, anyway'."[1]

On the surface, this seems to have been the main reason, according to general historical accounts at least, why Liu Yin 劉因 (Ching-hsiu 靜修) (1249–93) repeatedly resisted pressure to take office under Mongol rule. Like the sensible Raphael, who, having come across a mixture of conceit, stupidity, and stubbornness in the leadership of sixteenth-century Europe, refused to become a member of any privy council,[2] Liu found the world of politics in his lifetime too harsh and humiliating to merit his service. Liu's repeated defiance of the summons of the Yüan court may have been significantly different from Raphael's philosophical aloofness. But it seems that they both cherished a sense of personal integrity and were determined to retain their purity as thinkers and scholars.

However, Raphael, the student of philosophy who tried to open people's eyes to the causes of social evils, was by and large a generic type created by More to occasion the discussion of a world that was "no place" (Utopia). By contrast, Liu Yin, one of the two most highly regarded Confucian masters

---

[1] Thomas More, *Utopia*, trans. Paul Turner (Middlesex, England: Penguin Books, 1975), 65. It is evident that, as Turner notes, "More's simile is a very free paraphrase of *Republic* 6:496d–e", see ibid., 140 n. 41.

[2] Ibid., 57–63.

of Khubilai's reign,[3] was a historical figure with all the specificities of birth, education, and vocation. Although our knowledge of his life history is extremely scanty, we have a twelve-*chüan* 卷 collection of his writings and some supporting information from contemporary official documents and miscellaneous notes.[4] We learn that Liu was born into a scholar-official family of Jung-ch'eng 容城 in Pao-ting 保定 (modern Hopei 河北). For generations, the family had been known for its Confucian studies and distinguished government services. As Sun K'o-k'uan 孫克寬 notes in his informative study of Yüan Confucianism, the Liu clan can be characterised as a "gentry family" (*shih-chu* 士族) of the Jurchen Chin 金 dynasty (1115–1234).[5] Yin's grandfather (Ping-shan 秉善) moved the whole family to the south in the Chen-yu 貞佑 period (1213–17), obviously as a result of the decision of the Chin government, under Mongol pressure, to move its capital from Yen-ching 燕京 (modern Beijing) to Pien 汴 (Kaifeng 開封) by 1215. Not until 1232, two years before the Mongols extinguished the Chin dynasty, did Yin's father (Shu 述) manage to have the family returned to Hopei.[6]

Spiritual Self-definition

At the time of Yin's birth in 1249, his father was already in his forties. According to Yin's biography in the dynastic history, the aging patriarch of the Liu clan had actually offered a pledge to heaven, promising that if he should be blessed with a son, he would give him a fine eduation. Since Shu himself is said to have dedicated much of his life to scholarship (*wen-hsüeh* 文學) and, in particular, to the study of Confucian moral philosophy (*hsing-li chih shuo* 性理之説), his commitment is quite understandable. The seeming hyperbole in the description of Yin's intellectual precociousness may, against

---

[3] The other Confucian master, who seems to have exerted a much wider influence on Yüan politics than Liu Yin did, was Hsü Heng. For an anthology of Hsü's writings, see *Lu-chai i-shu* 魯齋遺書, various editions. For a recent study of Hsü Heng, see Yüan Chi, 袁冀, *Yüan Hsü Lu-chai p'ing-shu* 元許魯齋評述 (Taipei: Commercial Press, 1972).

[4] See *Ching-hsiu hsien-sheng wen-chi* 靜修先生文集 (hereafter abbreviated as *Wen-chi*; 1879); YS (Beijing: Chung-hua shu-chü 中華書局, 1976) 171:4007–10; *Hsin Yüan shih* 新元史 (Tientsin, 1930) 170:13a; SYHA 宋元學案 (1846) 91:1a–11b; and T'ao Tsung-i, *Cho-keng lu* (TSCC 叢書集刊) 2:37. For a recent addition to scholarship on Liu Yin, see Yüan Chi, "Yüan ming-Ju Liu Ching-hsiu hsing-shih pien-nien", 元名儒劉靜修行實編年 in his *Yüan shih lun-ts'ung* 元史論叢 (Taipei: Lien-ching 聯經 Publishers, 1978), 19–76. Also see his interpretive essay on Liu's literature and personality and his annotation on and addition to Liu's biography in the SYHA, in ibid., 77–105, 107–27.

[5] Sun K'o-k'uan, "Yüan-Ju Liu Ching-hsiu hsüeh-hsing shu-p'ing" 元儒劉靜修學行述評, in his *Meng-ku Han-chün yü Han wen-hua yen-chiu* 蒙古漢軍與漢文化研究 (Taipei: Wen-hsing Book Co., 1958), 75.

[6] YS 171:4007.

this background, appear credible: he acquired an ability to read books at three, learned several hundred words a day as a young boy, began to compose poems at six and essays at seven, and at twenty, when he was "yet to be capped"(*jo-kuan* 弱冠), had already earned a wide reputation as a promising scholar. He was soon recognised as the best student of Yen Mi-chien 硯彌堅 (1212–89), a reputable teacher from the South.[7] As he became more deeply immersed in classical scholarship, he began to raise serious questions about the then-prevalent methods of philology and exegetics. He strongly suspected that the "essential meanings" (*ching-i* 精義) of the sages must be more than what the standard commentaries conveyed. This intense concern for self-development as a scholar impelled him to search for other interpretations of the Confucian Way.[8]

The kind of scholarship that Liu Yin had been exposed to, we may surmise, consisted of standard works such as the *Correct Meanings of the Five Classics* (*Wu-ching cheng-i* 五經正義) with commentaries and subcommentaries by Han–T'ang 漢唐 textual analysts who were particularly concerned about philological and exegetical matters. It was unlikely that in his formative years he had ready access to the writings of the Sung 宋 Neo-Confucian masters, and especially to the philosophical essays and conversations of Chu Hsi 朱熹 (1130–1200). It is commonly believed that Sung Learning was first introduced to the North when Mongol armies took the famed scholar Chao Fu 趙復 (c. 1206–c. 1299) and brought him, against his will, from Te-an 德安 of modern Hupei 湖北 to the Mongol capital in 1235. Even assuming that the cultural enthusiast Yao Shu 姚樞 (1203–80), who was instrumental in arranging this unusual feat, succeeded only a few years after his arrival in persuading Chao to lead the T'ai-chi 太極 (Great Ultimate) Academy, the newly created centre of learning, the initial instructions on Sung Learning to the students of the North would have had to wait until the 1240s. Liu Yin must have gained a considerable mastery over the classics before he first learned about the great Sung masters.[9]

---

[7] For an account of Yen Mi-chien's biography, see Su Tien-chüeh 蘇天爵, *Tzu-hsi wen-kao* 滋溪文稿 (Taipei: National Central Library, 1970) 7:287–93, and SYHA 90:14b–15a. Since he is classified as a *t'ung-tiao* 同調 (similar tune) of the Chiang-han 江漢 school in SYHA, his philosophical ideas were viewed as compatible with those of the more famous Confucian master from the South, Chao Fu.

[8] YS 171:4008.

[9] For Chao Fu's life and thought as well as the devleopment of the Chiang-han school alleged to have been founded by him, see SYHA 90:1a–23b. It should be noted, however, that although Liu Yin was indebted to Chao for his exposure to Sung Learning, he was not, in a strict sense, a follower of Chao Fu. Sun K'o-k'uan argues against the supposed claim in SYHA that Liu belonged to the Chiang-han school. But a careful reading of the SYHA interpretation seems to show that the authors are aware of this. Although they note that Hsü Heng was a follower of Chao Fu, they actually put Liu Yin

An essay entitled "On Aspiring to Become a Sage" ("Hsi-sheng chieh" 希聖解), dramatically and poetically constructed, provides us with a rare opportunity to see how, in Liu Yin's spiritual self-definition, the Sung masters actually guided him to pursue the Way of the Sages. Historically it may also be taken as Liu's "rite of passage" into the Confucian world. Since the main part of the essay has been admirably translated by Frederick W. Mote,[10] I shall quote only the most relevant passages here. The essay begins with a vivid description of a full-moon night in autumn. The word *wang* 望, indicating the fifteenth day of the lunar month and also a sense of longing and hope, immediately imparts a mood of anticipation to the reader. Liu tells us that as he sits in the central court, a melancholy feeling arises. Wine becomes tasteless and the lute tuneless. He is now both so puzzled and so fascinated by the lofty ideas in Master Chou Tun-i's 周敦頤 (1017–73) *Penetrating the Book of Change*[11] (*T'ung-shu* 通書) that he takes it out again to read it in the moonlight. When he encounters the line "The scholar aspires to become a worthy, the worthy aspires to become a sage, and the sage aspires to become heaven", he can only sigh and feel terribly perplexed. How can anyone really aspire to become heaven, he asks. This kind of absurdity may have been intended to take an unfair advantage of unsophisticated students like himself, he ponders. Then, in a spirit of complete release, he "hums a poem to the pure breezes, fondles the bright moon, raps on the big earth, drinks the 'Great Harmony' [*t'ai-ho* 太和] and chants the line, 'How vast and empty the primordial beginnings.'" This trancelike experience evokes in him a song of the *Ch'u-tz'u* 楚辭 style, which is reminiscent of Ch'ü Yüan's 屈原 (338–277 B.C.) helpless appeal to the Supreme Being for meaning and direction. Just then, he reports, three divine elders appear.

One of them, with an untrammelled demeanour like a "pure breeze and

---

in a different category. The subtle difference between *Chiang-han so-ch'uan* 江漢所傳 in the case of Hsü and *Chiang-han pieh-ch'uan* 江漢別傳 in the case of Liu is particularly relevant here. See SYHA 90:1a and 3a. For Sun's observation, see "Yüan-chu ju-hsüeh" 元初儒學, in his *Yüan-tai Han wen-hua chih huo-tung* 元代漢文化之活動 (Taipei: Chung-hua shu-chü 中華書局, 1968), 185.

[10] Frederick W. Mote, "Confucian Eremitism in the Yüan Period", in *The Confucian Persuasion*, A. F. Wright, ed. (Stanford: Stanford University Press, 1960), 213–15. The conclusions Mote arrived at almost three decades ago concerning the salient features of Confucian eremitism in the Yüan period provide an excellent background for the present inquiry.

[11] For a translation of this important Confucian document, see Wing-tsit Chan, trans. and comp., *A Source Book in Chinese Philosophy* (Princeton: Princeton University Press, 1973), 465–80. I would like to acknowledge my indebtedness to Professor Chao Tzu-ch'iang 趙自強 for translating *I ching* as the *Book of Change* rather than as the *Book of Changes*.

clear moon",[12] identifies himself as the Plain Old Man (Cho-weng 拙翁). The others introduce themselves as the nameless Elder (Wu-ming kung 無名公) and the Master of Sincerity, Brilliance, and Centrality (Ch'eng-ming-chung tzu 誠明中子). In a mixture of joy and fear, Liu Yin asks their reasons for such an unexpected visit. He wonders why he is honoured with their majestic presence. Surely the humble abode of a self-imposed meditator is not the vast space for them to roam freely with the spirit of the universe. The nameless Elder remarks first that he comes in response to the song of the "Great Void" and the chant of the "primordial beginnings". Is it possible that Liu's selfish desires have now so beclouded his heavenly principle that he has already forgotten what he called out for just a moment ago? The Master of Sincerity, Brilliance, and Centrality joins in, noting that he cannot bear to see Liu, as a younger brother of his fellow human beings, fail to realise "his 'superior talents'" (ying-ts'ai 英才) and fall into the moral snares of the unworthy. "I wish that you should be nourished to fruition," the master continues, "How can you forsake me and forget all about it?"

However, the most pertinent and extensive instructions come from the Plain Old Man, who, after a long pause, enters into a dialogue with Liu:

> "The scholar aspires to become a worthy, the worthy aspires to become a sage, and the sage aspires to become heaven — these are my words that you have doubted, haven't you, my young friend?"
> "Can one really become a sage?"
> "Yes."
> "Is there any essential way?"
> "Yes."
> "Please explain it to me."
> "The essential way is singleness."
> "What is singleness?"
> "No desire."
> "Who can [attain the state of] 'no desire'?"
> "All people under heaven can [attain the state of] 'no desire'."
> "Does this mean that all people under heaven can become sages?"
> "Yes."[13]

---

[12] The phrase was originally coined by the well-known Northern Sung poet Huang T'ing-chien in characterising the lofty personality of Chou Tun-i. Chu Hsi's teacher Li T'ung was particularly fond of this expression. It seems that by Chu Hsi's time, it had already been widely recognised among Confucian literati as a sort of poetic reference to Master Chou. For a brief discussion of this, see Ch'ien Mu 錢穆, *Chu Tzu hsin hsüeh-an* 朱子新學案 (Taipei: San-min 三民 Book Co., 1971), 3:49. See also Chu Hsi, "Shu Lien-hsi kuang-feng chi-yüeh t'ing" 書濂溪光風霽月亭, in *Chu Wen-kung wen-chi* 朱文公文集 (i.e., *Chu Tzu ta-chuan* 朱子大全) (SPPY ed.), 84:29b–30a.

[13] Most of this conversation is quoted from two sources in Chou Tun-i's *Penetrating the Book of Change*. The first statement is from *ch.* 10, "The Will to Learn" and the rest are from *ch.* 20, "Learning to Be a Sage". Cf. Chan, *Source Book*, 470 and 473.

"If so, then I am absolutely confused. I really don't
understand this."

"Please sit down. I will explain it to you. Listen carefully."

With this rhetorical device, Liu introduces the Plain Old Man's metaphysical justification for universal sagehood. There is only one principle
(*li* 理) in the universe. Although the principle manifests itself in the myriad
things, it is the ultimate source to which all of them eventually return. Therefore, in the perspective of the principle, heaven and earth are human beings
and human beings are heaven and earth. Similarly, the sages and worthies are
myself and I am the sages and worthies. However, what human beings have
gathered from the principle is complete and all-pervading, whereas what the
myriad things have obtained are partial and blocked. Surely what is partial
and blocked cannot be transformed, but what is complete and pervasive,
once communicated, can reach everywhere. The sage aims to become heaven.
If he can, he will be heaven; if not, he will still be a great sage. The worthy
aims to become a sage. If he can go beyond that, he will be heaven; if not,
he will still be a great worthy. Similarly, the scholar aims to become a
worthy. If he can go beyond that, he will be a sage or if he just reaches
that, he will be a worthy; if not, he will still preserve his good reputation
as a scholar. Based upon this general observation, the Plain Old Man then
focuses his attention on Liu himself:

> You have received the centrality [the highest excellence] of heaven
> and earth and have been endowed with the wholesome and harmonious
> material forces [*ch'i* 氣] of the Five Constancies [*wu-ch'ang* 五常].
> Your talents are the essence of the sages and your learning is the
> achievements of the sages. You are like the sages and the sages are
> like you. Now you have offended yourself and yet you consider me
> [my words] absurd. Are you absurd, or am I, your teacher, absurd?
> If you cultivate [*hsiu* 修] yourself and dwell in tranquility [*ching* 靜],
> encourage yourself and take comfort in doing so, realise your design,
> fully develop your nature, improve from thought to wisdom, and
> progress from brilliance to sincerity, then will you really aspire to
> become a sage, or the sages aspire to become you? Now you have
> forsaken yourself and yet you think that I have taken mean advantage
> of you. Is it you who have cheated your teacher, or I, your teacher,
> who have cheated you?

The essay ends with a line revealing Liu Yin's self-image. He fully acknow-
ledges his narrow-mindedness and accepts the instructions of the Plain Old
Man. The Nameless Elder and the Master of Sincerity, Brilliance, and Centrality then pat him on the back and urge him to live up to their expectations

They express the wish, "Some day if we hear about 'an exemplar of purity' in the world, it will be you!"

There are a few features of this deceptively simple essay that merit further discussion. Philosophically the argument in it mainly consists of digested statements from Chou Tun-i's *Penetrating the Book of Change* and *Diagram of the Great Ultimate Explained* (*Tai-chi-t'u shuo* 太極圖説). Indeed, virtually all of the instructions of the Plain Old Man are from the writings of Master Chou. But since there is internal evidence to show that the Nameless Elder refers to Shao Yung 邵雍 (1011–77) and the Master of Sincerity, Brilliance, and Centrality refers to Chang Tsai 張載 (1020–77), Liu Yin seems to have constructed his thesis on a general appreciation of Northern Sung Confucian moral metaphysics rather than on a limited exposure to the works of one master.[14] This is particularly significant in view of the fact that Sung Learning was still in a preliminary stage of development among Yüan scholars of Liu's generation. Especially noteworthy in this regard is the date of the essay. The *ting-mao* 丁卯 year in traditional Chinese chronology that appears in the first line of the essay corresponds to either the third year of Hsiench'un 咸淳 of the Sung or the fourth year of Chih-yüan 至元 of the Yüan 元 (1267) when Liu was only eighteen years old. This seems to substantiate the claim of Liu's biographer in the dynastic history that he had established himself as a significant interpreter of Sung Learning prior to his capping ceremony. According to the same account, after he had read extensively the writings of Chou Tun-i, Ch'eng Hao 程顥 (1032–85), Ch'eng I 程頤 (1033–1107), Chang Tsai, Shao Yung, Chu Hsi, and Lü Tsu-ch'ien 呂祖謙 (1137–81), he confidently remarked that he had long suspected that such a tradition ought to have existed.

Liu Yin's acceptance and promulgation of Sung Learning, recognised and appreciated by a number of his contemporaries, amounted to a commitment to an ethico-religious tradition, a phenomenon believed to have become more prevalent among late Ming students of Confucian thought. This, however, must not give the impression that Liu uncritically surrendered himself to the authority of the Sung masters. On the contrary, since his

---

[14] It is not difficult to figure out that the "Nameless Elder" refers to Shao Yung and the "Master of Sincerity, Brilliance, and Centrality" refers to Chang Tsai. For one thing, all the references to the former are from Shao's work, such as the *Huang-chi ching-shih shu* 皇極經世書 (Supreme principles governing the world) and *I-ch'uan chi-jang chi* 伊川擊壤集 (A collection of [poems] striking the earth at the I River) and the latter from Chang's *Hsi-ming* 西銘 (Western inscription) and *Cheng-meng* 正蒙 (Correcting youthful ignorance). In fact, Shao Yung's autobiography is called "Wu-ming kung chuan" 無名公傳, the biography of a nameless elder. See Michael D. Freeman's unpublished essay, "From Adept to Sage: The Philosophical Career of Shao Yung", p. 18. For a survey of philosophies of Shao and Chang, see Chan, *Source Book*, 481–517. Actually, in one of Liu Yin's poems, he specifically notes that Shao Yung styled himself as the "Nameless Elder". See *Wen-chi* 9:1a.

dissatisfaction with the philological and exegetical approaches to the classics preceded his discovery and confirmation of the "essential meanings" of Sung Learning, he was predisposed to the spiritual directions of the Sung masters by his own intellectual struggle. "On Aspiring to Become a Sage", in this connection, is as much a statement of his own faith in self-perfectibility as an acknowledgment of his indebtedness to the three Northern Sung Confucian teachers. Indeed, he is said to have been able to elucidate the subtleties of their teachings as soon as he was exposed to their writings. Liu's independence of mind is further shown by his succinct characterisations of the strengths of the philosophies of each of the three Northern Sung masters: the encompassing nature of Shao, the refined quality of Chou, and the authenticity of Chang. Only Chu Hsi, he further observed, was capable of reaching a great synthesis.[15]

In the light of Liu Yin's spiritual self-definition, it seems that Liu's decision not to accept an official position to serve the Yüan court was not an outright rejection of politics. It may have been a commitment to something else that was, to him, more meaningful in a deep, personal way. Yet it is difficult to believe that the idea of "purity", as he used it, did not imply a negative attitude toward the politics of his time. His contemporaries certainly read political significance into his actions. Even the ruler is alleged to have interpreted them in this way. It may not be far-fetched to suggest that Liu Yin could, to a certain extent, subscribe to Raphael's reasons for a sensible person to steer clear of politics. Yet the *Problematik* involved is more complex. For one thing, how can Liu Yin's apparent eremitism be justified in terms of his faith in Confucian teachings?

Public Image and Personal Choice

Liu Yin's official biography, which provides extremely limited information about his life history, tells us that his father died when Liu was young, probably in his early teens. For quite a while, he was not able to perform proper burial rites for either his grandfather or his father because of poverty. Only with the financial help of an influential friend did he finally manage to fulfill his wishes and obligations as a filial son. We learn from his poems that his mother died when he was only six years old;[16] he was probably

---

15 YS 171:4008.

16 See his poem, which was obviously inspired by a dream he reports to have taken place on the twenty-eighth day of the ninth month of 1279. He notes in the poem that his mother has been dead for twenty years; see *Wen-chi* 11:9–b. Based upon evidence of this kind, Yüan Chi also arrives at the same conclusion, see his *Yüan shih lun-ts'ung*, 25.

raised by a stepmother. His biography also tells us that he earned a meagre living for his family, including his stepmother, by teaching. Although his seriousness of purpose attracted several outstanding students, he did not have a large following. And his strong sense of propriety inhibited him from meeting influential scholar-officials. Even after he had gained a considerable reputation as one of the foremost Confucian masters of his time, he still declined to receive admirers of high official status. Those who were disappointed by his refusal to grant them an audience criticised him as "arrogant" (*ao* 傲). Perhaps it was for this reason that the power elite tended to ignore him.

Nevertheless, it is not entirely true that Liu never accepted any official appointment. In 1282, when he was thirty-three years old, he was unexpectedly recommended for a respectable position and served briefly as a tutor for the imperial clan in the capital, Yen-ching 燕京. But within a month or so he resigned and returned home to attend to his ailing stepmother who died the following year. In 1291, he turned down a summons from the court inviting him to become an academician of the Imperial College. It was this event that attracted a great deal of attention in the scholar-official circle. Probably as an attempt to silence the further spread of rumours about his alleged "arrogance", which could easily anger the court, he wrote a famous letter to the highest authority in the government, giving poor health as the real reason for his inability to accept the invitation.[17] This, on the surface at least, seems credible, for he died only two years afterward. But the significance of the letter as a clue to his self-description cannot be overestimated. Indeed, almost half of his biography in the dynastic history consists of the letter in its entirety.

Liu died on the sixteenth day of the fourth month of the thirtieth year of Khubilai's reign (1293). He had no male progeny. Nor did he have enough of a discipleship to carry on his mode of scholarship. However, he is recorded to have composed a thirty-*chüan* study of the "essential points" (*ching-yao* 精要) of the Four Books and five *chüan* of poems. His students and friends compiled another collection of his articles and conversations in more than ten *chüan*, which includes an essay on the "Great Commentary" of the *Book of Change*; it was completed after he had become gravely ill.[18] Most of his writings are probably no longer extant, but an anthology of his works

---

[17] The letter entitled "Yü cheng-fu shu" 與政府書 is found in *Wen-chi*, 3:7b–9b.

[18] Although we have only limited evidence for Liu's scholarship on the *Book of Change*, he was recognised by his contemporaries as an expert on the book. See YS 171:4010; see also Sun, "Yüan-ch'u ju-hsüeh", 185. Sun claims that precisely because of Liu's profound knowledge of *Lao Tzu* and the *Book of Change*, his spiritual orientation was significantly different from that of the so-called Chiang-han scholars.

in twelve *chüan* is still readily available. It includes eight miscellaneous articles, ten essays, seventeen prefaces, twelve memoirs, ten epilogues, fifteen letters, four memorials, two biographical sketches, fifteen obituaries, eight funeral odes, eleven inscriptions, and over eight hundred poems.[19]

During the Yen-yu 延佑 reign (1314–20) of Emperor Ayurbarwada (Jen-tsung 仁宗, r. 1311–20), more than a decade after Liu's death, Liu was post-humously enfeoffed as the Duke of Jung-ch'eng and given the honorific name of Wen-ching 文靖 (Cultured Tranquillity). He also received the title of academician of the Imperial College. Although it was not unusual for the court to recognise outstanding scholars in this way, its belated action in this case seems to have been taken in response to Liu's growing reputation among a select group of influential scholar-officials. The great literary figure Yü Chi 虞集 (1272–1348), for example, unequivocally characterised Liu as the foremost scholar in the North in terms of his "loftiness, brilliance, steadfastness, and courage". He also contended that Liu was the authentic transmitter of Sung Learning, for he had learned the teachings of Chu Hsi from Chao Fu and, through them, fully understood the philosophies of the Northern Sung masters.[20] Yüan Chüeh 袁桷 (1266–1327), another eminent literatus, praised Liu's writing as "refined and profound" and his ideas as "single-minded and truthful". He particularly noted Liu's serious commit-ment to the Confucian Way and his independence of mind in arriving at a critical appreciation of Chu Hsi.[21] In the same spirit, Ou-yang Hsüan 歐陽玄 (1283–1357), the director-general of the dynastic histories of Sung, Liao 遼, and Chin, depicted Liu as the embodiment of the best in two of Confucius' esteemed disciples: the freedom of Tseng Tien 曾點 without his wildness and the courage of Tzu-lu 子路 without his militancy.[22]

The public image of Liu Yin, as it was formed in the literary world of the time, presents us with several intriguing questions. Why did a Con-fucian eremite such as Liu emerge as a culture hero for the generation of the 1310s? Since the aforementioned Yü, Yüan, and Ou-yang were all south-erners, what could have been their motivation for lavishing such high praise

---

[19] For a readily available edition of Liu's literary works, see *Ching-hsiu hsien-sheng wen-chi* (TSCC ed.), *mu-lu* 目錄 (table of contents).

[20] See Yü Chi, "An Ching-chung wen-chi hsü" 安敬仲文集序, in his *Tao yüan hsüeh-ku lu* 道園學古錄 (1730), 6:4b–6b.

[21] See Yüan Chüeh, "Chen-ting An Ching-chung mu-piao", in *Ching-jung chü-shih chi* 清容居士集 (SPTK) 四部叢刊, 30:22a.

[22] See Ou-yang Hsüan, "Ching-hsiu hsien-sheng hua-hsiang tsan" 靜修先生畫像贊, in his *Kuei-chai wen-chi* 圭齋文集 (SPTK), 15:3b–4a. Also see his "An hsien-sheng ssu-t'ang chi" 安先生祠堂記, ibid. 5:11b–12a.

on this particular nothern scholar? Was Liu's reputation used for some political end? These questions seem to have prompted Sun K'o-k'uan to offer his "conspiracy" thesis. A simplified version of it goes something like this: The intellectual circle of the North was at the time dominated by the followers of another highly regarded Confucian master, Hsü Heng 許衡 (1209–81). When the great southern classicist Wu Ch'eng 吳澄 (1249–1333), who later received critical acclaim as the most distinguished Confucian scholar of the Yüan dynasty as a whole, visited the capital, he was poorly treated by the northern scholars. As the rivalry between the North and the South intensified, Wu's students, such as Yü Chi, decided to launch a campaign to elevate the status of Liu Yin in the Confucian legacy as a challenge to the overpowering influence of the Hsü school.[23]

In addition to the "conspiracy" thesis, Sun offers us a "promotion" thesis. The principal actor in this connection was Su T'ien-chüeh 蘇天爵 (1249–1352), famous for his systematic attempt to compile anthologies of representative writings of the Yüan era. As the compiler of a voluminous collection of Yüan literary works, Su created early in his career an ever-widening circle of literary talents around him. His close friends, Yü Chi and Yüan Chüeh, were among the examiners who ranked him first in the 1316 provincial examination. Ou-yang Hsüan was for some time his colleague in the Hanlin 翰林 Academy. This partly explains his ability to influence the climate of opinion in which Liu's reputation soared. The immediate occasion for his promotional efforts, however, came from a different connection. Su was a northern scholar with long and extensive associations with many prominent literati in the North, mainly because he himself came from a scholarly family with an impressive tradition of Confucian studies. Su was also a disciple of the Neo-Confucian master An Hsi 安熙 (1270–1311), whose admiration for Liu Yin led him to identify himself as Liu's "privately cultivated" (*ssu-shu* 私淑) student.[24] Even though An Hsi never met Master Liu, he is listed in the *Sung-Yüan hsüeh-an* 宋元學案 as one of Liu's students, which, by association, makes Su a follower of Liu's Ching-hsiu 靜修 school as well. It seems reasonable then for Su to have advocated the significance of Liu and to have rallied his influential literary friends to Liu's support. The very fact that both Yü's and Yüan's laudatory remarks on Liu are found

---

[23] Sun, "Yüan-Ju Liu Ching-hsiu", 77.

[24] The expression is found in *Mencius* 7A:40. Mencius claims that one of the five ways that the "profound person" (*chün-tzu* 君子) instructs is to set an example so that those who have no direct access to education can emulate his mode of life. By implication, the "privately cultivated" student is one who follows the example of the teacher, even though he does not have any immediate contact with him.

in their writings honouring Su's teacher, An Hsi, seems to give further weight to this line of reasoning.[25]

We encounter in both the "conspiracy" and the "promotion" thesis an implicit assertion that Liu Yin was not only different from but adversary to Hsü Heng. A most revealing story about this is found in T'ao Tsung-i's 陶宗儀 *Cho-keng lu* 輟耕錄. When Hsü was summoned to the court by Khubilai in 1260, the story tells us, he paid a special visit to Liu. As he was criticised by Liu for his apparent alacrity in serving the Mongol ruler, Hsü replied that if scholars like themselves did not respond with eagerness to the imperial calls, the Confucian "Way could not prevail" (*tao pu-hsing* 道不行). More than two decades later, in 1283, the story continues, when Liu first resigned from a respectable official position after an extremely short tenure and then declined to accept an even more prestigious position, he was asked for an explanation. Liu stated that if scholars like themselves did not decline such offers, the Confucian "Way would not be respected" (*tao pu-tsun* 道不尊).[26] It is true, as Sun has pointed out, that T'ao was also a southerner. But in the *Cho-ken lu* story there is no indication that Liu's attempt to dignify the Way was necessarily superior to Hsü's attempt to put it into effect. The moral seems to suggest that, given the circumstances and the personal sense of involvement in them, both choices were righteous and fitting. The gap between the North and the South notwithstanding, both the effectiveness and the respectability of the Way were vital to all concerned Confucian scholars.

In fact, the likelihood of Hsü's having met Liu in 1260 seems slim. For one thing, it is highly improbable that the already well-known Hsü would have consulted an eleven-year-old boy about his new appointment.[27] However, the story does symbolise a real existential conflict between two radically different, if equally acceptable, modes of life faced by virtually all eminent Confucians under the Mongol conquest. Paradoxically, during the Yen-yu years, when Liu Yin's dignity as a scholar was formally recognised by the court, the reopening of the examination system actually attracted a number

[25] It is interesting to note that as an obvious recognition of An Hsi's intellectual self-identification, the authors of SYHA list him as a follower of Liu Yin and qualify the description with the term *ssu-shu*. For a short anthology of An Hsi's surviving works, see *An Mo-an hsien-sheng chi* 安默庵先生集, (TSCC ed.). An account of An's philosophical ideas is found in "Chai-chü tui-wen" 齋居對問, ibid 3:15–17. For An's commitment to Liu Yin, see "Chi Ching-hsiu hsien-sheng wen" 祭靜修先生文 in ibid. 4:26. A very informative account of Liu Yin's life history is found in Su T'ien-chüeh, "Ching-hsiu hsien-sheng Liu-kung mu-piao" 靜修先生劉公墓表, in *Tzu-hsi wen-kao* 滋溪文稿 8:295–305. According to Su, the great southern scholar Wu Ch'eng singled out Liu Yin as the only Yüan Confucian master of the previous generation whom he truly respected, see ibid 8:304–5.

[26] This often-quoted statement is found in T'ao Tsung-i's *Cho-keng lu* 2:37.

[27] For a persuasive argument on this issue, see Sun, "Yüan-Ju Liu Ching-hsiu", 77–78.

of Confucian literati to government service. Those who were instrumental in formulating a powerful public image for Liu were themselves officials and thus were, more or less, emulating Hsü's approach to politics. In 1349, an imperial dispatch was issued, instructing local educational authorities throughout the country to make the writings of Liu Yin readily available for students. The rationale behind this unusual action is instructive. It is true that Liu only served the government briefly, the dispatch states, but his "purity and integrity" (*ch'ing-chieh* 清節) exerted such a remarkable influence on the country that the circulation of his works would "assist in the moral transformation of the government above and provide a model for the students below".[28] When the court failed to recruit Liu in 1291, Khubilai is alleged to have said that there had been "unsummonable ministers" (*pu-chao chih ch'en* 不召之臣) and that Liu must have been a follower of them.[29] He would have been pleased to know that Liu inadvertently performed a good service to the government after all.

The exemplariness of Liu's life and thought takes on new meaning in the light of his own justification for his existential choice. The letter that he submitted to the highest authority in the government is particularly relevant here. As already mentioned, he gave poor health as the reason for refusing to serve. But his strategy of presentation and the manner in which he presented himself to the court merit a more focused investigation. Needless to say, he was aware of the gravity of the situation when he decided that he was not able to respond to the imperial summons. Especially noteworthy was his reference to mounting rumours that he was actually motivated by a desire for fame. He must have known well that any indication that his choice was intended to defy the authority of the court could easily infuriate the emperor and bring disastrous consequences to him and his family. Furthermore, since the power of a newly founded dynasty to attract the services of hermits had long been considered in traditional Chinese historiography as an important index of the spread of its legitimacy, he could not argue his case simply in terms of a personal preference.[30]

---

[28] See "Yüan Chih-cheng chiu-nien chiu-yüeh shih-i-jih tieh" 元至正九年九月十一日牒, in *Wen-chi, tieh-wen* 牒文, 1b.

[29] YS 171:4010.

[30] The idea of "voluntary eremitism of protest" as developed by Frederick W. Mote should perhaps be understood as a subtle way of mobilising the symbolic resources available to the Confucian eremite, not as bases for a "free" choice but as the necessary condition for asserting one's personal integrity on grounds different from political loyalty but still endorsed by the imperial authority. See Mote, "Confucianism Eremitism", 209–12. For contrasting the Confucian eremites with those Confucians who chose to transform politics from within, see John W. Dardess, *Conquerors and Confucians: Aspects of Political Change in Late Yüan China* (New York: Columbia University Press, 1973), 53–94.

Thus, in the very beginning of the letter, Liu states that even as a young boy he learned and understood from his father and his teacher the meaning of the "righteous relationship between ruler and minister" (*chün-chen chih i* 君臣之義). Since the security and livelihood of the people are direct concerns of the ruler that the people themselves share in, they must use their physical labour or their mental strength to exert themselves in his service. This is the inevitable course of history for thousands of years, which Chuang Tzu 莊子 called "that which is inescapable between heaven and earth".[31] With this introductory statement, Liu explains that in forty-three years he has not yet contributed a modicum of energy to the service of the country (*kuo-chia* 國家) that has protected and reared him. Now with this extraordinary opportunity at hand, how can he continue to betray his country by indulging in self-imposed isolation? If he does, it will amount to committing a serious transgression against the teachings of "centrality and commonality" (*chung-yung* 中庸) in the tradition of the sages. Liu then makes it clear that he has never entertained the thought of becoming a hermit or a recluse; in fact, we may add, he has always set his heart on the Confucian Way. This is why, he further states, he immediately responded to the imperial summons of 1282. Although his service was abruptly cut short because of his stepmother's illness and death, it was not at all an excuse to go into seclusion. The letter concludes with a detailed description of his own deteriorating health and his inability, rather than unwillingness, to accept the new appointment.

There is no reason for us to believe that the letter was written in bad faith. But it also seems that, given the circumstances, it could not have been composed otherwise. This sense of inevitability implies a twofold meaning. On the surface, Liu admitted that he was to blame for his failure to serve. He was probably aware that he might have appeared unreasonably arrogant to his contemporaries when he turned down an offer from the mighty ruler, Khubilai. Therefore self-criticism seems to have been the only way out. Once he made his philosophy of life clear, it seems that he had to resort to poor health as the real reason. Actually, he promised, he would embark on the journey to the capital as soon as he became well. On the other hand, he may have had something else in mind. To be sure, the first appointment had ended briefly and the second offer could not be honoured. Yet almost ten years had elapsed from 1282 to 1291. The government could have enlisted his service after he had fulfilled his mourning rite and before his health deteriorated. This interpretation seems compelling in light of his plea toward the end of the letter. After all, he argues, unlike the central figures in the

---

[31] *Chuang Tzu* (SPPY ed.), *ch.* 4.

court, he is but a remote and lowly official. It in fact matters very little whether he enters into or withdraws from the government. Indeed, the court can afford to "allow him to complete what he is from beginning to end".[32]

The expression "allow him to complete what he is from beginning to end" is most suggestive. It may simply refer to an earlier statement in which he requested the highest authority of the government to find a way to protect and save him. Since the letter was sent to the government (*cheng-fu* 政府) and was specifically addressed to the prime minister (*tsai-hsiang* 宰相), Liu was gingerly trying to win the sympathy of the leadership of the scholar-official class so that his case would not be misinterpreted by the court (*ch'ao-t'ing* 朝庭). The fact that he was not futher pressured to accept the appointment indicates that the strategy worked. Thus Liu subtly conveyed his wish to lead an alternative way of life. To be sure, this life was not that of a hermit or of a recluse. But neither was it "political" in the sense that the lives of all scholar-officials who joined the government inescapably were. It seems that Liu opted for a way to "complete" himself that was neither a conscious design to escape from official service nor an unquestioned attachment to it. It was in many respects the solitary struggle of an independent mind. And yet undeniably, because of his profound sense of purity and integrity, he not only developed enough inner strength to make this particular form of the Confucian Way meaningful to him and to his small group of students but also symbolically opened the way for later scholars who wished to cultivate their sense of dignity without any direct reference to politics.[33]

We may say that, to a certain extent, Liu sincerely regretted that as a Confucian he had failed to fulfill one of the five basic human relationships, the righteous relationship between ruler and minister. He must have suffered even more intensely at the death of his only son in 1290.[34] In addition, his father and mother had died when he was very young, so far as we know, he did not have any brothers or sisters. Thus, at the time he wrote the letter, he could have maintained at most only one of the five basic human relationships defined in Confucian teachings. We are not even sure that even this

---

[32] See "Yü cheng-fu shu", *Wen-chi* 3:8b–9b.

[33] This may have been the main reason that scholars such as Yü Chi, Yüan Chüeh, and Su T'ien-chüeh wholeheartedly supported him in the first decades of the fourteenth century.

[34] His intense feelings of joy mixed with a realistic sense of doubts at the birth of his son when he was already forty *sui* 歲 are vividly captured in his poem entitled "Sheng-jih" 生日, in *Wen-chi* 8:2b. It seems that his son died an infant of no more than two years. According to Su T'ien-chüeh's biographical account, Liu had three daughters and all of them married into prominent scholar-official families. See Su's "Ching-Hsiu hsien-sheng Liu-kung mu-piao", in his *Tzu-hsi wen-kao* 8:301.

relationship existed because there is no reference to Liu's wife in the extant sources. Therefore, his wish to face death alone, also alluded to in the letter, should have conveyed a sense of tragedy to those who had any idea of the brute realities of life that he had experienced.

Liu's conscious choice not to participate directly in governmental service and his ineluctable fate not to be blessed with familial ties in the last years of his life may appear diametrically opposed to the ideal image of a Confucian. Furthermore, since most of his students emulated him in refusing to take an active political role, the direct influence he had on his times was relatively small. As a result, the school of thought that he is alleged to have founded has often been labelled as a form of "quietism". His style name, Ching-hsiu (Quiescent Cultivation), which has been widely used to designate his teachings, may also give the impression that there is a strong Taoist element in his Confucianism. It is perhaps in this sense that his Confucian eremitism has sometimes been interpreted as a kind of Confucian-Taoist syncretism.[35]

Politics, Poetry, and Intellectual Identity

We noted earlier that Liu might have cherished the hope of serving the state in an official capacity in the intervening years between the first and second summonses from the court. A poem written by him in 1278 to record a dream that he had on the twenty-fourth day of the eleventh month of that year is of particular interest in this connection.[36] Liu states that in the dream he has been recommended to the court by a joint memorial sponsored by a group of more than ten elderly persons all formally dressed in magnificent attire. In the memorial, he is addressed as "Chin-wen shan-jen" 金文山人 (the mountain man of "golden" literature). Among many of the laudatory phrases that the elders lavish on him, he remembers two in particular. One obviously refers to a statement by Confucius in the *Analects*, "Only when the year grows cold do we see that the pine and cypress are the last to fade."[37] The other, taken at its face value, does not convey a

---

[35] Needless to say, his profound knowledge of the *Book of Change* further gives the impression that his mode of thought was somewhat in conflict with the Confucian learning of Yao Shu and Hsü Heng. For an example of Liu's interpretive position on the *Book of Change*, see his discussions of the hexagrams *Chieh* 節 (no. 60) and *Chung-fu* 中孚 (no. 61), in *Wen-chi* 1:16b–18a. For a brief reference to this, see Sun, "Yüan-ch'u ju-hsüeh", 185. This was probably also the reason that Ou-yang Hsüan characterised him as an exemplar of the spirit of Tseng Tien; see "Ching-hsiu hsien-sheng hua-hsiang tsan", in his *Kuei-chai wen-chi* 15:3b–4a.

[36] See "Chi-meng" 記夢, in *Wen-chi* 9:9a–b; see especially the preface to the poem.

[37] *Analects* 9:27.

sense of praise at all: "The evening scene of the mulberry tree" ordinarily suggests the fading years of old age because the dying rays of the sun often light up the tops of these trees. It is not difficult to surmise that in the dream Liu was recommended by those dignified senior statesmen as a person who has proven his incorruptibility and whose service must be sought immediately, lest a rare chance be missed. Since the dream actually preceded his first appointment by three years, it seems to convey a persistent concern rather than simply an isolated occurrence.

Even his choice of a style name, Ching-hsiu, reflects a similar concern. It is not true, as one would suspect, that by "Quiescent Cultivation" he meant to convey a Taoist preference for quietism. The evidence shows that the phrase was in fact based on Chu-ke Liang's 諸葛亮 (181–234) famous statement, "Quiescence wherewith to cultivate the self" (*ching i hsiu-shen* 靜以修身).[38] The delicate difference lies partly in divergent motivations. Of course, Taoist quietism is also a form of self-cultivation, but what Chu-ke had in mind was primarily a spiritual preparation for a great political task. As the legend goes, only after the ruler of the State of Shu 蜀 had visited him in person three times at his straw-thatched hut did Chu-ke consent to reemerge from his self-imposed isolation to serve as the prime minister of Shu. Recalling Liu's alleged criticism of Hsü Heng, it was not governmental service itself but the manner in which it was requested and rendered that made all the difference. Far from being a kind of ritualism, what was involved had far-reaching political implications. The scholar must maintain his dignity not only as an adviser but, more important, as a critic. And in order to maintain his critical judgment, he must be able to distance himself from the centre of power. Only then can he really perceive and influence politics from a broad cultural base. The scholar-official, by implication, must subscribe to a set of value priorities significantly different from the status quo. "Quiescence wherewith to cultivate the self" as Chu-ke, and for that matter Liu, would have it, was a political as well as a personal dictum.

Liu Yin's relationship to and perception of the existing structure of power under the domination of the Mongol court were further complicated by what may be called his loyalist sentiments toward the extinguished Chin dynasty. The rise of the Jurchen in northeastern Manchuria and their rebellion against the state of Liao (947–1125) in 1114, which resulted in the establishment of the Chin (Golden) dynasty in the following year, is a story widely known

---

[38] Liu notes in one of his poems that he was so fond of Chu-ke Liang's phrase "Quiescence wherewith to cultivate the self" that he named his studio "Quiescent Cultivation". See the eighth verse in his "Ho tsa-shih", in *Wen-chi* 12:10a. It seems that this was the main reason that his students later referred to him as Ching-hsiu hsien-sheng (the master of quiescent cultivation). See also Mote, "Confucian Eremitism", 213.

to students of Chinese history. Also known is the military expansion of the Chin in northern China: the capture of the Sung capital of Kaifeng, together with its emperor and the abdicated former emperor Hui-tsung 徽宗 (r.1100–25) in 1126, the consolidation of its power base in the North by moving the capital from Manchuria to Yen-ching in 1153, and the maintenance of a large mobile nomad cavalry that presented a continuous threat to the survival of the Southern Sung (1127–79). Less known, however, is the whole story of Chin's development into an increasingly sinicised state and the Confucian influences, including the examination system and the court rituals, that were exerted upon it.[39]

When the Mongols conquered the Chin capital in 1215 and destroyed the Chin state in 1234, the North had already developed its own style of learning independent of the flowering of Neo-Confucian thought in the South, for it had been cut off from the South for almost a century. A synoptic view of Yüan Hao-wen's 元好問 (1190–1257) biographical sketches of some of the eminent ministers of the Chin[40] gives us an indication of the range of cultural activities that the Chin political elite had been engaged in. Yüan himself had profound knowledge of Chinese culture, and his literary works made him one of the great writers of all time in Chinese poetry and prose. Yeh-lü Ch'u-ts'ai 耶律楚材 (1189–1243), from a highly cultured ruling house of the Khitan Liao, may have been unique as an influential adviser in the court of Chinggis Khan. But his literary competence seems to reflect the norm of cultural attainments among the Chin political elite. It was people of Yeh-lü's background, such as the Yeh-lü A-hai-t'u-hua 耶律阿海秃花 brothers, Marshal P'u-ch'a 蒲察, Wang Chi 王檝, Li Pang-jui 李邦瑞, and Kuo Pao-yü 郭寶玉, who were instrumental in introducing "Confucian consciousness" as a way of government to the Mongol ruler.[41] Liu Yin, as we have already mentioned, came from such a tradition.

---

[39] For one of the most comprehensive studies of the history of the Chin dynasty in modern scholarship, see Toyama Genji 外山軍治, *Kinchōshi kenkyū* 金朝史研究 (Kyoto: Society of Oriental Researches, 1964). However, even in such a broad coverage, the cultural history of the Chin is not adequately discussed. For a welcome monograph on this issue in English, see Jing-sheng Tao 陶晉生, *The Jurchen in Twelfth-Century China: A Study of Sinification* (Seattle: University of Washington Press, 1976).

[40] See Yüan Hao-wen, *I-shan hsien-sheng wen-chi* 遺山先生文集 (SPTK ed.) *ch.* 16–30.

[41] See Sun, "Yüan-ch'u Ju-hsüeh", 143. For an informative discussion of the sinicised Western Asians in the Yüan, see Ch'en Yüan 陳垣, *Yüan Hsi-yü jen Hua-hua k'ao* 元西域人華化考 (reprint; Taipei: Chiu-ssu 九思 Publishers, 1977), *ch.* 2. See also the English translation by Ch'ien Hsing-hai 錢星海 and L. C. Goodrich, *Western and Central Asians in China under the Mongols* (Los Angeles: Monumenta Serica at U.C.L.A., 1966), 18–80. For a useful background reading on this subject, see Hsiao Ch'i-ch'ing 蕭啓慶, *Hsi-yü-jen yü Yüan-ch'u cheng-chih* 西越人與元初政治 (Taipei: Faculty of Arts, National Taiwan University, 1966).

Classical scholarship in the Chin was limited in scope and, by comparison with that of Southern Sung, lacked sophistication. This was the reason that Chao Fu's arrival in the North marked the beginning of a new era for the northern scholars. And this was also the reason that Liu Yin's initiation into Sung Learning was through Chao. But the Chin intellectual world was so rich in literary and artistic expression that the warfare accompanying the Mongol conquest can easily be interpreted as the annihilation of a superior civilisation by a brutal force of destruction. This was certainly Liu's view of what happened to the culture in which he was raised. His great admiration for Yüan Hao-wen,[42] his emotional response to the paintings of the Chin prince Wan-yen Yün-kung 完顏允恭 (1146–85),[43] and his frequent references to words and ideas associated with the character *chin*[44] in his writings seem to show a nostalgic identification with a faded cultural world that still remained meaningful to him. Indeed, he claims in one of his poems that "literary brilliance does not perish together with scorched earth".[45] This

[42] See his poem "Chin t'ai-tzu Yün-kung mo-chu" 金太子允恭墨竹, in *Wen-chi* 7:10b–11a, especially the last six lines. However, Sun's claim that Liu's literary style was consciously modelled on that of Yüan Hao-wen needs further exploration. To be sure, as Sun notes, Liu seems to have established a friendly relationship with Hao Ch'ung-ch'ang 郝仲常, whose brother Hao Ching 郝經 (1223–75), a well-known literatus and an important Confucian master, was an influential disciple of Yüan Hao-wen. But the evidence seems to show that Liu was not particularly impressed by Hao Ch'ung-ch'ang's literary talents. See Liu's preface entitled "Sung Hao Chi-ch'ang hsü" 送郝季常序, in *Wen-chi*, 7b–8a. For Sun's contention, see his "Yüan-Ju Liu Ching-hsiu", 79–80. Yet it is beyond doubt that Liu himself greatly admired Yüan Hao-wen. See Liu's poem lamenting the fact that he had not had the fortune of meeting the literary giant, "Pa I-shan mo-chi" 跋遺山墨蹟, in *Wen-chi* 7:27b.

[43] See "Chin t'ai-tzu Yün-kung mo-chu", in *Wen-chi* 7:10b–11a. The other two seven-line verses bearing the same title are equally informative; see *Wen-chi* 11:13a–b. Also see his poem "Chin t'ai-tzu Yün-kung T'ang-jen ma" 金太子允恭唐人馬, in *Wen-chi* 7:7a–b.

[44] A most revealing case is, of course, the one mentioned in n. 36 where he identified himself as Chin-wen shan-jen. However, there are several cases in his poems where the use of the word *chin* seems to convey special meanings. For example, see his poem "Kan-shih" 感事, *Wen-chi* 11:8b. For his emotional response to a copy of the *Veritable Record* of the Chin, (*Chin-ch'ao shih-lu* 金朝實錄), see the aforementioned poem "Chin t'ai-tzu Yün-kung mo-chu", in *Wen-chi*, 7:11b.

[45] See "Chin t'ai-tzu Yün-kung mo-chu", in *Wen-chi* 7:11b. A preliminary study of three outstanding literary figures of the Chin period clearly indicates that the "literary brilliance" of the Jurchen dynasty has yet to be fully explored in Chinese cultural history. It is interesting too that classical scholarship and historical learning were particularly emphasised by these literati. See Wang Jo-hsü 王若虛, *Hu-nan i-lao chi* 滹南道老集 (SPTK ed.), *ch.* 11–29; Chao Ping-wen 趙秉文, *Hsien-hsien lao-jen Hu-shui wen-chi* 閑閑老人滏水文集 (SPTK ed.), *ch.* 1 and 14; and Yüan Hao-wen, *I-shan hsien-sheng wen-chi*, ch. 32–37. For an overview of numerous Chin studies on T'ang historical and literary studies, see Yang Chia-lo 楊家駱, "Hsin-pu Chin shih i-wen chih" 新補金史藝文志, in *Chin shih* (Taipei: National War College, 1970), vol. 2; and Hsü Wen-yü 許文玉, "Chin-yüan ti wen-yu" 金源的文囿, in Cheng Chen-to 鄭振鐸, ed., *Chung-kuo wen-hsüeh yen-chiu* 中國文學研究 (reprint; Hong Kong: Lung-men 龍門 Book Co., 1963), 677–714. See also Hok-lam Chan 陳學霖, *The Historiography of the Chin Dynasty: Three Studies* (Wiesbaden: Franz Steiner, 1970), chap. 2. For a brief survey of art history in the Chin, see Susan Bush, "Literati Culture Under the Chin (1122–1234)", *Oriental Art* 15 (1969): 103–12.

reminds us of the honorific title by which the elderly statesmen referred to him in his dream. Although Chin-wen has been rendered as "golden literature", it is not unlikely that it may have also been intended to suggest "the literature of the Chin". Liu's "loyalist sentiments" had little to do with the Chin state. Although the Liu clan of his grandfather's generation had figured prominently in politics, his father had only served briefly as a local official. There certainly was no impelling reason for Yin to feel obligated to the conquered dynasty. However, the Mongol takeover had been so devastating to the general population and the Mongol government so harsh on the literati, we can easily surmise, that he felt utterly disgusted with the conquerors. These sentiments pervade his poems.

It is difficult to summarise Liu's poetic production in terms of themes and subjects. Their quantity alone prevents us from generalising about them. We can of course acquire a sense of the mood pervading the majority of his poems. Even a limited exposure should call to our attention a deep feeling of melancholy that underlies both the tranquillity of his five-line poems and the virility of his seven-line poems. Through his verses composed explicitly in the style of T'ao Yüan-ming 陶淵明 (365–427), Liu Yin[46] expressed himself not in a soaring spirit of detachment and transcendence but in a sad awareness of fateful inevitability. Similarly the knightliness in his poems, reminiscent of the works of frontier poets in the T'ang 唐 (618–907) such as Ts'en Ts'an 岑參 (715–770) and Kao Shih 高適 (d. 765),[47] far from being an expression of romantic heroism, seems to signify a lament for the deaths of many strong and courageous men. Indeed, several of his powerful historical accounts, including the funerary inscriptions, give us a vivid, sometimes even graphic, picture of the horrible last decade of the Chin dynasty.[48] Liu's proficiency and sensitivity in other highly refined cultural activities, such as painting and calligraphy, must have made the dehumanising effects on all forms of cultural life under the Mongol conquests unbearable.

We therefore encounter in Liu's poems a fascinating paradox. At first it appears that he wished to lead a way of life reminiscent of the carefree spirit of T'ao Yüan-ming, but on closer examination we discover that his "withdrawal" was also meant to deliver a political message. Undeniably, when

---

[46] As an example of this, see his nine poems after the style of T'ao Yüan-ming entitled "Ho ni-ku" 和擬古, in *Wen-chi* 12:7a–8b.

[47] Sun, "Yüan-Ju Liu Ching-hsiu", 81. For a historical account of the frontier poets in the T'ang, see Liu Ta-chieh 劉大杰, *Chung-kuo wen-hsüeh fa-chan shih* 中國文學發展史 (reprint; Taipei: Chung-hua shu-chü, 1957) 1: 347–53.

[48] For example, see "Hsiao-tzu T'ien-chün mu-piao" 孝子田居墓表, in *Wen-chi* 4:22a–24a. Also see his poems "Chai chieh-fu shih" 翟節婦詩, in *Wen-chi* 6:10b–11b and "Wang I-ching" 望易京, in *Wen-chi* 9:17a.

T'ao decided to retire to his country cottage to cultivate his own vegetable garden, enjoy wine, and read books for pleasure, he too delivered a political message: "Never bow for a mere five pecks of rice."[49] Yet although T'ao had several times been forced to take office in order to provide a minimum livelihood for his family, once he left the political arena (so the legend goes), his heart never again returned to the mundane world. Instead it found a permanent home in the Taoist arcadia. What Liu found in T'ao, however, was not only a personality ideal but also poetic inspiration. A number of Liu's poems are modelled on the style of T'ao. Time and time again, T'ao's celebrated themes, such a chrysanthemums and "the Peach-blossoms Source", struck a sympathetic chord in Liu's imagination. One entire category of Liu's poetry consists of some eighty elegantly constructed poems devoted to the single task of rhyming with some of Tao's well-known verses ("Ho T'ao" 和陶).[50] However, it would be a mistake to assume that Liu's fascination with the aesthetic world of perhaps the greatest master of Taoist lyric poetry reflects his personal identification with the Taoist view of life.

Liu Yin's attitude toward Taoism has been well documented by Frederick W. Mote. He was "clear-minded about Taoist thought and its implications", rejecting the teachings of Chuang Tzu and Lao Tzu 老子 on the grounds of illusory escapism and manipulative distortion. What Liu found most objectionable in the Taoist tradition was not the original philosophical intention but the manner in which lofty ideas were put into effect. His subtle discussion of the butterfly metaphor in the chapter "Ch'i-wu lun" 齊物論 ("Equalisation of Things") in the *Chuang Tzu* is a case in point.[51] By asking, "Am I Chuang Chou who dreamed I was a butterfly, or am I really a butterfly dreaming I am Chuang Chou?" after he has awakened from a dream in which he was a butterfly, Chuang Tzu poses a fundamental question about our perception of reality. In principle, Liu accepts Chuang's idea of "equalising" (*ch'i* 齊) and his desire to "move freely without constraint" (*wu shih er pu-k'o* 無適而不可; literally, "no end cannot be reached" or "nothing will not do"). But he argues that the creation of a world of fantasy (*huan* 幻) will not get us very far. The problem with Chuang is his inability to see through that fantasy as a tactic, a psychological device, to lessen the painful realisation that one is "adrift among all the innumerable and motley things of this world for but a brief moment of time". The ideal

---

[49] See Hsiao T'ung 蕭統, "T'ao Yüan-ming chuan" 陶淵明傳, in *Ching-chieh hsien-sheng chi* 靖節先生集 (1840) preface, 5b. the same reference is found in T'ao's biographies in both *Chin shu* and *Nan shih*.

[50] *Wen-chi* 12:1a–14b.

[51] "Chuang Chou meng-tieh-t'u hsü" 莊周夢蝶圖序, in *Wen-chi* 2:4a–5b.

way of being human, Liu seems to contend, must not be sought in the escapist illusion of being transformed into a different being. Real freedom lies in the courage to face up to the actual conditions of one's life.

The real existential choice, then, is to opt for Mencius' idea of a "profound person" (*chün-tzu* 君子). "[What he] follows as his nature is not added to when he holds sway over the Empire, nor is it detracted from when he is reduced to straitened circumstances."[52] The self-sufficiency of what the profound person follows as his nature is, according to Mencius, "rooted in his heart, and manifests itself in his face, giving it a sleek appearance. It also shows in his back and extends to his limbs, rendering their message intelligible without words."[53] Liu identifies this inner strength as "righteous destiny" (*i-ming* 義命). Following the Neo-Confucian, in particular the Ch'eng-Chu 程朱, teachings on the matter, Liu insists that a step-by-step effort of "exhaustively appropriating the principle inherent in things" (*ch'iung-li* 窮理) is absolutely necessary for learning to be fully human. The difficulty of the task is obvious. Even among the leading Confucians there are those who, on suffering extreme hardships, fall back on Taoist fantasies for solace and diversion. To cultivate a true sense of one's own "righteous destiny" is thus a great challenge.[54]

This line of thinking reminds us of Liu's essay "On Aspiring to Become a Sage". His initial uneasiness with Chou Tun-i's assertion in *Penetrating the Book of Change* is comparable to what he believes to be the trouble with Taoists: "They see how vast the world is, and how great the span of time from the past to the present. They observe how comprehensive and how abundant are the achievements of the Sages and Worthies, and how tiny and insignificant they themselves are."[55] The belittling of one's true self and, by implication, one's humanity, accounts for much of the escapism in Taoist thought. Escapism may seem to be a failure of nerve, but according to Liu's observations, it also results from narrow-mindedness. A limited perception or understanding of reality in its fullest manifestation often ends in a failure to act in accordance with one's "righteous destiny". This is not simply an epistemological problem, because the application of what one knows ultimately determines the quality and the correctness of one's knowledge. Liu's

---

[52] *Mencius* 7A:21. For this translation, see D. C. Lau, trans., *Mencius* (Middlesex, England: Penguin Classics, 1976), 185.

[53] *Mencius* 7A:21; Lau, *Mencius*, 186.

[54] For references to *i-ming*, see *Wen-chi* 2:4a and 5a.

[55] Ibid. 2:4a.

essay explaining the name of "The Studio of Withdrawal" is most instructive in this connection.[56]

The essay begins with an observation. If read out of context, it could easily be taken as unqualified support for the Taoist point of view:

> The substance of the Tao is originally tranquil. It produces things but is not produced by things and governs things but is not governed by things; it governs the myriad with singleness and it transforms but is never transformed. If this is perceived from the mutuality of the Principle [*li* 理], the interaction of the Power [*shih* 勢] and the circulation of the Number [*shu* 數], all those that emulate the substance of the Tao are free from constraints with an inexhaustible potential for creative adaptation.[57]

Yet Liu is quick to point out that Lao Tzu does not really understand the substance of the Tao because what he describes as the Tao is, according to Liu, a perversion, a self-serving tactic. Liu then gives us a long list of examples: humility becomes a means to gain and weakness to conquer; selflessness turns out to be an insidious form of egoism, and withdrawal a camouflage for aggression. Lao Tzu's manipulative intentions are further shown in his practices of disguising cleverness behind the façade of dullness and hiding eloquence under the appearance of inarticulateness. The image of a Taoist in Liu's depiction is therefore the embodiment of a calculating mind who places himself in a strategic position so that he can advance or retreat at will, "anticipate the end as he begins, plan the exit as he enters, occupy the centre in order to seek for profitable returns and read the incipient signs of conflict so as to benefit from it".[58] He takes advantage of others without leaving a discernible trace. Since for him personal gains and losses outweigh all other considerations, his action is detrimental to the state and harmful to the people, although he himself manages to remain aloof and beyond reproach.

A critic may argue that Lao Tzu's great ability to manipulate the world should also be considered a reflection of his profound knowledge of the Tao. Ironically it seems that Liu himself has, to a certain extent, advanced such a thesis. He admits that the Taoist "strategy" (*shu* 術) fully exploits natural as well as human forces. And it is extremely difficult to comprehend the mysterious pivot from which the Taoist turns the world around his fingers.

---

[56] See his "T'ui-chai chi" 退齋記, in *Wen-chi* 2:22b–24b. The essay was composed in the eighth month of 1276.

[57] *Wen-chi* 2:22b.

[58] *Wen-chi* 2:23b.

Liu comes close here to a political appropriation of Taoist values and symbols. By characterising Lao Tzu in this fashion, he seems to suggest that unlike Chuang Tzu's Taoists who prefer to dwell in fantasies, Lao Tzu's Taoists are really skillful strategists in the government who manipulate politics for selfish ends. We have no way of determining historically what group of individuals his criticism is directed against. It seems likely, however, that he has in mind influential politicians in the court who have long forsaken their ethical principles for personal expediency, since he suggests in his brief remarks toward the end of the essay that these manipulators now style themselves champions of the righteousness of Confucius and Mencius and of the principle of Ch'eng I and Chu Hsi. Nevertheless, it is difficult to substantiate the Ch'ing 清 historian Ch'üan Tsu-wang's 全祖望 (1705–55) claim that this essay contains an implicit critique of Hsü Heng.[59]

We encounter here another fascinating paradox. Liu finds in Lao Tzu's manipulative perversion of the Tao a deliberate attempt to exercise a kind of deceitful cunningness. It is not the choice of "withdrawal" itself but the insincere psychology behind it that really bothers him. By contrast, Chuang Tzu's philosophy of life seems more acceptable. At least his quest for inner spirituality points to a realm of value where the standards of this world are no longer applicable. What the Taoist manipulators effect in the court, on the other hand, is a total relativisation of ethical norms, which leads to great confusion in moral conduct. The isolated individuals who set high standards of personal integrity in the wilderness can still have a salutary influence on society and indirectly contribute to the respectability of the Tao. On the other hand, those who corrupt the government from within can never put the Tao into effect because they have perverted it from the very beginning. The distinction between Confucianism and Taoism assumes a different meaning in the light of this. The genuine Taoist can have a wholesome influence on society that the Confucian ought to appreciate, but the false Confucian, who distorts and manipulates Taoist ideas in politics, is destructive on all accounts.

Liu is understandably appreciative of some of the outstanding Taoist personalities in history, although he clearly does not subscribe to their modes of life. In addition to the aforementioned T'ao Yüan-ming, who seems to have inspired unreserved admiration from scholars of all philosophical persuasions, Liu, in two poems and several references, praises the famous

---

[59] For Ch'üan's interpretation, see SYHA 91:3b–4a. It seems also possible that Liu's critique was directed against scholar-officials such as Liu Ping-chung 劉秉忠. See Hok-lam Chan, "Liu Ping-chung (1216–74): A Buddhist-Taoist Statesman at the Court of Khubilai Khan", *T'oung Pao* 53, nos. 1–3 (1967): 98–146.

Former Han recluses known as the "four white-haired ones" (*ssu-hao* 四皓).[60] We also find in his poetry a highly laudatory comment on the cordial relationship between Emperor Kuang-wu 光武 (r. A.D. 25–57) of the Later Han and the much honoured hermit Yen Kuang 嚴光 (37 B.C.–A.D. 43).[61] In addition, he asserts that the accommodating Hui 惠 of Liu-hsia 柳下 was narrow-minded and that Po I 伯夷, the "pure sage" who was absolutely uncompromising in his sense of personal integrity, was really receptive to the idea of human equality.[62] This rather unconventional view that Po I's quest for personal purity was more socially efficacious than Hui of Liu-hsia's political flexibility could ever become further contributes to the impression that for Liu self-respect, as an overarching concern, is a precondition for social service. This thesis can of course be taken as a consistent and sophisticated argument for morality and culture over politics.

Self-development as a Calling

Another central concern in Liu Yin's life and thought was to demonstrate that morality and culture are essential to politics because they are the prerequisites of responsible service in the government. Obviously Liu was not simply making a general comment on politics. He understood well that the Mongol conquerors styled their rulership on entirely different principles. He knew that the majority of the people were victims of the most ruthless imposition of military and economic controls China had ever experienced. And he could also see the necessity for virtually all scholar-officials to muddle through an extremely dangerous situation. His sense of purity was definitely not what Mencius took the purity of Po I to have been. This was perhaps the reason that he reversed the Mencian critique of Po I as "narrowminded" and used it to characterise the seemingly flexible Hui of Liu-hsia. In what sense, then, could Liu justify his sense of purity as a universal value rather than merely as a personal preference?

Liu must have been aware that the audience to whom his message was delivered constituted a small coterie of like-minded friends and students in the intellectual world, in other words the tiny minority of a tiny minority.

---

[60] See the two poems entitled "Ssu-hao", in *Wen-chi* 6:10a–b. Also see his poem inspired by an artistic imagining of the portraits of the "four white-haired ones" entitled "Ssu-hao t'u" 四皓圖, in *Wen-chi* 10:2a.

[61] See his poem "Yen Kuang", in *Wen-chi* 6:10b.

[62] See the fourth of his seven poems entitled "Ho yung p'in-shih" 和詠貧士, in *Wen-chi* 12:11a–b. For a perceptive analysis of this poem, see Mote, "Confucian Eremitism", 225–27.

From the viewpoint of the sociology of knowledge, Liu seems to have been inescapably caught in a kind of moral and cultural elitism. By setting up an extremely high standard in personal conduct, Liu had already excluded himself from the "main stream" of scholar-official activities. His feeling of alienation, not unlike the solitariness in Ch'ü Yüan's "Encountering Sorrow" (*Li-sao* 離騷), is captured in a poem probably occasioned by insomnia on a spring night:

> People are all soundly asleep as I sit alone
> And peruse the spring in the cosmic tranquillity.
> If perchance for a moment everyone rests,
> Who will tell the time and count the watches?[63]

Many other poems of similar spirit are found in his collection. Among them, several earlier ones focused on the heroic personality of Ching K'o 荊軻, whose abortive attempt to assassinate the first emperor of the Ch'in dynasty (r. 221–210 B.C.) made him the archetype of the impassioned knightly figure from the state of Yen 燕.[64] As a native of the same region, Liu, in his youth, sometimes styled himself as the man from the I 易 River,[65] obviously referring to the place where Ching K'o said an emotional farewell to his best friends before he embarked on his fateful journey. Liu's youthful fascination with Ching K'o even brought him to the I River in the tenth month of 1266 to deliver a funeral ode in memory of the pre-Ch'in hero.[66] Liu's enthusiasm for unusually courageous persons was more than a reflection of his adventurist spirit as a young man. His poems and essays clearly indicate that he was continuously impressed by them and that he believed their idiosyncratic modes of behaviour had a universal appeal.

Consistent with this line of thinking was his choice of exemplary teachers in the Confucian tradition as a whole. Among Confucius' disciples, he singled out Yen Hui 顏回 and Tseng Tien.[67] Philosophically he was indebted to Mencius for his view of human nature and his attitude toward politics. He was not very much impressed by Han-T'ang thinkers. Prior to

---

[63] See his poem "Ch'un-yeh pu-mei" 春夜不寐, in *Wen-chi* 11:32b.

[64] See his poem "Teng Ching K'o shan" 登荊軻山, in *Wen-chi* 7:3b.

[65] For example, in the aforementioned essay "Hsi sheng-chieh", Liu refers to himself as the Liu of the I River; see *Wen-chi* 1:1a. Also see his poem "Tz'u-yün ta Liu Chung-tse" 次韻答劉仲澤, in *Wen-chi* 9:41a.

[66] See his essay "Tiao Ching K'o wen" 弔荊軻文, in *Wen-chi* 5:1a–2b.

[67] See his two poems entitled "Yen Tseng" 顏曾, in *Wen-chi* 11:13b–14a. Also see his two poems probably written on his personal fan, "Tseng Tien shan-t'ou" 曾點扇頭, in *Wen-chi* 11:18b.

the emergence of Neo-Confucianism in the Sung, he mentions prominently only Tung Chung-shu 董仲舒 (176–104 B.C.) and Han Yü 韓愈 (768–824).[68] The Northern Sung Confucian master that inspired him most was Shao Yung,[69] but he seems to have learned more from Chou Tun-i and Chang Tsai. He had a great admiration for the Ch'eng brothers, whom he describes in a poem as instrumental in helping us to understand heavenly truth and to appropriate fully the meaning of the principle in things by examining the minuteness of one hair.[70]

Liu's veneration for Ch'eng Hao is further shown in a poem where he praises the Elder Ch'eng as "propitious sun and auspicious clouds"[71] This may have prompted Sun K'o-k'uan to contend, in response to the eminent Ming thinker Liu Tsung-chou's 劉宗周 (1578–1645) claim that Liu Yin reminded him of Shao Yung, that Yin's style of life was closer to that of Ming-tao 明道 [Ch'eng Hao]. And it suggests that Liu would have been sympathetic to Lu Hsiang-shan 陸象山 (1139–93), if he had heard of him.[72] We know that although Liu may not have read Lu Hsiang-shan's collected works, he certainly knew about Lu's philosophical challenge to Chu Hsi. Yet Liu completely identified himself with the Chu Hsi school;[73] he even characterises Chu's teacher Li T'ung 李侗 (1093–1163) in one of his poems as "iced pot and autumn moon" (*ping-hu ch'iu-yüeh* 冰壺秋月),[74] a conventional way of describing an exemplar of clarity and purity. Nevertheless, despite Liu's whole-hearted devotion to Chu Hsi and, for that matter, to Sung Learning in general, he was committed to the idea of an independent mind as the ultimate judge of relevance and value. He not only remarked that a thousand

---

[68] See his essay "Hsü-hsüeh", in *Wen-chi* 1:8a. Also see the ninth of his nine poems entitled "Kuei-yu hsin-chü tsa-shih" 癸酉新居雜詩, in *Wen-chi* 11:15b.

[69] The following poems from the *Wen-chi* are particularly revealing in this connection: "Chou Shao" 周邵, 8:6a; "Kan-shih", 8:11a; "Shui-pei tao-kuan" 水北道館, 9:21b; and "Hsin-chü" 新居, 11:22a. I take the expression *Yü-ch'iao* 漁樵 (fisherman and woodcutter) in the latter two poems as a reference to Shao Yung's celebrated essay on the conversation between a fisherman and a woodcutter.

[70] See the first of his three poems entitled "Hsieh-chen shih" 寫真詩, in *Wen-chi* 11:18a.

[71] See his poem "Yu-huai" 有懷, in *Wen-chi* 9:9a.

[72] Actually Su T'ien-chüeh also thought that Liu's personality was most compatible with that of Shao Yung. See Su's "Ching-hsiu hsien-sheng Liu-kung mu-piao", in *Tzu-hsi wen-kao* 8:296–98. For Sun's observation, see "Yüan-Ju Liu Ching-hsi", 85–86.

[73] See Liu's essay "Ho-t'u pien" 河圖辨, in *Wen-chi* 1:10b–16b, and his essay "*T'ai-chi-t'u* hou-chi" 太極圖後記, in *Wen-chi* 1:18a–20a.

[74] See his poem "Yu-huai", in *Wen-chi* 9:9a.

years of "divinational wisdom" really resides in the human mind[75] but insisted that one's "innate knowledge" (*liang-chih* 良知) must not be swayed by opinions from outside, even if they are as authoritative as the teachings of the Sung masters.[76]

Again, we encounter here an obvious conflict. The historical personages to whom Liu attached great cultural and moral significance were well-known "loners". All of them remained marginal to the centre of power and some, by deliberate choice, detached themselves from it. Their source of strength did not come from political participation but from learning and self-cultivation. With the exception of Ching K'o, they all made their reputation as scholars and teachers. And even Ching K'o evoked sympathy in literary minds mainly because of his poetlike passion. Ironically, his clumsiness in handling an assassin's dagger enhanced his reputation as a tragic loner who met his death by confronting the most powerful tyrant of his times. However, unlike the Taoists who preferred either to create a realm of value completely outside politics or to develop a personal sanctuary within it by subtle manipulations, Liu's heroes sought to improve the political situation and their critical judgments never allowed them to become totally independent of it. Instead of seeing their position as a failure to differentiate morality and culture from politics, it is possible to view the dilemma in which virtually all of them were caught as the result of a conscious decision to transform politics through morality and culture. The language of the whole conceptual scheme employed here is foreign to Liu Yin's linguistic world, but its validity as a heuristic device can be shown by focusing on Liu's perception of scholarship.

Liu himself was aware of the distinction between culture and politics. His refusal to serve in a manner deemed perfectly acceptable by the scholar-officials of his time can also be understood as a means of demonstrating that the respectability of the Tao, a cultural idea to be sure, could not be preserved simply by political participation. In an essay on a Confucian temple located near his home town, Liu argues that since what Confucius intended to accomplish was to "establish the Way to be human" (*li jen-tao* 立人道), the right to honour him is open to all villagers and cannot be monopolised by authorised educational officials.[77] In a poem dedicated to a Taoist hermit he says, with a touch of irony, that while in officialdom rats are all taken as tigers, in the lives of certain people (Taoist hermits)

---

[75] See his poem commenting on a line from the *Analects*, "Man is born with uprightness" (6:17), in *Wen-chi* 11:4b.

[76] See his essay "Hsü-hsüeh", in *Wen-chi* 1:5b.

[77] "Kao-lin ch'ung-hsiu K'ung Tzu miao chi" 高林重修孔子廟記, in *Wen-chi* 2:21b–22b.

dragons are taught to become fish.[78] If it is deplorable that courageous tigers are really timid rats and that talented dragons merely learn to disguise themselves as evasive fish, what is the way Liu himself recommends? Rather than a delicate balance of the two, he offers a different approach: "Strenuous efforts at the classics, philosophy, and history for ten years. Then allow one's painting, poetry, and calligraphy to flourish forever." This sense of immortality through cultural activities is a common motif in Liu's writings. We shall later examine in some detail his "ten-year plan" of learning for his students; in his view, access to the most profound and lasting influence on the human community lay in culture rather than in politics.

It would be wrong to suppose, however, that Liu's commitment to culture was apolitical in the sense that he saw little political relevance in what he did, and only a general sort of human relevance. His deliberate disclaimer in one poem is revealing: "There are real Confucians in the court. Please do not say that this culture (*ssu-wen* 斯文) would depend on me for support!"[79] His awareness that "this culture" would have to depend on people like him for survival was probably the main reason that he often referred to his vocation metaphorically as putting the fragmented texts in order.[80] He also discussed frequently in his poetry the difficulty of the task and the loneliness one had to bear in order to fulfill it.

> Broken slips and fragmented texts interrupted the appreciated sound;
> Who would manifest the genuine gold through a hundredfold of smelting?
> Now after the Dragon Gate has lost its song for a thousand years,
> More so do we feel the great lonely pains of the fine artisan.[81]

But Liu's single-minded attempt to rescue the culture from oblivion was much more than the scholarly ambition of a private citizen. It was also intended to challenge those who presumed to be cultural transmitters as well as political participants, namely the scholar-officials who were actively in support of the Mongol government.

Liu seems to have been perfectly capable of sarcastic remarks when it came to his perceived or real competition with the gentlemen in the court. In an obvious attempt to silence those who still thought that he could be won over, he says in a poem, "As for the great peace, there are you

[78] "Shou T'ien ch'u-shih" 壽田處士, in *Wen-chi* 9:40a.

[79] "Tz'u-yün ta Shih Shu-kao" 次韻答石叔高, in *Wen-chi* 9:40b–41a.

[80] See his poem "Min han" 憫旱, in *Wen-chi* 9:23b–24a. Also see his poem "P'ing-hsi" 平昔, in *Wen-chi* 9:12b–13a.

[81] The sixth of his seven poems entitled "Kan-hsing" 感興, in *Wen-chi* 11:16b.

gentlemen to take care of it / Who would have need of turning to the direction of Nan-yang 南陽 and asking K'ung-ming 孔明 [Chu-ke Liang] for advice?"[82] Sarcasm it was, especially in the light of his remark about rats in officialdom, but Liu's main concern was not so much to humiliate those whom he despised as to perfect his own studio. Although he deeply regretted that he had no teachers and friends and that his students were few,[83] a sense of self-possession, suggesting inner repose and tranquillity, underlies many of his poems. For example, he meditates on a winter day that Chu Hsi hardly enjoyed any earthly comfort and that Confucius came to realise the mandate of heaven as he went around in mufti.[84] As neither of them had necessarily been better-off than he was, the idea that he too was personally responsible for the continuity of the cultural tradition must have crossed his mind numerous times.[85] A poem written in the first month of 1279 when he had just turned thirty shows the intensity of this concern:

> As I silently sit in the autumn breeze of the Confucian Temple,
> A thousand years of antiquity overwhelmingly enter into my
>   deep meditation.
> I offer myself totally [to the great task], noticing still the presence of
>   the primordial mind —
> Nowadays who will truly continue the Tao?[86]

This seemingly subjective assertion would have been no more than hubris, had Liu Yin refused to divulge the actual process by which he intended to complete his self-assigned task. The "presence of the primordial mind" may refer to his decision at the age of eighteen to "aspire to become a sage". However, the attempt to continue the Tao required a long and strenuous process of learning. He saw no possibility of a shortcut such as "sudden enlightenment". The key phrase in the title of what was probably his last essay, composed in 1292, is particularly apt in this connection, "planting virtue" (*shu-te* 樹德).[87] The development of oneself, the purpose of Confucian learning, is like the growth of a tree. A tree has to be planted, watered,

---

[82] "Tz'u-yün k'ou p'an-kung" 次韻叩泮宮, in *Wen-chi* 9:41b.

[83] See his poem "Chih ts'ai-lin" 示彩鱗, in *Wen-chi* 9:29a.

[84] See his poem "Tung-jih" 冬日, in *Wen-chi* 9:12a–b.

[85] For example, see his poem "Tz'u-yün ta Shih Shu-kao" cited in n. 79.

[86] The second of the two poems entitled "Chi-mo yüan-jih" 己卯元日, in *Wen-chi* 11:9a. *Chi-mo yüan-jih* means New Year's Day of the *chi-mo* year (1279).

[87] "Chung-te t'ing chi" 種德亭記, in *Wen-chi* 2:25b–26b.

and nourished. The persistence with which one must work at one's learning may have prompted Liu to confess that since he dared not emulate Shao Yung in the sky, he might as well follow Ssu-ma Kuang 司馬光 (1019–86) on the solid ground.[88]

Liu Yin's recommendations for learning "on the solid ground" are detailed in a long essay.[89] Although we do not know when it was written, internal evidence shows that it must have been composed after he had been teaching for several years. It thus reflects his mature thought on the subject. Entitled "On Learning" ("Hsü-hsüeh" 叙學), the essay consists of a short introductory note and four main parts. Following the balanced style of examination prose, the material is introduced, explained, developed, and eventually concluded with a summary statement. The thematic approach incorporates two contrasting sets of ideas along with some secondary thoughts. One major theme is developed by Liu's constant return to the main structure of the presentation, which is a rather formal instruction on the exact sequence by which one masters the basic literature in the Confucian tradition. Another set of ideas seems to argue that at every juncture of this learning process there is infinite possibility for creative adaptation. The primary concern here is to develop a sense of direction. The interplay between self-discipline and self-discovery gives the essay a dynamism that distinguishes it from ordinary manuals for learning.

At the beginning, Liu asserts that inherent in the nature (*hsing* 性), mind (*hsin* 心), and material force (*ch'i* 氣) of every human being is an irreducible potential for self-completion. Learning means the process by which this potential is realised. Since each person is originally endowed with the capacity to learn, it is inconceivable that the task of self-completion is not open to all people. However, the present state of scholarship (*hsüeh-shu* 學術) has deviated much from the norm, its pattern (*p'in-chieh* 品節) is confusing, and it has suffered a great deal from the attacks of heterodox traditions (*i-tuan* 異端). This is the reason that learning to be fully human requires a systematic inquiry into the best of the cultural heritage, which Liu outlines as follows:

1. *Six Classics, Confucian Analects, and Mencius.* Clearly intending to depart from Chu Hsi's pedagogy, Liu insists that learning should commence with the Six Classics.[90] Only after the student has been extensively exposed

[88] See the first of a group of nine poems entitled "Kuei-yu hsin-chü tsa-shih", in *Wen-chi* 11:14b. These poems were composed in the *kuei-yu* year (1273).

[89] "Hsü-hsüeh", in *Wen-chi* 1:3b–10b.

[90] Ibid., 4a–b.

to classical scholarship, he argues, can he really appreciate the refined expressions of the *Analects* and *Mencius*. Since the wisdom in these two books crystallises many years of sagely efforts, the student must be well prepared before a fruitful encounter is possible. Among the classics, the *Odes* should be on top of the list because it not only properly channels basic human feelings but also opens up new areas of human sensitivity. The *Odes* and the *Documents*, alleged to be a written account of sagely sentiments, are said to have established the great foundation. The *Rites*, both the *Book of Rites* and the *Rites of the Chou*, can be seen as social and political applications of the great foundation. The *Spring and Autumn Annals* are then studied for their historical judgments, which may be considered a moral reflection on human activities.

Only after these classics have been carefully learned can one begin to understand the subtle meanings of the *Book of Change*, a task that leads to the culminating point of classical scholarship. Following the Sung thinkers, Liu notes that an exhaustive appropriation of the principle in things and a full appreciation of human nature can eventually lead to a comprehension of the mandate of heaven. All these, he believes, must precede the study of the *Change*. He also insists that a balanced classical education must involve intensive work on the Han commentaries, the T'ang subcommentaries, and the Sung interpretations. However, he urges his students to maintain the independence of their own "innate knowledge" (*liang-chih*)[91] in the whole process.

2. *History.* Quoting from *Mencius*, Liu says that to master classical education is to "establish that which is great",[92] suggesting a centre of gravity and a sense of priority. With the established standards of conduct in the classics as a guide, the student should proceed to the study of history. Liu states that in ancient times there was no distinction between classics and history and that "the *Odes*, the *Documents*, and the *Spring and Autumn Annals* were [originally] all history". It is interesting to note that this perceptive observation, which is commonly attributed to the Ch'ing scholar Chang Hsüeh-ch'eng 章學誠 (1738–1801) as a bold attempt to see history as on a par with classics, is here formulated and presented as a matter of fact by Liu several centuries earlier.[93] Liu's recommendation for the study

[91] Ibid., 5a–b.

[92] Ibid., 6a. Also see *Mencius* 6A:15.

[93] Wang Yang-ming 王陽明 (1472–1529) also made it clear that he believed that the Five Classics are history (*shih*) as well as classics (*ching*). See his *Ch'uan-hsi lu* 傳習錄 in *Yang-ming ch'üan-shu* 陽明全書 (reprint; Taipei: Cheng-chung 正中 Book Co., 1955) 1:8. It is important to note, however, it was Chang Hsüeh-ch'eng who for the first time offered persuasive arguments to show that the Six Classics

of history is again a remarkable demonstration of his balanced approach to scholarship. As expected, he puts a great deal of emphasis on Ssu-ma Ch'ien's 司馬遷 (145–86? B.C.) *Records of the Historian (Shih chi 史記)* as the major source of inspiration for all subsequent Chinese historians in terms of organisation, style, and narrative art. Liu also singles out the *History of the [Former] Han (Han shu 漢書)* and the *History of the Later Han (Hou-Han shu 後漢書)* for praise. Although he makes some scathing criticisms on Ch'en Shou's 陳壽 (233–297) biased approach in the *Chronicles of the Three Kingdoms (San-kuo chih 三國志)*, he believes that P'ei Sung-chih's 裴松之 (372–451) commentaries serve as useful correctives.[94]

He feels that the *History of the Chin (Chin shu 晋書)* under the compilation of a group of famous high scholar-officials in T'ang Tai-tsung's 唐太宗 (r. 627–649) court is unduly complex. He observes, too, the shortcomings of the *History of the Southern Dynasties (Nan shih 南史)*, *History of the Northern Dynasties (Pei shih 北史)*, and *History of the Sui (Sui shu 隋書)*, all completed in the first few decades of the T'ang dynasty. He then compares the two versions of the *History of the T'ang (T'ang shu 唐書)* and the *History of the Five Dynasties (Wu-tai shih 五代史)*. His admiration for Ou-yang Hsiu 歐陽修 (1007–72), who was responsible for both new versions, does not lead him to conclude that the old ones are outdated. In fact, he argues that precisely because Ou-yang and his colleagues had a particular viewpoint to convey, their interpretations may have significantly departed from the factual basis. Thus the old versions should still be read for countervailing effect. Since the Sung and Chin histories have not yet been compiled, he further observes, the student should take advantage of the *Veritable Records (Shih-lu 實錄)* and miscellaneous notes of informed literati.[95] His general recommendation is to obtain an overview of Chinese history first, to sharpen one's judgment by a continuous application of the principles in the classics as a second step, and finally to compare what one has learned from the primary sources with the opinions expressed in Ssu-ma Kuang's *Comprehensive Mirror for Aid in Government (Tzu-chih t'ung-chien 資治通鑑)* and in the writings of Sung Confucians. In short, Liu considers it imperative that the student confront history as a holistic structure rather than as isolated events.

---

should be taken as historical records. See Chang Hsüeh-ch'eng, *Wen-shih t'ung-i* 文史通義 (reprint; Hong Kong: T'ai-p'ing Book Co., 1973) 1:1–33. For a stimulating interpretation of this, see Yü Ying-shih 余英時, *Lun Tai Chen yü Chang Hsüeh-ch'eng* 論戴震與章學誠 (Hong Kong: Lung-men 龍門 Book Co., 1976), 45–53.

[94] "Hsü-hsüeh", in *Wen-chi* 1:6b.

[95] Ibid., 7b.

3. *Philosophy.* Liu's open-mindedness is best seen in his approach to the philosophical schools in early China. He recommends that, after studying history, the student should read *Lao Tzu, Chuang Tzu*, the late Han Taoist classic *Lieh Tzu* 列子, and the T'ang religious Taoist work *Yin-fu Ching* 陰符經 because they contain many remarkable insights into principle. Furthermore, he recommends for careful reading books in medicine and military sciences, such as *Su-wen* 素問 for the former and the treatises attributed to Sun Pin 孫臏, Wu Ch'i 吳起, Chiang Tzu-ya 姜子牙, and Huang Ti 黄帝 for the latter.[96] He criticises Hsün Tzu's 荀子 theory of human nature but praises it for its sophistication in argumentation. Although he regards the *Kuan Tzu* 管子 as a book advocating the way of the hegemon, he still thinks that it should be studied. Among the Han Confucians, he mentions Yang Hsiung 揚雄, (53 B.C.–A.D. 18), Chia I 賈誼 (201–169 B.C.), Tung Chung-shu, and Liu Hsiang 劉向 (77–6 B.C.) in particular; he asserts that Tung's celebrated views on the mutuality of heaven and man are second only to the thought of Mencius. During the eight-century interval between the Han and the Sung, he only mentions Wang T'ung 王通 (Wen-chung Tzu 文中子, 584–618), the famed Confucian teacher of the Sui dynasty who is alleged to have trained a generation of outstanding scholar-officials for the T'ang, and Han Yü. Among the Sung thinkers, he groups together Chou Tun-i, Ch'eng Hao, Ch'eng I, and Chang Tsai as philosophers of "human nature and principle" (*hsing-li* 性理). Shao Yung is singled out as the founder of the school of "form and number" (*hsiang-shu)* 象數. And Ou-yang Hsiu, Su Shih 蘇軾, (1036–1101) and Ssu-ma Kuang are characterised as exponents of "statecraft" (*ching-chi* 經濟). Nevertheless, he does not even mention Buddhism, and he refuses to recognise Moist and Legalist texts as legitimate subjects in this highly selective list of basic philosophical readings for the confirmed Confucian.

4. *Poetry, Prose, Calligraphy, and Painting.* Liu begins his discussion of the arts with a quote from the *Analects*: "Set your will on the Way, have a firm grasp on virtue, rely on humanity, and roam among the arts."[97] He admits that the meaning of "arts" (*i* 藝) has undergone a fundamental change since the time of Confucius: while the Master used it to refer to the practices of rituals, music, archery, charioteering, calligraphy, and arithmetic,[98]

---

[96] Ibid., 7b. For his interest in and knowledge of medicine, see "*Nei-ching lei-pien hsü*" 內經類編序, in *Wen-chi* 2:5b–6b; "Shu shih yang-i" 書示疴醫, in ibid. 3:11b–12b; and "Ta i-che Lo Ch'ien-fu" 答醫者 難謙父, in ibid. 3:16b–17a.

[97] *Analects* 7:6; trans. Chan, 31.

[98] For a brief account of the "six arts" (*liu-i*) in Confucian learning, see Tu Wei-ming, "The Confucian Perception of Adulthood", *Daedalus* 105, no. 2 (Spring 1976): 115.

nowadays the arts mainly include poetry, prose, calligraphy, and painting. Since these cultural activities are essential for further self-completion, Liu continues, the student ought to study them in a systematic way. He then offers precise suggestions for undertaking a comprehensive programme of learning. In the area of poetry, Liu gives a six-point instruction, identifying his choices in practically all the major genres available to a Yüan scholar: (1) an understanding of the "six meanings" (*liu-i* 六義) in the *Book of Odes*; (2) an exposure to the *Ch'u-tz'u* style, especially the "Encountering Sorrow" of Ch'ü Yüan; (3) an awareness of the rhymed prose of the Han, in particular of pieces such as the "Three Cities" and the "Two Capitals"; (4) an acquaintance with the Wei-Chin tradition, notably the writings of the Ts'aos (Ts'ao Ts'ao 曹操 [155–220] and Ts'ao Chih 曹植 [192–232]), Liu Chen 劉楨 (d. 217), T'ao Yüan-ming and Hsieh Ling-yün 謝靈運 (385–433); (5) a knowledge of the Sui-T'ang poetic transformation, with emphasis on the works of Li Po 李白 (699–762), Tu Fu 杜甫 (712–70), and Han Yü; and (6) a familiarity with the Sung poets such as Ou-yang Hsiu, Su Shih, and Huang T'ing-chien 黃庭堅 (1045–1105). This seemingly comprehensive list is, again, highly selective. For one thing, Liu has deliberately deleted virtually all of the romantic poets. His "classicism" is also reflected in his choices for the study of prose, and, although his instructions for calligraphy and painting are much briefer, they are basically in the same spirit.

Toward the end of the essay, Liu Yin remarks confidently that if his students learn to educate themselves in this way, they will be ready either for the most active roles in the government or for a complete withdrawal to the wilderness. Indeed, all three well-known paths to immortality will be open to them: morality, politics, and scholarship. In the case of Liu Yin himself, we may surmise, his self-development or, more specifically, his quest for "purity" was not simply an attempt to steer clear of politics. Like the "sensible person" in More's *Utopia*, he wisely decided to work on the Confucian texts indoors rather than to get soaked in the pouring rain.

In retrospect, Liu Yin's Confucian eremitism seems to symbolise more than a rejection of and a protest against the Yüan dynasty. Nor did Liu's decision not to serve the Mongol government have much to do with loyalism, despite some nostalgic sentiments he expressed over the collapse of the Chin state. Frederick W. Mote has noted that Liu was not engaged in any "compulsory" eremitism that was theoretically binding on all servitors of a fallen dynasty.[99] But in what sense can Liu's refusal to serve be understood as a kind of "voluntary" eremitism? Of course, his decision was "clearly an expression of protest against impossible conditions of service, and more or

---

[99] Mote, "Confucian Eremitism", 229–32.

less directed against the ruler and his government",[100] but the grounds on which the decision was made were not exclusively political, for the Confucian demand that a man serve society is primarily an ethico-religious one. Moreover, the basic Confucian commitment is to morality and culture rather than to any particular structure of power.

It is therefore quite understandable that Liu Yin should not have been particularly interested in what is alleged to have been Confucian historiography in the writings of Ou-yang Hsiu. Although Liu praised Ou-yang for his *New Histories* of the T'ang and the Five Dynasties, it seems that Ou-yang's highly politicised attempt to rally ideological support for the threatened Sung state was to Liu no more than a personal historical judgment.[101] Furthermore, despite Liu's admiration for Ssu-ma Kuang as a historian, there is no indication that he subscribed to Ssu-ma's view on political legitimacy. Liu's decision to withdraw from politics was surely not imposed on him as a moral duty in the name of what Ou-yang and Ssu-ma characterised as "loyalty".[102] Nor was it what Nemoto Makoto 根本誠 refers to as a kind of "subjectively determined"[103] loyalism because he was impelled to choose morality and culture over politics by a profound sense of mission, an ultimate concern for personal purity and dignity out of respect for the Confucian Tao. Since his purpose in life was to become an exemplary teacher and a cultural transmitter through the effort of self-realisation, Liu Yin's eremitism not only challenged a well-established convention of identifying Confucian service with political participation but also reenacted a powerful Confucian practice, inspired by the example of Mencius: the great man carries out the Way alone, when the times do not permit him to join the government. "He cannot be led into excesses when wealthy and honoured or deflected from his purpose when poor and obscure, nor can he be made to bow before superior force."[104]

---

[100] Ibid., 209.

[101] For a survey of the political thought of this important scholar, see James T. C. Liu 劉子健, *Ou-yang Hsiu, An Eleventh-Century Neo-Confucianist* (Stanford, Calif.: Stanford University Press, 1967). See Liu Yin, "Hsü-hsüeh", in *Wen-chi* 1:7a–b; Mote, "Confucian Eremitism", 209–12.

[102] For a critical examination of interpretive positions on the Classics, such as Ssu-ma Kuang's attack on Mencius, see Hsiung Shih-li 熊十力, *Tu-ching shih-yao* 讀經示要, (reprint; Taipei: Kuang-wen Book Co., 1960) 2:1–22. It is interesting to note that Hsiung's own sense of "loyalty" led him to a severe criticism of Wu Ch'eng and Liu Yin. See ibid., 25.

[103] Nemoto Makoto, *Sensei shakai ni okeru teiko seishin* 專制社會における抵抗精神(Tokyo: Sogensha, 1952), 51–54, quoted in Mote, "Confucian Eremitism", 209.

[104] *Mencius* 3B:2; Lau, *Mencius*, 107.

6
Subjectivity in
Liu Tsung-chou's
Philosophical Anthropology

Before approaching the complex issue of the relationship between individualism and holism in Neo-Confucian thought, it is necessary to identify an appropriate point of entry, one that neither introduces a totally alien conceptual scheme nor confines the discussion to an internal dialogue. The point of entry I propose to use in this essay is the thought of Liu Tsung-chou 劉宗周 (1578–1645), one of the most brilliant original thinkers of seventeenth-century China. Since Liu's thought, like that of many of his predecessors in the Neo-Confucian tradition, can be categorised as "self-cultivation" philosophy, its main concern is self-knowledge. This stress on self-knowledge may give the impression that the solitary individual is the primary datum for analysis. In reality, however, the matter requires a twofold approach. There is the individualist side, which deals with the self in a state of solitariness. The dignity, autonomy, and independence of the self are predicated on the ability of the self to know, to feel, and to will as a moral agent. There is also the holistic side: the necessity to transcend self-centredness, to enter into meaningful communication with others, and to experience the common spring of humanity. Self-knowledge, so conceived, reveals not one's own private desires, feelings, and thoughts but the uniqueness of being human, which is shared by all members of the human community.

The whole idea of learning for the sake of the self, which is prominent in Neo-Confucian literature, addresses issues not only of individualism but also of holism. Yet the clear preference in Liu Tsung-chou's philosophical anthropology, his systematic and fundamental reflection on the ceaseless process of learning to be human, is to build his case on the idea of subjectivity. Lest we take Liu's emphasis on subjectivity as a preference for individualism, it is important to note, from the onset, that subjectivity in the Neo-Confucian context is both individualist and holistic. For the sake of convenience, we may first take the idea of subjectivity to be a movement from individualism to holism. In the course of our discussion, I want to show how insights gained from critical reflections on the Western concept of individualism[1] can be brought to bear on the Neo-Confucian idea of subjectivity. Of course, in so doing, it is essential that the integrity of the Chinese material — which, in the present case, means the shape of Liu's thought — be preserved. At the same time, I want to show that this kind of inquiry is in accord with the mode of reasoning inherent in Liu's logic. Since I have elsewhere explored the inseparability of subjectivity and onto-logical reality in Wang Yang-ming's 王陽明 (1472–1529) philosophy,[2] my focus here will be the Neo-Confucian claim that deep personal knowledge is the authentic way of making oneself whole. In other words, holism is achieved through deepened subjectivity.

T'ang Chün-i 唐君毅, in a thought-provoking article, analyses Liu Tsung-chou's philosophy as a critique of Wang Yang-ming's *hsin-hsüeh* 心學 ("learning of the mind"), especially the later developments of Wang's teaching on *liang-chih* 良知 ("conscientious consciousness", "innate knowledge", "knowledge of the good", or "primordial knowing").[3] Fang Tung-mei 方東美, on the other hand, characterises Liu as "an exponent of modified idealism based upon Wang Yang-ming".[4] Mou Tsung-san 牟宗三, while endorsing T'ang's general analysis, maintains that Liu's "internal criticism" can be understood as a refinement of Wang's formulation of the idea of *liang-chih*.[5] All of these writers seem to share the view that through critical interpretation Liu made explicit what was implicit in Wang's thought and thus brought the "learning of the mind" to its fruition.

---

[1] For a critical analysis of the idea of individualism in the West, see Steven Lukes, *Individualism* (Oxford: Blackwell, 1973). For a sociopsychological study of the idea of the self, see David L. Miller, *Individualism: Personal Achievement and the Open Society* (Austin: University of Texas Press, 1967). See also Charles A. Moore, ed., *The Status of the Individual in East and West* (Honolulu: University of Hawaii Press, 1968).

[2] "Subjectivity and Ontological Reality: An Interpretation of Wang Yang-ming's Mode of Thinking", *Philosophy East and West* 23, nos. 1–2 (January–April 1973: 187–205.

[3] T'ang Chün-i, "Liu Tsung-chou's Doctrine of Moral Mind and Practice and His Critique of Wang Yang-ming", in Wm. Theodore de Bary et al. eds., *The Unfolding of Neo-Confucianism* (New York: Columbia University Press, 1975), 305–31.

[4] Thomé H. Fang (Fang Tung-mei 方東美), *Chinese Philosophy: Its Spirit and Its Development* (Taipei: Linking Publishing Co., 1981), 471–76.

[5] Mou Tsung-san, *Ts'ung Lu Hsiang-shan tao Liu Chi-shan* 從陸象山到劉蕺山 (From Lu Hsiang-shan to Liu Chi-shan; Taipei, Taiwan: Hsüeh-sheng Shu-chü 學生書局, 1979), 451–88.

I intend, in this exploratory essay, to probe the underlying structure of Liu's thinking, viewing it not merely as a response to Wang Yang-ming's challenge but also as an articulation of a philosophical anthropology in its own right. The focus will be Liu, the original thinker who has something profound to say about moral self-cultivation, rather than Liu, a major intellectual figure of the late Ming period. Methodologically, I propose to discuss Liu's philosophical claims as if they were addressed to a timeless and spaceless human community, while assuming that the Neo-Confucian world in the seventeenth century, with all of its cultural and social specificities, was the particular locale in which Liu philosophised in the spirit of universal moral concepts.

Since a person never thinks in a vacuum, the context in which he consciously responds to challenges provides a necessary background for understanding the meaning of the expressed thought. Thus, a familiarity with the general "discourse" by which a style of thinking has been shaped is immensely helpful for an appreciation of those subtle ideas that give the content its unique contour. If we want to know how a thinker creates a new way of perceiving reality, we need to acquire a knowledge of the intellectual world in which the presumed "new way" is both a continuation of and a departure from shared assumptions. But even the availability of a kind of "mental map" of the age can provide no more than an indication of where the thinker's difficulties arise. An appreciation of the actual process by which the thinker comes to terms with his *Problematik* requires an explanation significantly different from influence studies or contextual analyses.

The primary aim of this essay is to show how subjectivity emerges as a central issue in Liu's conception of selfhood, that is, the inner core of the personality, which defines the quality of one's existence in a subtle and yet fully conscious way. Such an inquiry may help us to understand the problem, the background, and the method of addressing the perennial Confucian concern for making an ultimate commitment to the process of the goal of learning to become a sage. Furthermore, an appreciation of Liu's recommendation for "realising humanity" may shed some light on the Neo-Confucian ideal of the unity of all things, which is predicated on a belief in the great human potential for sympathy rather than on the romantic notion of "embracing the universe".

The Problem

The difficulty in understanding Liu's philosophical anthropology as an integral part of the Confucian quest for self-knowledge arises from two sources: his fidelity to the classical tradition, centring on the *Great Learning* (*Ta-hsüeh* 大學), and his unusual penchant for probing human frailty as a way of asserting personal dignity. T'ang Chün-i's description of Liu's *Problematik* is insightful:

> In Liu Tsung-chou's critique of Wang Yang-ming's thought, it is a contest for "priority or primacy" of conscientious consciousness as "willing only the good" over the "primacy or priority" of the same consciousness as "knowing good and evil". In Wang's thought, this consciousness starts with knowing good and evil; then, second, liking the former and disliking the latter; and, third, doing the former and avoiding the latter. This seems to be a psychological order conforming to common experience. However, according to Liu, this order must be converted into one which recognises the primacy or priority of the good will as an original function of mind which is connected with another original function of mind – feeling. The knowing function is essentially determined by the orientation of the original will and its accompanying feeling, and is posterior to the will and feeling in an ontological order.[6]

T'ang's description, simply put, identifies Liu's major dissatisfaction with Yang-ming's doctrine of *liang-chih* and with his Four-Sentence Teaching – namely, the issue of the priority or primacy of willing (*i* 意) over knowing (*chih* 知) in the structure and function of the mind.

In Yang-ming's Four-Sentence Teaching, which represents his final statement on Confucian self-cultivation, the centrality of *liang-chih* is evident: "There is neither good nor evil in the mind-in-itself. There are both good and evil in the activation of intentions. Knowing good and evil is the [faculty] of *liang-chih*. Doing good and removing evil is the rectification of things".[7]

For Yang-ming, moral effort begins when one is aware of the distinction between good and evil. At that moment, one's *liang-chih* takes cognisance of the situation and initiates the process of self-cultivation. Since Yang-ming advocates the unity of knowing and acting, to know is simultaneously to act. Yet from Liu's point of view, this process of self-cultivation presupposes that knowing rather than willing is the foundation of morality. As a result, Yang-ming's "final statement" still falls short of grasping the root of Confucian self-cultivation.

---

[6] T'ang Chün-i, "Liu Tsung-chou's Doctrine of Moral Mind", 313.

[7] Wing-tsit Chan, trans. and comp., *A Source Book in Chinese Philosophy* (Princeton: Princeton University Press, 1963), 86.

The *locus classicus* for this issue is the text of the *Great Learning*: "When things are investigated, knowledge is extended; when knowledge is extended, the will becomes sincere; when the will is sincere, the mind is rectified; when the mind is rectified, the person is cultivated." In this brief passage, five basic concepts in Confucian thought are ordered in a specific way: *wu* 物 (thing), *chih* 知 (knowledge), *i* 意 (will), *hsin* 心 (mind), and *shen* 身 (person). Yang-ming's attempt to underscore the primacy of knowing as an ontological ground for moral action suggests a way of reading the passages not as four discrete steps to self-cultivation but as four integrated perspectives in the same process. If we take the text of the *Great Learning* to mean four discrete steps to self-cultivation, we envision the process as a sequential development. We investigate things first in order to acquire knowledge; as knowledge is acquired, we learn to make our wills sincere; through the moral effort of making our wills sincere, we then try to rectify our minds. Only after we have rectified our minds can we begin to cultivate our persons. Thus, the investigation of things, the extension of knowledge, the sincerity of the will, and the rectification of the mind are perceived as four necessary steps by which we cultivate ourselves. Yang-ming, however, proposes that these "steps" are actually integrated in a holistic process, symbolising different degrees of refinement and subtlety in self-cultivation.

This interpretive stance, based on his theory of the "unity of knowing and acting" (*chih-hsing ho-i* 知行合一) impels Yang-ming to depart significantly from the exegetical tradition that takes the "investigation of things" as a precondition for the "extension of knowledge". In Yang-ming's thought, *ke-wu* 格物 ("investigation of things") is understood as "rectification of affairs" *cheng-shih* 正事, and *chih-chih* 致知 ("extension of knowledge") is understood as the "full realisation of primordial knowing". Thus, in taking "knowing" to mean more than cognition (because "knowing" entails "doing"), Yang-ming underscores the affective and conative aspects of the mind. Indeed, a distinctive feature of his "dynamic idealism" is its emphasis on the power of the will.[8] On the surface, what Liu objects to is not so much the original formulation of Yang-ming's position as the fallacious applications of the Four-Sentence Teaching in the writings of his disciples, notably Wang Chi 王畿 (Lung-hsi 龍谿; 1498–1583) and Wang Ken 王艮 (Hsin-chai 心齋; 1483–1541).[9] Liu's insistence on the primacy of willing over knowing can thus be interpreted as a return to and a confirmation of Yang-ming's philosophical intention. However, we must not ignore the fact that Liu's intellectual self-definition

---

[8]   Ibid., 654–91.

[9]   Mou Tsung-san, *Ts'ung Lu Hsiang-shan*, 451–52.

is significantly different from Yang-ming's. For one thing, he believes that the "fallacious applications" are rooted in the teaching of *liang-chih* itself.[10]

As T'ang notes, Liu's theoretical work is inseparable from his practical concern for providing a concrete plan for self-cultivation. The primacy of willing over knowing is, for him, "most crucial for the moral practice of becoming a sage".[11] While Liu shares with Yang-ming, and virtually all other Neo-Confucian thinkers, a faith in the perfectability of human nature through self-effort, he strongly doubts that the illumination of the mind is all that is needed. The process he envisions requires a much more subtle appreciation of the human propensity for evil. Liu's *Problematik*, in this connection, is as follows: according to Yang-ming's interpretation of the *Great Learning*, knowing good and evil entails not only liking good and disliking evil but also doing good and eradicating evil. If this is the case, the existence of evil is presupposed, and the knowledge of its existence therefore follows the experience of it. Thus, the eradication of evil can never precede the experience of it. Efforts at moral self-cultivation "are one step behind the evils already done", and to pursue human perfection is no more than "to catch the tail of those evils".[12] As a result, sagehood as the most authentic manifestation of humanity is an unrealisable ideal, and the assumption that every human being is potentially a sage is unprovable.

Liu Tsung-chou's strategy to improve on Yang-ming's teaching of *liang-chih* involves two basic assumptions. He insists, on the ontological level, that human nature is ultimately good and, on the existential level, that it is absolutely necessary for each person to engage in a continuous and strenuous moral struggle against evil. In his view, the approach that combines these two basic assumptions can open a path to sagehood that avoids the two serious fallacies of the Yang-ming school: relativism (as seen in those who are overly enthusiastic, who confuse *liang-chih* with passions and claim that the dictates of all desires must be accepted as good); and absolutism (as evidenced by those who are excessively lofty, who identify *liang-chih* with a sort of objectless "sudden enlightenment" and disregard the actual growth

---

[10] "Liang-chih shuo 良知説" (An essay on *Liang-chih*) in *Liu Tzu ch'üan-shu* 劉子全書 (The complete works of Master Liu; 1822 ed.), 8.24a–26a. Hereafter cited as LTCS. See also *Yang-ming ch'üan-hsin lu* 陽明傳信錄 (A record of the truthful transmission of Yang-ming's teaching), in *Liu Tzu ch'üan-shu i-pien* 劉子全書道編 (Supplementary edition of the complete works of Master Liu; 1850 ed.), 13.23b–24a. I am indebted to Wing-tsit Chan for calling my attention to this important text and for his kindness in making available to me his personal copy of this work, perhaps the only copy in North America. For an informative discussion of "Liang-chih shuo", see Okada Takehiko 岡田武彦, *Ryū Nen-dai bunshū* 劉念台文集 (Literary works of Liu Nien-t'ai; Tokyo: Metoku 明德, 1980), 187–99.

[11] T'ang Chün-i, "Liu Tsung-chou's Doctrine of Moral Mind", 313.

[12] Ibid., 314.

of the moral self).[13] But Liu's concern with the perceived extremes is not merely diagnostic. He goes further, criticising the later developments of the Yang-ming school in order to establish a more refined and more balanced way of self-cultivation.

Theoretically, Liu's intellectual enterprise begins with an inquiry into the "three major precepts" of the *Great Learning*, particularly the third one, which states that the way of learning to be fully human consists in one's ability to "dwell in the ultimate good" (*chih yü chih-shan* 止於至善). This statement might simply mean that in one's quest for perfection, one should try to the best of one's capacity to reach the optimal standard of performance in a given moral situation. Liu, however, interprets the "ultimate good" as the basis for self-cultivation. It is not merely an ideal for emulation, but the practical reason that moral action can be initiated in the first place. Moral action is possible because the ability to dwell in the ultimate good is inherent in our nature. It is our birthright, as moral agents, to manifest the ultimate good in our daily affairs. Since our nature is endowed by heaven, it is in its original state heavenly and thus divine in the fullest sense of the word. We are heaven's co-creators: "Heaven cannot fulfill itself without human participation."[14] Thus, Liu advances the Mencian thesis that if one knows one's own human nature, one knows heaven.[15]

The idea that human nature is good in a transcendental sense underlies virtually all traditions of Neo-Confucian thought. Liu's assertion that "human nature is originally heaven",[16] however, goes beyond the Ch'eng-Chu 程朱 belief that "human nature is principle"[17] in bringing to the fore human creativity. To say that "human nature is originally heaven" implies that human nature, as originally decreed by heaven, is also generative because it is an integral part of heaven. Heaven has an infinite power of generativity. Although the idea that human participation in the cosmic transformation of heaven and earth is central to the philosophy of the *Book of Change* and the *Doctrine of the Mean*, Liu's assumption that heaven also depends upon human activity for its own fulfillment seems unusually explicit. Therefore, for Liu, the ability to dwell in the ultimate good is not only humanly possible but morally imperative.

---

[13] "Cheng-hsüeh tsa-chieh 正學雜解" (Miscellaneous notes on verifying learning), item 25, in LTCS 6.14a.

[14] "I-yen 易衍" (Expansive notes on the *Book of Change*), chap. 7, in LTCS 2.14a.

[15] *Mencius* 7A:1.

[16] "I-yen" 2.14a.

[17] Ch'eng I 程頤, *I-shu* 遺書 (Posthumous works), in *Erh Ch'eng ch'üan-shu* 二程全書 (Complete works of the two Ch'engs; SPPY ed.), 18.17b.

By establishing the claim that human nature, rather than a transcendent source, is the basis for morality, Liu's philosophical anthropology remains very much a part of the mainstream of Neo-Confucian thinking on the matter. The rhetorical context in which he articulates this particular notion is so common that even the distinction between the Ch'eng-Chu and the Lu-Wang 陸王 schools, two diverging trends in Neo-Confucian thought, cannot be clearly made at this level of generality. In order to pinpoint Liu's unique contribution to this ongoing discourse, a brief discussion of what may be called the "principle of subjectivity" in Neo-Confucianism seems in order.

The Background

In an attempt to characterise the distinctive features of their spiritual quest, the Sung–Ming 宋明 (tenth- to seventeenth-century) Confucians defined their Way as the "learning of human nature (*hsing* 性) and heavenly decree (*ming* 命)", the "learning of mind (*hsin* 心) and human nature", or the "learning of body (*shen* 身) and mind". These four key concepts – *hsing*, *ming*, *hsin*, and *shen* – constitute the basic problem in understanding the principle of subjectivity in Neo-Confucian thought.

The Neo-Confucian quest for the realisation of the true self begins with the learning of the "body and mind". The juxtaposition of body and mind may give us the impression that the Neo-Confucians are aware of the distinction between body as the physical self and mind as the mental self. However, a distinctive feature of their mode of thinking is to transcend the distinction rather than to accept it as self-evidently true. As a result, the language of the body is laden with symbolic significance for understanding how the concept of mind (or, more appropriately, "mind-and-heart") is formulated; at the same time, the mind, as the master of the body, is never conceived as a disembodied spirit. The mutuality of body and mind defines the Neo-Confucian idea of the self and, indeed, the Neo-Confucian principle of subjectivity.

The body is a realm of existence in which ethico-religious values are created, maintained, and crystallised. The body is perceived not only as a gift from one's parents (hence the centrality of "filial piety" [*hsiao* 孝] in Confucian symbolism) but also as the highest form among sentient beings endowed by heaven. Self-cultivation (*hsiu-shen* 修身) means trimming, nourishing, and disciplining (*hsiu* 修) the body, rather than denying the bodily sensations through ascetic practices. The belief that the body has to be somehow surrendered and surpassed in order to permit the emergence of higher mental and spiritual values fundamentally conflicts with the Confucian assumption that human perfection is tantamount to the full realisation of one's "bodily form".[18] The project of self-cultivation, in concrete terms, necessarily involves the training of the body. Rites, music, archery, charioteering, calligraphy, and arithmetic are as much physical exercise as intellectual discipline.[19] It is through the "ritualisation of experience", in Erik Erikson's sense,[20] that the body matures in self-understanding and in its communicativeness.

It is true that when Chou Tun-i 周敦頤 (1017–73) describes human beings as receiving the "highest excellence" in the creative process of the cosmos, his main purpose is to place humanity in the pivotal position of metaphysics – as creator rather than creation in the "great transformation" (*ta-hua* 大化).[21] But implicit in his metaphysical outlook is the assertion that the defining characteristic of being human is sensitivity, a subtle and pervasive sense of consanguinity with all modalities of being. This enables Chang Tsai 張載 (1020–77) to make the seemingly romantic observation: "Heaven is my father and earth is my mother, and even such a small being as I find an intimate place in their midst. Therefore that which fills the universe I regard as my body and that which directs the universe I consider as my nature. All people are my brothers and sisters, and all things are my companions."[22] The metaphor of the body is extended by Ch'eng Hao 程顥 (1132–85): "The man of humanity regards heaven and earth and all things as one body. To him there is nothing that is not himself. Since he has recognised all things as himself, can there be any limit to his humanity? If things are not part of the self, naturally they have nothing to do with it. As in the case of the paralysis of the four limbs, the *ch'i* 氣 [material force, vital force] no longer penetrates them and therefore they are no longer parts of the self."[23]

---

[18] *Mencius* 6A:14, 7A:38.

[19] For a brief discussion on this aspect of Confucian education, see Tu Wei-ming, 杜維明, "The Confucian Perception of Adulthood", in his *Humanity and Self-Cultivation: Essays in Confucian Thought* (Berkeley: Asian Humanities Press, 1980), 44.

[20] Erik H. Erikson, *Toys and Reasons: Stages in the Ritualisation of Experience* (New York: Norton Press, 1978).

[21] Chou Tun-i 周敦頤, "T'ai-chi t'u-shuo 太極圖說" (Essay on the diagram of the Great Ultimate), in *Chou Tzu ch'üan-shu* 周子全書 (Complete works of Master Chou; SPPY ed.), 1.2.

[22] Chang Tsai 張載, "Hsi-ming 西銘" (The Western Inscription), in *Chang Tzu ch'üan-shu* 張子全書 (Complete works of Master Chang; SPPY ed.), 1.1a; trans., 497.

[23] Ch'eng Hao 程顥, "Selected Sayings", in *I-shu* 遺書, 2A:2; Chan, *Source Book*, 530.

On the basis of these accounts, the body can perhaps be conceived as the "house" where the human spirit dwells. The idea that the body through its sensitivity forms a communion with the myriad things can thus be understood as a concrete manifestation of the human spirit. The body, as a result, becomes an instrument for realising spiritual values. This optimism about the intrinsic goodness of the body is predicated on an assumption that basic feelings, such as joy, anger, sorrow, and delight, are indications of our response to stimuli from the outside, signifying our human sensitivity toward the world around us. The notion that appears in common parlance, that it is human to experience pain and itch, may have been derived from Ch'eng Hao's medical characterisation of paralysis of the four limbs as the "absence of humanity" (*pu-jen* 不仁) in the four limbs.[24] As the most sentient beings, humans are therefore endowed with the most sensitive bodies. And it is in this sense that "to embody all things in one's sensitivty is not only humanly possible but necessarily human".[25]

The self, as the human body, is thus a feeling, a caring, and loving self, constantly interacting and communicating with the total environment. It responds, adapts, and internalises the symbolic as well as physical resources that surround it, mobilising biological as well as affective energies for its survival, development, and fulfillment. Mencius' statement that only the sage can bring his human form to the full realisation of its potential is laden with ethico-religious implications, but in actual practice it also signifies that the "completion" of the body is an ultimate concern. Aging is perceived as a natural process of self-realisation that eventually and inevitably leads to the concluding chapter of one's life history. Premature death is regrettable; the ripe age of seventy calls for communal celebration.

Unlike the body, the mind is formless and spaceless. According to Hsün Tzu 荀子, it is vacuous, unitary, and tranquil.[26] The mind can be filled with external impressions, but it never loses its capacity for receiving new information from the outside. The mind can be attracted to a variety of subjects at the same time, but temporal fragmentation does not injure its internal coherence. And even though the mind can be easily perturbed by stimuli from the immediate environment, there is always an underlying quiescence. Hsün Tzu's attempt to emphasise the cognitive function of the mind, however, represents only a minor current in Confucian thought.

---

[24] Ch'eng, "Selected Sayings", 2A:2; Chan, *Source Book*, 530.

[25] Tu Wei-ming, "The Neo-Confucian Concept of Man", in *Humanity and Self-Cultivation*, 74.

[26] "Chieh-pi 解蔽" (Dispelling delusions), in *Hsün Tzu yin-te* 荀子引得 (Index to the *Hsün Tzu*; Cambridge: Harvard-Yenching Institute, 1950), 80.34-41.

The predominant intellectual tradition, under the influence of Mencius, designates the mind as the creative centre of morality. A primary function of the mind is thinking (*ssu* 思).[27] But thinking, in the Mencian sense, is a transformative act, involving the total person. This is part of the reason that Mencius characterises the mind as the "great body" (*ta-t'i* 大體).[28] As the creative centre of morality, the mind not only thinks but wills; and it is by willing that the mind authenticates the truthfulness of its thinking. As Mencius points out, the will is the directionality of the mind; when the mind directs, a "bodily energy" follows.[29] Actually, the conative and affective dimensions of the mind take precedence over its cognitive function. For the mind feels and wills more often and more immediately than it thinks, cogitates, and reflects.

Etymologically, the Chinese word *hsin* can also be rendered as "heart". To convey both senses, it is sometimes translated as "heart-mind".[30] Even though *hsin* is ineffable, it is directly accessible through bodily sensations. The feeling of commiseration, the sensation of being unable to bear the sufferings of another human being, is cited by Mencius to show that humaneness (*jen* 仁) is an intrinsic quality of *hsin*. Analogously, *hsin* by nature is capable of making righteous judgments, intelligent choices, and appropriate social decisions. According to Mencius, the feelings of shame, of right and wrong, and of deference are natural manifestations of *hsin*. Respectively, each of them serves as the affective basis for realising the moral will in righteousness (*i* 義), intelligence (*chih* 知), and propriety (*li* 禮). Needless to say, the Mencian conception of the heart-mind is diametrically opposed to the claim that the external environment through socialisation determines the shape of human conscience and consciousness.

It is also misleading, however, to characterise the Mencian position as a kind of immanentism, claiming that moral ideas are innate in the mind. Although Mencius maintains that humaneness, righteousness, intelligence, and propriety are not drilled into us from outside, he never undermines the importance of the environment and the necessity of experiential learning. In fact, a distinctive feature of Mencian thought is its commitment to the "learning of the mind" as a comprehensive project of self-cultivation.

[27] *Mencius* 6A:15.

[28] Ibid.

[29] Ibid. 2A:2.

[30] See Wm. Theodore de Bary, "The Neo-Confucian Learning of the Mind-and-Heart", in his *Neo-Confucian Orthodoxy and the Learning of the Mind-and-Heart* (New York: Columbia Press, 1981), 67–185.

Techniques of concentration and yogalike practices do not feature prominently in this particular approach. The ethico-religious concern for establishing what is great in each of us, commonly known as "establishing the will" (*li-chih* 立志), serves as the starting point.[31] The primary concern of such a task, which means "to make a total commitment to self-realisation", is to purify the will so that it can be exclusively focused on personal cultivation. Concretely, Mencius proposes that the best way to nourish the mind is to make desires few.[32] This seeming platitude is predicated on the belief that whenever the mind encounters a thing, it confronts the danger of being inadvertently led astray. More desires dictate contact with more things. As things interact with things, the mind becomes incapable of returning to its original state of equilibrium. It becomes "lost" in the changing landscape of the external world. Therefore, the minimum requirement for establishing the will is to search for the "lost mind".[33]

One of the major debates in Sung–Ming Confucianism is whether or not the mind can independently and automatically establish its own will. If the mind can, the act of willing is all that is needed as the initial step in moral self-cultivation. Lacking this capacity, methods of disciplining the mind with the explicit purpose of firming up the will must be devised. In either case, the underlying assumption of the perfectability of human nature through self-effort remains unchallenged. The difference, in Neo-Confucian terminology, lies in the relationship between mind and human nature. If human nature is such that the mind as a feeling, willing, and thinking faculty spontaneously creates moral values, then in the ultimate sense the mind defines what human nature truly is. There should not be an essential distinction between mind and human nature. On the other hand, if the mind is the actual faculty whereby one can learn to be moral but is not necessarily the ontological ground of morality, a significant distinction between mind and human nature must be recognised.

Confucians who hold the view that mind and human nature are identical stress the centrality of inward illumination and self-enlightenment of the mind as the direct and immediate path of perfecting one's nature. To them, the ontological ground for human beings to be moral is not a static structure but a dynamic process. As a process, human nature and mind can be automatically engender the necessary strength for the realisation of the moral

---

[31] *Mencius* 2A:6; 6A:15. Lu Hsiang-shan's philosophical anthropology can be said to have centred around this Mencian thesis. See Mou Tsung-san, *Ts'ung Lu Hsiang-shan*, 3–25.

[32] *Mencius* 7B:35.

[33] Ibid. 6A:11.

self. To establish the will is perceived by them as the most efficacious way of initiating the whole process of self-realisation. They further claim that the mind has no original substance of its own: its substance is shaped, as it were, by the moral effort of the will. In other words, will as the directionality of the mind defines the quality of the mind. We have a sort of paradox here. If the mind in itself is the defining characteristic of the goodness of human nature, why is there any need for moral self-cultivation? On the other hand, if it is essential to exert moral effort so that the goodness of human nature can be fully realised, does not the mind fall short of being totally self-enlightening?

This difficulty may have impelled Confucians who hold the view that mind and human nature are separable to maintain that the mind must be cultivated so that it can eventually be identified with human nature. The mind is not automatically self-illuminating. If it becomes so, it is because it has learned the art of self-mastery through a rigorous discipline. It is not enough to rely on the power of the will. Moral self-cultivation involves at least ritual learning, reading, and social practice. The possibility of perfecting oneself through the enlightenment of the mind without the mediation of carefully internalised methods of acquiring self-knowledge is limited. It is neither necessary nor desirable to engage oneself in the highly elusive project of bringing to fruition the moral propensity of human nature by working directly through the inner qualities of the mind; for the mind is often amorphous and the subtlety of the mind in its original state can hardly reveal itself in ordinary human existence.[34]

Although they do not agree on whether the mind can independently establish its own will, all major Neo-Confucian thinkers accept the view that human nature, as the ordaining principle, is endowed by heaven. The *raison d'être* of human existence can thus be understood as the manifestation of the "heavenly principle" (*t'ien-li* 天理) inherent in our nature. On the surface, this line of thinking seems compatible with the idea that human beings are divinely circumscribed. Indeed, the principle inherent in our nature is metaphorically a gift of the heavenly decree. However, unlike the circumscribed divinity that is only a pale reflection of the real divine, the principle (either as the Great Ultimate [*t'ai-chi* 太極] or as human nature) remains the same. Implicit in this assertion is the belief that the human principle, like the ultimate principle, is a full manifestation of the heavenly decree. Since the separation of divine and mundane, sacred and secular,

---

[34] An example of this line of thinking is found in Chu Hsi's philosophy of mind; see Mou Tsung-san, *Hsin-t'i yü hsing-t'i* 心體與性體 (The substance of mind and nature; Taipei: Cheng-Chung 正中 Book Co., 1969), vol. 3.

creator and creation, and so on, is not entertained even as a rejected possibility in Confucian symbolism, the heavenly decree can never become the
"wholly other". On the contrary, it is immanent in the basic structure
of being human: if one can fully realise one's mind, one can understand
human nature; by understanding human nature, one knows heaven.

The Method

Huang Tsung-hsi's 黃宗羲 (1610–95) influential book *Ming-Ju hsüeh-an* 明儒
學案 (Scholarly synopses of the Ming Confucians), provides us with an
overview of Liu's "learning of the heart-and-mind". It is well known that
Huang, the most famous, if not the most intimate, student of Master Liu,
did much to shape the historical image of his teacher as the last towering
figure of the Sung–Ming Confucian tradition. In Huang's judgment, Master
Liu's teaching of "vigilant solitariness" (*shen-tu* 慎獨) crystallised the essential
meaning of the Confucian Way as interpreted by the Sung philosophers and
by Wang Yang-ming. By focusing on the idea of the "root of intention" (*i-ken*
意根), Liu significantly improved on Yang-ming's theory of *liang-chih* by
developing a new understanding of the critical Neo-Confucian concept of
the "substance of nature" (*hsing-t'i* 性體), the ultimate justification for human
uniqueness. Since Huang's discussion of Liu's contribution in the *Ming-Ju
hsüeh-an* is relatively brief, however, even though his selection of Liu's writings and recorded conversations is quite extensive, we have little knowledge
of the reasoning underlying his assessment. It will therefore be more fruitful
to approach Liu's thought through Mou Tsung-san's attempt to pinpoint the
precise area in the "learning of the heart-and-mind" of Liu's original insight.

Liu was trying to combine the insights of the two Confucian traditions
mentioned above. To be specific, he wanted to reformulate the idea of the
unity of mind and human nature in Wang Yang-ming's thought so that it
might successfully defend itself against the criticism of being one-sidedly
committed to the self-enlightening capacity of the mind. Following Mou
Tsung-san's suggestion, we can perhaps characterise Liu's strategy as reformulating Yang-ming's "explicit teaching" (*hsien-chiao* 顯教) of the mind in the
spirit of the "esoteric teaching" (*mi-chiao* 密教) of "vigilant solitariness".[35]
The centrality of the idea of solitariness in Liu's concept of the concrete
process by which one learns to be human should become clear in the course
of our discussion.

Despite Liu's critique of Yang-ming's philosophy of *liang-chih*, he fully
endorses Yang-ming's emphasis on the centrality of inward illumination and

---

[35] Mou Tsung-san, *Ts'ung Lu Hsiang-shan*, 453–57.

self-enlightenment of the mind. He also shares with Yang-ming the belief that the mind can independently and automatically establish its own will. However, Liu is suspicious of the view that the knowing faculty of the mind, even with its implicit affective and conative dimensions, can really be trusted with the whole enterprise of self-cultivation. It is not what one knows but what one does not know at a given juncture of moral development that matters. The discriminating function of knowledge presupposes the dichotomy of good and evil. Such a presupposition conditions the moral agent in a divided world. Being alienated from his own nature, which is ultimately good, the moral agent can only pursue the good life in a fragmented and incremental style.

The belief that by "sudden enlightenment" the moral agent can, once and for all, dwell in the eternal bliss of the ultimate good does not provide a viable alternative either. For one thing, the supposed inward illumination of the mind can in actuality turn out to be no more than an empty vision. Yang-ming's first precept in his Four-Sentence Teaching — "the mind-in-itself is beyond good and evil" — thus begins in Liu's opinion with a wrong turn. If the substance of the mind is human nature, it should be taken as where the ultimate good dwells. The mind should not be perceived as *liang-chih*, or pure consciousness, as if the willing to be good were somehow external to its original structure. Yang-ming's second and third precepts, "in the movement of the will, there is good and evil" and "knowing good and evil is *liang-chih*", are also problematic, especially in the sense of priority. If the dichotomy of good and evil occurs in the movement of the will, primordial knowing can never precede the existence of evil. Furthermore, there is no guarantee that the act of knowing itself necessarily eradicates what the will engenders. As a result, "knowing becomes enslaved in the will; where does the good reside?"[36]

To rectify the wrong turn, Liu proposes a fine distinction between two forms of knowing. To know good and evil resembles knowing love and respect, but the resemblance is superficial. While the knowledge of love and respect is intrinsic to the feelings of love and respect, the knowledge of good and evil is extrinsic to the intuitive sense of good and evil. *Liang-chih*, in regard to love and respect, means that our primordial awareness is not adulterated by feelings of hatred and disrespect. *Liang-chih* is therefore always good. By contrast, since the knowledge of good and evil depends on a value judgment issuing from *liang-chih*, it is inevitably a secondary procedure. Liu further proposes a more refined discrimination of the idea of the will. He believes that it is vitally important to differentiate two kinds of will.

[36] "Liang-chih shuo" 良知說 8.25a.

For the sake of expediency, we shall call the first "volition" (*nien* 念) and the second "intention" (*i* 意). Liu argues that Yang-ming is hampered by two problems: a misconception of the idea of the will as intention, which compels him to search for the good in the faculty of knowing, and an unsophisticated comprehension of the idea of knowledge, which compels him to search for the most refined manifestation of the good in the mind.[37]

Liu's strategy significantly reformulates Yang-ming's Four-Sentence Teaching as follows:

> In the movements of the mind, there is good and evil.
> In the tranquillity of the will, there is liking the good and disliking
> the evil.
> Knowing good and evil is primordial knowing.
> Doing good and eliminating evil is the principle of things.[38]

In this reformulation, even though the sequence of *mind, will, knowing*, and *thing* remains unchanged and the third sentence is identical to Yang-ing's original, the meaning undergoes a profound transformation. Instead of positing as a transcendental principle that the "substance of the mind" is beyond good and evil, the mind is taken in its commonsense idea as consciousness. The will, on the other hand, assumes an active role in moral self-cultivation. Primordial knowing, accordingly, functions not as a posterior reflection on the good and evil engendered by the motions of the will; it knows as the will transforms. Liu characterises the will as "where the mind dwells rather than what the mind issues forth" and knowing as "implicated in the will rather than what the will gives rise to".[39] It is in this sense that Liu takes the will as the substance of the mind and contends that the act of willing, especially in the most subtle manifestation of such an act, defines the true function of the mind.

The centrality of the will in Liu's philosophical anthropology is evidenced in his distinction of the two kinds of will mentioned above. For him, volitional ideas, conditioned and shaped by past experiences, personal tastes, and instinctual demands, are not manifestations of the "pure will". Pure will, in its original state of intending, is the function of pure consciousness. As T'ang Chün-i notes, "consciousness is pure when it withdraws itself from outer or inner empirical objects, purifies itself from what is mixed

---

[37] Ibid. 8.25b.

[38] "Hsüeh-yen 學言" (Words on learning), pt. 1, in LTCS 10.26b. See also Huang Tsung-hsi, *Ming-ju hsüeh-an* (SPPY ed.), 62.7b.

[39] Ibid. 8.25a.

with, and sees itself as a pure subjectivity or a pure spiritual light".[40] On the other hand, if consciousness is oriented toward an object, impacted with external impressions, or mixed with ideas of the outside world, it is no longer pure. The assumption that consciousness, in its pure form, means not being conscious of something and that human beings, as their birthright, are all potentially capable of this kind of "intellectual intuition" is a salient feature of Neo-Confucian thought, indeed, of all Three Teachings in Chinese philosophy.[41] Liu's unique contribution, to quote from T'ang again, is to take pure consciousness "not merely as a pure knowing, like a light, but also as a pure feeling and a pure willing like the heat of light. Thus, pure consciousness has a life".[42]

In a deeper sense, however, Yang-ming and the majority of his followers also take pure consciousness as a vital force for ultimate self-transformation. To them, *liang-chih* as a form of pure knowing entails pure feeling and pure willing. *Liang-chih* is a transformative act as well as a reflective knowing. In the structure and function of *liang-chih* , to know involves not only "knowing that" and "knowing how" but also the evocative acts of enlightening, transforming, and, indeed, realising. Since a defining characteristic of *liang-chih* is the unity of knowledge and action, pure consciousness is also a form of creativity. The knowing subject is thus a full-fledged creator. This seemingly Berkeleyan assertion is further predicated on a belief that each human being is endowed with a godlike faculty to create through intellectual intuition. The known object becomes a living thing rather than an external fact, because the knowing subject, by an act of intention, has brought life to its existence. Yang-ming's idea that a thing is where the will resides points directly to the "idealistic" character of his thought, which seems compatible with Liu's insistence that the will as intention is a life-giving force.[43]

In what sense, then, are we to understand Liu's philosophical anthropology as reformulating Yang-ming's "explicit teaching" of the mind in the spirit of the "esoteric teaching" of "vigilant solitariness"? Mou Tsung-san suggests that we take Liu's idea of the will as a transcendental principle.[44]

---

[40] T'ang Chün-i, "Liu Tsung-chou's Doctrine of Moral Mind", 315.

[41] Mou Tsung-san, *Chih ti chih-chüeh yü Chung-kuo che-hsüeh* 智的直覺與中國哲學 (Intellectual intuition and Chinese philosophy; Taipei: Commercial Press, 1971).

[42] T'ang Chün-i, "Liu Tsung-chou's Doctrine of Moral Mind", 316.

[43] Wang Yang-ming, *Ch'üan-hsi lu* 傳習錄 (Instruction for practical living), in *Wang Yang-ming ch'üan-shu* 王陽明全書 (Complete works of Wang Yang-ming; Taipei: Cheng-Chung Book Co., 1955), 1:5.

[44] Mou Tsung-san, *Ts'ung Lu Hsiang-shan*, 465–66.

To be specific, the will as volition is empirical and thus operates *a posteriori*. The problem with volition so conceived is the implicit predisposition underlying the choices of the moral agent. The will as volition is so much intertwined with the habits of the past and the partiality of the present that it can become an indulgence rather than a liberation. If we simply act according to our volition, we may find ourselves predisposed to a behavioural pattern contrary to our moral well-being. On the other hand, the will as intention is thought to be the manifestation of the pure will. The pure will, in Liu's terminology, never strays from the "ultimate good", for it is an expression of the mind as natural as the waves of the ocean. The pure will operates in its own intuitive way totally independent of knowledge of the senses and yet never commits an intellectual fallacy. There is, therefore, absolute certainty in doing the right thing in the right situation at the right time. The main concern, however, is to see to it that the transcendental principle is concretely applied to effect the most desirable result. In other words, there is a guarantee that the transcendental principle becomes an experienced reality rather than simply a theoretical postulate. The concept of "vigilant solitariness" speaks directly to this point.

The word *tu* 獨, rendered here as "solitariness", also means uniqueness and absoluteness. The concept of "vigilant solitariness" occurs in both the *Great Learning* and the *Doctrine of the Mean*, denoting a method of self-cultivation with far-reaching ethico-religious implications. Although *shen-tu* is often translated as being "watchful over oneself when alone",[45] the commonsense reading of *shen* as "watchful" and *tu* as "alone" does not do justice to Liu's deliberate attempt to assign a pivotal position to the concept of *shen-tu* in his philosophical anthropology. To him, the self-discipline of being watchful over oneself when one is physically alone only scratches the surface of moral cultivation. The real challenge is to learn to be in tune with one's innermost being, the centre of moral creativity, which is solitary, unique, and absolute. As we have already noted, Liu takes human nature to be ultimately good, and man to be heaven's co-creator. The concomitance of heaven and man provides an ontological justification for according humanity a godlike power of creative self-transformation.

Solitariness, in this sense, denotes an ontological substance and an experienced reality. As an ontological substance, it is the heaven-endowed nature, the original mind, and the "root of intention"; as an experienced reality, it is both the unmanifested "centrality" (*chung* 中) and the manifested

---

[45] Chan, *Source Book*, 89.

"harmony" (*ho* 和) of the mind.[46] Although this aspect of Liu's thinking is compatible with the identity of mind and principle in the Lu-Wang tradition, the main thrust of his argument is deliberately more subtle and paradoxical. The "solitariness" (or, if you will, the uniquely human capacity for critical self-examination) inherent in our nature is a sufficient as well as a necessary cause for our moral self-perfection. Yet the concrete procedure by which we can initiate the process of realising fully what we essentially are is by no means straightforward. For one thing, what we existentially are falls short of what we morally ought to be, which is tantamount to what our human nature ontologically is.

Since Liu rejects the claim that the mind can by its enlightening knowledge directly bring about an ultimate moral transformation of the person, "vigilant solitariness" is not simply a form of introspective knowing. Rather, it is an attempt to create an experiential basis for a penetrating, comprehensive, and continuous scrutiny of the deepest layer of one's motivational structure. The scrutiny, in this particular connection, functions both as a focused investigation of all the underlying reasons for one's action and as an overall confirmation of the unlimited possibility for personal moral growth. Self-criticism and self-respect are thus two integrated dimensions of the same process. To be thoroughly critical of everything one does, big or small, obvious or hidden, is to be totally committed to the singularity of oneself as a dynamic moral agent. This seemingly insurmountable task of self-scrutiny cannot be carried out merely at the behavioural and attitudinal levels. Unless a linkage, indeed, a channel, is established with the centre of moral creativity to bring forth an inexhaustible supply of energy for self-cultivation, there is no hope of any qualitative improvement. Sporadic efforts certainly will not do; even systematic and programmatic endeavour is not enough, if it remains in an ethical realm that fails to account for the ultimate source of morality.

In Liu's terminology, "vigilant solitariness" involves a twofold process: to "transform volitional ideas into the mind" (*hua-nien kuei-hsin* 化念歸心)[47]

---

[46] "*Chung-yung* shou-chang shuo中庸首章證" (An essay on the first chapter of the *Doctrine of the Mean*), in LTCS (1824–35 ed.), 8.9a–12a. The first part of the essay (9a–10b) is missing from the Chung-hua Wen-shih Ts'ung-shu中華文史叢書 edition published in Taipei. The Chung-hua edition is supposed to be a photocopy of the 1822 Tao-kuang 道光 edition of the LTCS. The two pages are missing in one version of the Tao-kuang edition. The Chung-hua edition, intent on emending the defective text, supplies two handwritten pages for 9a–10b. Unfortunately, the two handwritten pages have taken material from 8.7b–9a and have thus added further confusion to the defective text. I have examined two versions of the LTCS (1824–35 ed.) in the Harvard-Yenching collection. One of them is defective in the same way.

[47] The expression *hua-nien kuei-hsin* is found in "Hsüeh-yen", pt. 2, in LTCS 11.11b. For an investigation of this issue, see "Chih-nien shuo治念説" (Theory on dealing with volition), in LTCS 8.24a–b.

and to "manifest nature through the mind" (*i-hsin tso-hsing* 以心著性).[48]
The former is predicated on the belief that intention is not an expression
of the mind but where the mind dwells.[49] In other words, the "root of
intention" defines the "substance of the mind" (*hsin-t'i* 心體). To transform
"volitional ideas" into the mind, therefore, means to restructure volition so
that it becomes totally transformed into intention. Whether or not volition
or volitional idea conveys the essential meaning of *nien*, the distinction Liu
makes is subtle but unequivocal. Using the etymological tactic of splitting
the character *nien* into the two scriptural components – *chin* 今 (today, present)
and *hsin* (mind-heart), Liu defines *nien* as *yü-ch'i* 餘氣 ("residual material
force") of the mind.[50] T'ang Chün-i characterises this aspect of Liu's thought
as follows:

> Actually, what *yü-ch'i* denotes is the potentiality of an activity when
> it is gone. This is the origin of habits. Every habit, as it comes
> from man's past activity of consciousness, has some residual effect
> to compel the present consciousness to take the habitual form, called
> *hsi* 習. *Hsi* may be quite different from nature. When the present
> consciousness takes the habitual form of its past activity, which is
> different from nature, it withdraws itself backward to the habitual
> form and solidifies in that form, becoming partial and noncreative.
> This is the origin of error and evil.[51]

Nien can thus be seen as "a solidification of consciousness controlled by
partial habitual form".[52]

Liu is aware that *nien* can be either good or bad and that it is desirable
to develop the good and eliminate the bad. But he is, in principle, dissatisfied
with the whole enterprise of initiating self-cultivation at this relativistic
level. His quest for an absolute standard of moral excellence impels him to
probe beyond objectifiable patterns of behaviour, no matter how good they
appear to be. He proposes that unwilled autonomous acts be thoroughly
scrutinised so that one can gradually learn to act in perfect accord with the

---

[48] The expression *i-hsin tso-hsing* is coined by Mou Tsung-san; see *Ts'ung Lu Hsiang-shan*, 458. The claim
is fully substantiated by Liu's interpretation of human nature; see "Yüan-hsing 原性" (On the origin
of nature), in LTCS 7.1b–3a.

[49] "Hsüeh-yen", pt. 2, in LTCS 11.6b.

[50] Ibid. 11.11a.

[51] T'ang Chün-i, "Liu Tsung-chou's Doctrine of Moral Mind", 318.

[52] Ibid.

full intention of pure consciousness.[53] In practice it is unlikely that one can ever reach such a high level of intentional self-motivation that the problem of the weakness of the will is dissolved and every act is the consequence of the mind's self-illumination. To strive for it, however, is not only a possibility for each human being but a moral imperative for those who take the "learning of the body and mind" seriously.

The second part of the twofold process of "vigilant solitariness" bring us to Liu's unique contribution to Neo-Confucian thought, namely, his "esoteric teaching". The suggestion that true human nature can be revealed only through the intentional acts of the mind is a widely shared assumption in Sung–Ming Confucian learning. Liu's unusual move, as a response to Yang-ming's precept of *liang-chih*, is to probe the innermost structure and function of the mind. This requires an experiential understanding of the mind at the moment when its manifestation of human nature is still an incipient (*chi* 幾) form. The possibility for an incipient manifestation to go astray is so great that unless one encounters the subtlety of one's own mind time and again as a lived reality at the source, one cannot ensure its full development. Although the mind is potentially capable of realising human nature fully, a frustrated manifestation rarely indicates what humanity really is. It is therefore vital to exert moral effort at the "root of intention".

However, unlike the enlightening functions of the mind, which can at least be noticed in times of introspection, the root of intention is too subtle to be fully recognised. It can easily escape our attention if we are not in tune with the basic rhythm of the creative life of pure consciousness. The cultivation of the root of intention, comparable to Mencius' recommendation for nourishing the mind, must be "unforgetful" (*wu-wang* 勿忘) and "unhurried" (*wu-chu* 勿助).[54] While fully endorsing the Mencian belief that making desires few is the best method of nourishing the mind, Liu further suggests, in the spirit of the *Doctrine of the Mean*, a continuous interplay between the "unaroused" and "aroused" states of the mind. Specifically, he proposes that we constantly follow the ebb and flow of our feelings and emotions, mapping out the seasonal changes, as it were, in order to acquire a comprehensive understanding of where we are in our stages of moral growth.[55] As we gain awareness of our inner lives, the moral effort should be directed toward an appreciation of the inseparability of the substance and

---

[53] An example of this can be found in Liu's discourse on *hsi* (habit); see "Hsi-shuo 習說" (On habits), in LTCS 8.19b–20b.

[54] *Mencius* 2A:2.

[55] "Tu *I* t'u-shuo 讀易圖說" (A diagrammatic note on reading the *Book of Change*, in LTCS 2.8B–9a. See also "Hsüeh-yen", pt. 2, in LTCS 11.9a–10b.

function of the mind. The more we act in accordance with the autonomy and spontaneity of the mind, the more we experience our nature as an authenticating activity rather than merely as an imagined possibility.

We must not be misled into believing, Liu cautions, that since our true nature is accessible to us through the spontaneous and autonomous functions of the mind, we are guaranteed a safe passage to dwelling on the ultimate good. The root of intention is so subtle that as soon as the strenous effort of "making the will sincere" (*ch'eng-i* 誠意) is discontinued, it disappears as an experienced reality. On the other hand, even though one never ceases to refine the art of bringing about the "sincerity of the will", there is always a dimension of abstruseness in the root of intention that we cannot penetrate.[56] Therefore, Liu considers "vigilant solitariness" the best approach to self-cultivation. The elaborate project of correcting mistakes in his seminal treatise, *Schematic of Man* (*Jen-p'u* 人譜), can thus be interpreted as his strategy for learning to be human by putting "vigilant solitariness" into practice as a daily ritual.

Realising Humanity

Liu's *Schematic of Man* is, on the surface, a map, a diagram, a score, or a manual for teaching people to "change to the good and reform faults"[57] in order to become fully developed moral persons. The underlying structure of the treatise, however, is a holistic vision of self-cultivation by the practice of "vigilant solitariness". Human beings, as the most sentient beings in the universe, are "decreed" by heaven to embody the "centrality" of the cosmic transformation as their nature. They are "created" not as creatures but as co-creators for the task of providing necessary assistance in the cosmic transformation of heaven and earth.[58] As a full member of this trinity, humanity is divine by definition, and it is human to be divine. However, although human nature is ultimately good, its way of self-manifestation is by no means transparent. The naive belief that one can become a sage by sudden enlightenment, without the strenuous effort of self-cultivation, is based on a misunderstanding of the abstruseness of the original design: human nature can be manifested only through the willing, knowing, and feeling activities of the mind.

---

[56] "Kai-kuo shuo 改過説" (On correcting mistakes), pt. 1, in LTCS 1.13a–b.

[57] *Jen-p'u*, in LTCS 1.6b.

[58] *Doctrine of the Mean*, secs. 29–31. See Chan, *Source Book*, 111–12.

The identity of the "substance of the mind" and human nature notwithstanding, the mind needs to be disciplined, cultivated, and nourished so that the "centrality" inherent in it can manifest itself without being obstructed by enclosed and limiting selfish ideas. To realise humanity is therefore to bring the actual functions of the mind into harmony with the constituents, such as the "four beginnings" (*ssu-tuan* 四端),[59] of human nature. Human nature so conceived is itself an activity, not merely a ground or an ideal of moral perfection. However, the form of activity human nature autonomously engenders is so subtle and incipient that it is hardly perceivable by the untutored mind. The incipient activity of human nature, known as the root of intention, is actually the substance of the mind. The failure of the untutored mind to recognise this means that the mind has yet to learn to listen to its own voice. The art of "vigilant solitariness", practised vigorously as a daily ritual, can purify one's sense perceptions and provide an experiential basis for the mind to be constantly responsive to the subtle signals of human nature.

The procedure, a ceaseless process of learning to be human, involves the following concrete steps: (1) dwelling in secluded retirement in order to experience the self in solitude; (2) divining the movement of thought in order to recognise incipient tendencies; (3) exercising caution in one's bearing in order to follow the decree of heaven; (4) strengthening the basic human relationships in order to crystallise the Way; (5) making complete the hundred practices in order to investigate one's conduct comprehensively; and (6) changing to the good and reforming faults in order to become a sage. These steps are further put in the context of a penetrating, comprehensive, and continuous project of self-criticism, which identifies moral failings in terms of six major categories: subtle faults, concealed faults, obvious faults, great faults, miscellaneous faults, and completed faults.[60]

Realising humanity, in Liu's philosophical anthropology, entails a thorough analysis of one's behaviour, attitude, motivation, and root of intention. The purpose is neither social adjustment nor personal integration in the ordinary psychological sense; it is rather the optimal manifestation of one's moral creativity as an ultimate concern. Human beings so defined are self-perfecting beings. Being human means to be ultimately self-transforming. To deepen one's subjectivity through "vigilant solitariness" is to open oneself up to the common spring of humanity. The deepened and deepening subjectivity is constantly in tune with the rhythmic pattern of heaven and earth; it is a

---

[59] *Mencius* 2A:6.

[60] *Jen-p'u* 1.3a–11b.

liberation from the constraints of "opinionatedness" (*i* 意, ironically, this is the same character that Liu later used to mean "intention"), "stubbornness" (*pi* 必), "arbitrariness" (*ku* 固), and "self-centredness" (*wo* 我).[61] Our dignity, autonomy, and self-sufficiency as human beings certainly lie in our possessing bodies and mind. Yet we really possess them when we have learned to recognise the true face of our human nature.

In the perspective of Liu Tsung-chou's philosophical anthropology, the relationship between individualism and holism assumes a particular meaning. The dignity and autonomy of the self is predicated on one's ability to go beyond the limitation and inertia of self-centredness because of one's deep personal knowledge. As a result, one does not assert one's independence as an individual vis-à-vis society. The central concern is the establishment and, more appropriately, the realisation of one's true subjectivity. True subjectivity, as the genuine will beyond the restrictions of selfish desires, is not simply a state of being but also a transformative activity. It is a dynamic movement toward the ultimate good. The realisation of one's true subjectivity, which can also be understood as a way of liberating oneself from obvious and insidious forms of egoism and subjectivism, necessarily involves the cultivation of a widening horizon of human understanding. The authentic way of making oneself whole is, therefore, not simply to search for that which is uniquely one's own but to acquire a taste for the quality that is uniquely human – ultimate self-transformation as a communal act. Only then can one really *know* heaven through one's own nature and thus form a trinity with heaven and earth. Holism, in this sense, is a natural outcome of subjectivity. As one authenticates one's "vigilant solitariness", one enlarges and refines one's sensitivity. The "embodiment" (*t'i* 體) of the universe holistically in one's subjectivity, far from being the expansion of the ego, signifies the openness, the transparency, and the spontaneity of the cultivated self.

---

[61] *Analects* 9:4. It should be noted that the character *i* used in this context, meaning "arbitrariness of opinion", is often rendered as "selfish ideas" in Neo-Confucian terminology. The same character, used in Liu's philosophical anthropology, is comparable in meaning to the Mencian idea of "will" in *Mencius* 2A:2.

7

Perceptions of
Learning (Hsüeh) in
Early Ch'ing Thought

Han Learning

It has often been assumed that Han Learning 漢學, as opposed to Sung Learning 宋學, is close to what academic people take to be the objectifiable standards of scholarship in basic research. For one thing, the Ch'ing 清 scholars who are thought to have been important practitioners of Han Learning were first-rate classicists, textual analysts, semanticists, and above all philologists. Most of them established their scholarly reputations by investigating one or several classical texts. Yen Jo-chü's 閻若璩 (1636–1704) critical study of the *Ku-wen Shang-shu* 古文尚書, for example, is a remarkable demonstration of methodological rigour in bringing virtually all available "sinological" techniques to bear upon the analysis of a single work. His *Shu-cheng* 疏證, the result of more than two decades of scholarly inquiry, is a combination of broad historical knowledge, highly refined philological skill, and unusually keen textual observations.[1] Yen's contemporary, Hu Wei 胡渭 (1633–1714), among other impressive accomplishments, brought new understanding to the ancient geographical treatise *Yü-kung* 禹貢, by his realistic reconstruction of the irrigational system in early China.[2] Chiang Fan 江藩 (1761–1831), in his controversial book on the transmission

---

[1] Yen Jo-chü, *Ku-wen Shang-shu shu-cheng* 古文尚書疏證 (Evidential commentary on the ancient text of the *Book of History*), 10 vols. (1796).

[2] Hu Wei 胡渭, *Yü-kung chui-chih* 禹貢錐指 (Pinpointing the *Tributes of Yü*), 20 *chüan* 卷, in Ch'ing ching-chieh 清經解 (Interpreting the classics in the Ch'ing), 20–47. Hu's work is still extensively used by modern specialists on the subject. See Hsin Shu-ch'ih 辛樹幟, *Yü-kung hsin-chieh* 禹貢新解 (A new interpretation of the *Tributes of Yü*; Hong Kong: Chung-hua 中華 Book Co., 1973), 2.

of the Han Learning in the Ch'ing dynasty, begins the genealogical line with Yen and Hu.[3]

Learning so conceived is directed toward the appropriation of empirical truth, literary knowledge, and ancient wisdom. Its main concern is neither internal self-cultivation nor the transformation of society by ritual acts but scholarship as a way to be human. Its method is inductive, its spirit critical, and its intention pragmatic. The underlying logic is not difficult to see: to use Ku Yen-wu's 顧炎武 analogy, the pursuit of scholarship is like mining copper. Without the actual endeavour in the fields, simply using recycled brass cannot produce top-quality coins. The problem with the lesser scholars is that they often satisfy themselves with the reminting of obsolete coins. As a result, their scholarship remains poor. Therefore it is absolutely necessary for the student to confront the primary sources with the critical eye of a skilful miner. Only then will he be able to come up with useful material.[4]

The learning of the "Han scholars" consists in a multidisciplinary approach to the written word. This deceptively simple methodological preference involves complex intellectual exercises, including palaeography, morphology, phonology, etymology, lexicology, and grammar. The questions posed and the answers provided by these scholars on the Chinese language remain influential in fields such as pragmatics, syntactics, and hermeneutics. Tuan Yü-ts'ai's 段玉裁 (1735–1815) systematic perusal of the first comprehensive dictionary of Chinese characters,[5] Chiao Hsün's 焦循 penetrating analysis of the *Book of Change*,[6] Wang Ming-sheng's 王鳴盛 (1722–97) massive research notes on the seventeen dynastic histories,[7] Wang Yin-chih's 王引之

---

[3] Chiang Fan, *Han-hsüeh shih-ch'eng chi* 漢學師承記 (The scholarly transmission of Han Learning), 8 *chüan* (preface, 1818). See an annotated version by Chou Yü-t'ung 周予同 (reprint; Hong Kong: Commercial Press, 1964).

[4] The statement was made by Ku in his response to a friend's query about his *Jih-chih lu* 日知錄 (Record of daily knowledge). See "Yü-jen shu 與人書" (Letters to people), no. 10, in *T'ing-lin wen-chi* 亭林文集 (Collected literary works of Ku Yen-wu), 4, quoted in Hsieh Kuo-chen 謝國楨, *Ku T'ing-lin hsüeh-p'u* 顧亭林學譜 (A scholarly chronology of Ku Yen-wu; rev. ed., Shanghai: Commercial Press, 1957), 53.

[5] Tuan Yü-ts'ai, *Shuo-wen chieh-tzu chu* 說文解字注 (Commentary on the *Explanation of Words*), 32 *chüan* (1808).

[6] Chiao Hsün, *Chiao-shih I-ku* 焦氏易詁 (Commentary on the *Book of Change* according to Master Chiao), ed. Shang Ping-ho 尚秉和 (reprint; Taipei: Chung-hua Book Co., 1971).

[7] Wang Ming-sheng 王鳴盛, *Shih-ch'i shih shang-ch'üeh* 十七史商榷 (A critical study of the seventeen standard dynastic histories), 2 vols. (punctuated ed., Shanghai: Chung-hua Book Co., 1958).

(1766–1834) major effort at the reconstruction of ancient Chinese phonetics[8] and Hung Liang-chi's 洪亮吉 (1746–1809) little-known commentaries on the *Spring and Autumn Annals*[9] have set such high scholarly standards that they have continued to evoke a sense of awe among serious students of sinology for almost two centuries.

The case of Tai Chen 戴震 (1723–77) is particularly noteworthy. His thought-provoking analysis of the *Book of Mencius*,[10] based on a firm belief that philology is the prerequisite for correct semantics and authentic hermeneutics, should rank as a watershed in Ch'ing scholarship as a whole. And his commitment to "evidential" learning both as a quest for deep understanding of the classical heritage and as a critique of the mode of thinking characteristic of Sung Confucian masters symbolises the intellectual preference, indeed the spiritual orientation of his generation. What Tai Chen advocated, however, was by no means simply a methodology. He was, of course, interested in determining the precise meanings of key words in the text of *Mencius*, but intent on a holistic appreciation of fundamental thrusts of Mencian thought, he regarded philological studies as points of departure. His aim was to interpret the Confucian tradition in a new light.

Tai Chen's approach, then, was meant to be a systematic inquiry into the underlying structure of classical Confucian thought. He rejected the possibility that the intentions of the sages could be comprehended as something independent of their linguistic articulations in the texts. Since the sagely messages contained in the surviving records had already fallen into oblivion, Tai contended, the student must seek them through philological studies of the classics. He therefore asserted, "Only if etymology is clear, can the ancient Classics be understood; and only if the Classics are understood, can the sages' philosophical ideas be grasped."[11] The seriousness with which he conducted his own philological study of *Mencius* is therefore an example

---

[8] Wang Yin-chih 王引之, *Ku-yün p'u* 古韻譜 (The schematic of ancient phenology), in *Kao-yu Wang-shih i-shu* 高郵王氏遺書 (Surviving works of Master Wang of Kao-yu), ed. Lo Chen-yü 羅振玉, 8 vols. (preface, 1925), vol. 3.

[9] Hung Liang-chi, *Tso-chuan ku* 左傳詁 (Philological study of the *Tso Commentary of the Spring and Autumn Annals*) in *Hung Pei-chiang ch'üan-chi* 洪北江全集 (Complete collection of Hung Liang-chi's works), 8 vols. (1877 ed.). Hung is well-known for his insightful observations on social and economic matters of his time. See *I-yen* 意言 (Intentional words), in *Hung Pei-chiang ch'üan-chi* 1:1a–25b.

[10] Tai Chen, *Meng Tzu tzu-i shu-cheng* 孟子字義疏證 (Evidential commentary on the meanings of words in *Mencius*), ed. Ho Wen-kuang 何文光 (Peking: Chung-hua Book Co., 1961).

[11] Tai Chen, "Yü Shih Chung-ming lun-hsüeh shu" 與是仲明論學書 (Letter discussing scholarly matters with Shih Chung-ming), in *Tai Chen wen-chi* 戴震文集 (Collected literary works of Tai Chen), punctuated and edited by Chao Yü-hsin 趙玉新 (Hong Kong: Chung-hua Book Co., 1974), 140. For this translation, see Yü Ying-shih 余英時 "Some Preliminary Observations on the Rise of Ch'ing Confucian Intellectualism", *The Tsing Hua Journal of Chinese Studies*, n.s. 10, nos. 1 and 2 (December 1975): 113.

of his personal "encounter" with Mencian philosophy as well as a demonstration of his application of the etymological method.

The method, according to Tai's theoretical formulation, involves at least three interconnected levels of analysis. The fundamental training focuses on the recognition of single characters, not as signs with one-dimensional references but as signs with complex life histories of their own. To perform this etymological task requires a highly specialised knowledge of palaeography, morphology and phonology, among other disciplines. Once words are recognised, the semantic quest begins. At this level, the student is instructed to make all kinds of intratextual comparisons so that associative meanings of key words can be established. Only then can sentences be fully appreciated as carriers of intentional utterances. The semantic quest necessitates what may be called a continuous exercise of "intertextural" analysis, the act of weaving together a variety of ideas and themes in the classical tradition. This is partly the reason behind Tai Chen's assertion that one of the three most difficult requirements for becoming a classicist is erudition.[12] Tai was himself, however, among the most erudite scholars of his generation. He was, besides being a leading classicist and philosopher of the Ch'ien-Chia 乾嘉 era (1736–1820), a noted mathematician, geographer, and astronomer.

Having mastered the etymological and semantic skills, one is then ready to engage in the interpretive art. Tai Chen showed that the ontological principle (*li* 理) in Sung Confucian thought is not only absent from but basically incompatible with the philosophical intentions of Confucius and Mencius.[13] In so doing, he attempted to reorient the spiritual direction of his age from metaphysical speculations on the ultimate reality to lived experiences of ordinary people. We will explore later the role of his profound concern for the political misappropriation of Confucian symbols for social control in motivating his "naturalist" and "empiricist" tendency in interpreting Mencius. Suffice it now to say that for decades Tai Chen has been studied and honoured as an original thinker because of his interpretive art. Hu Shih 胡適 may have exaggerated the claim about Tai's "pragmatism"[14]

---

[12] The other two difficulties are "insightful judgment" and "refined examination". See Tai, "Yü Shih Chung-ming lun-hsüeh shu", 141.

[13] Tai Chen did not deny the existence of the idea of *li* in classical Confucian thought; nor did he propose a total ban on the use of the word *li*. His interpretative strategy was to show that the attempt of the Sung masters to regard *li* as a metaphysical principle was extremely problematical. Indeed, one of Tai's sustained intellectual efforts was to establish an inseparable link between *li* and human feelings (*ch'ing* 情). See *Meng Tzu tzu-i shu-cheng*, 1–20, esp. 4–5.

[14] Hu Shih treated Tai's "pragmatic" contribution to Ch'ing scholarship against the background of Yen Yüan 顏元 on the one hand and Ku Yen-wu on the other. See his *Tai Tung-yüan te che-hsüeh* 戴東原 的哲學 (The philosophy of Tai Chen; Shanghai: Commercial Press, 1927), 1–21.

and Hou Wai-lu 侯外廬 about his "materialism",[15] but it is beyond dispute that Tai's encounter with Mencius is laden with far-reaching philosophical implications.[16]

Tai Chen is presented as the paradigm of a true Confucian scholar in Chiang Fan's influential book on the transmission of Han Learning in the Ch'ing dynasty. Even in terms of pure scholarship, Chiang ranked him as high as the well-known master Ch'ien Ta-hsin 錢大昕 (1728–1804).[17] However, Chiang's interpretation of Han Learning as the predominent intellectual trend in the Ch'ing has remained controversial ever since its publication in 1818. Chiang's interpretive position even drew criticism from Kung Tzu-chen (1792–1841) before the book was printed for wide circulation by Juan Yüan 阮元 (1764–1849) in Canton.[18] In Kung's 1817 letter to Chiang, the prominent thinker lists ten persuasive arguments against the characterisation of Ch'ing scholarship as Han Learning, noting that the dichotomy of Han and Sung is arbitrary and misleading. After all, Kung claims, some Sung scholars had been aware of the importance of philological studies and quite a few Han scholars had indulged in superstitious speculations. Kung thus recommends "Classical learning" as the appropriate label for Ch'ing scholarship.[19]

Kung's critical reflection on Chiang Fan's attempt to subsume the works of some of the most creative minds in early Ch'ing thought under the concept of Han Learning was by no means an isolated attack. His criticism was echoed by several nineteenth-century scholars. Ho Ch'iu-t'ao 何秋濤 (1824–62), Wu Ch'ung-yao 余重耀 (1810–63), and P'i Hsi-jui 皮錫瑞 (1850–1908), for example, all raised objections to this obviously one-sided appellation.[20]

[15] Hou Wai-lu, *Chung-kuo tsao-ch'i ch'i-meng ssu-hsiang* 中國早期啓蒙思想(History of early enlightenment thought in China), also known as the fifth volume of *Chung-kuo ssu-hsiang-shih* 中國思想史 (History of Chinese thought; Beijing: People's Publishers, 1958), 431–33. It should be mentioned that Hou also insisted that Tai's "intellectualism" was clearly in the idealist tradition, see p. 455.

[16] See Chung-ying Cheng 成中英, trans., *Tai Chen's Inquiry into Goodness* (Honolulu: The University Press of Hawaii, 1971), 3–53. Cheng's claim about Tai's successful critique of "Neo-Confucian" thought is debatable.

[17] In Chiang Fan's work, the chapters on Tai and Ch'ien are definitely among the most substantial both in terms of length and content. See *Han-hsüeh shih-ch'eng chi*, 202–75, 326–53.

[18] For information concerning the controversy over the publication of Chiang's study, see Chou's annotated version of the *Han-hsüeh shih-ch'eng chi*, 42–50.

[19] Kung Tzu-chen, "Yü Chiang Tzu-p'ing chien 與江子屏牋" (Letter to Chiang Tzu-p'ing), in *Kung Tzu-chen ch'üan-chi* 集自珍全集 (Complete works of Kung Tzu-chen), 2 vols., collated by Wang P'ei-cheng 王佩箏 (Hong Kong: Chung-hua Book Co., 1974), 346–47. For a brief discussion on the issue, see Yü Ying-shih, "Some Preliminary Observations", 223.

[20] See Chou, *Han-hsüeh shih-ch'eng chi*, 17–50.

They concluded that Chiang's glorification of Han Learning significantly restricted the actual range of scholarship in the Ch'ing. P'i in particular was annoyed by Chiang's seemingly innocuous decision to append the biographies of the two intellectual giants of the seventeenth-century, Huang Tsung-hsi 黃宗羲 (1610–95) and Ku Yen-wu (1613–82), to the end of the book.[21] The great prestige of Huang and Ku in the late Ch'ing intellectual scene must have enhanced P'i's impression that to put Yen Jo-chü and Hu Wei, instead of Huang and Ku, as the founding fathers of the new scholarship in early Ch'ing was a serious misjudgment.

By far the most systematic and powerful critique of Chiang's attempt to define Ch'ing studies in terms of Han Learning was developed by the T'ung-ch'eng 桐城 scholar, Fang Tung-shu 方東樹 (1772–1851).[22] Apparently under the influence of the prominent literary figure Yao Nai 姚鼐 (1732–1815), Fang directed scathing remarks against virtually all of the "Han scholars".[23] The polemical nature of Fang's *Han-hsüeh shang-tui* 漢學商兌 clearly indicates that his primary purpose was to appeal to his contemporaries for a redress of injustice done to Sung Learning. He repeatedly stressed Chu Hsi's 朱熹 (1130–1200) balanced approach to learning, which, he insisted, always required a commitment to philological studies. It was the Han Learning, he argued, that substantially restricted the rich resources of the Confucian tradition to the cultivation of fruitless examinations of "names, things, implements, and numbers". Although he severely denounced Wang Chung's 汪中 (1744–94) fascination with Moism and Liu T'ai-kung's 劉台拱 (1751–1805) refusal to take Sung commentaries on the classics into serious consideration, his critical reflections were centred on Tai Chen.[24] For he believed that Tai was instrumental in relegating Sung Learning to the background.

The essential points of Fang's all-out offensive against Tai can be summarised as follows: (1) Tai's claim that the study of the Six Classics depended on a systematic analysis of the meanings of words was no more than an affirmation of what the Sung scholars had taken for granted. (2) Tai's condemnation of the ontological principle and his emphasis of the lived experiences of the people was a "straw man" tactic because the Sung scholars never committed

[21] P'i Hsi-jui, *Ching-hsüeh li-shih* 經學歷史 (History of classical learning), annotated by Chou Yü-t'ung (Shanghai: Commercial Press, 1934), as noted in Chou, *Han-hsüeh shih-ch'eng chi*, 52 n. 8. A similar argument is advanced by Yeh Te-hui 葉德輝 in his *Ching-hsüeh t'ung-kao* 經學通告 (A comprehensive statement on classical learning), as also noted in Chou, *Han-hsüeh shih-ch'eng chi*.

[22] Fang Tung-shu, *Han-hsüeh shang-tui* (A critical discussion of Han Learning), 4 vols. (1882 ed.)

[23] See his preface to *Han-hsüeh shang-tui* 1:1a–2a.

[24] Ibid. 2:14a–15a may serve as an example.

what Tai depicted as "murder in the name of private opinions". (3) Tai's emphasis on "Elementary Learning" (*hsiao-hsüeh* 小學), far from being an innovation, substantially limited the scope of education as envisaged in classical Confucian thought. And (4) Tai's methodological procedure, from etymology to hermeneutics, was problematical; sometimes the semantic locus of a single word must be determined by a comprehensive understanding of the philosophical intention of the text as a whole.[25]

Fang's remarks, suggestive as they are, represented a minority point of view. His contemporary Juan Yüan, a high official and influential scholar, brought Han Learning to a powerful intellectual position. As a result, Sung Learning, in Fang's conception of it, further declined and Fang himself gained the reputation of a faultfinding critic. But despite the abortiveness of Fang's attempt, he did call into question the very concept of Han Learning as an adequate way to describe early Ch'ing thought in general and the intellectual orientations of the "Ch'ien-Chia masters" in particular. This leads us first to an examination of other equally prevalent perceptions of learning among the first generation of Ch'ing scholars.

Sung Learning and Ming Thought

Although it is widely accepted that Ch'ing Learning was a critique of Sung Learning, its emergence of a distinctive mode of scholarship in the eighteenth century marked a confluence of intellectual trends wherein Sung thought, especially the legacy of Chu Hsi, played a definitive role. Ku Yen-wu, who had exerted perhaps the single most profound impact on the development of the Ch'ien-Chia style of learning, was himself a committed thinker of the Ch'eng-Chu 程朱 persuasion which followed the teachings of Ch'eng I 程頤 (1033–1107) and Chu Hsi. His *Jih-chih lu* 日知錄, innovative as it is, can be understood as a systematic working out of the social and economic implications of the Ch'eng-Chu precept of *ke-wu* 格物 ("investigation of things").[26]

Of course, it is an oversimplification to assume that Ku's intellectual enterprise, centring on the broad Confucian concern of *ching-shih chi-min*

---

[25] My summary is based upon the following sources: ibid. 2:18b–24b, 3:3a–4a, 9a–13a, 14a–23b, 47a–48b.

[26] The title *Jih-chih lu* 日知錄 was based on Tzu Hsia's 子夏 statement, "He who from day to day knows [*jih-chih*] what he lacks, and from month to month never forgets what he has learned, may indeed be called a true lover of learning" (*Analects* 14:5). See *Jih-chih lu chi-shih* 日知錄集釋 (Collected commentaries on the *Record of Daily Knowledge*), comp. Huang Ju-ch'eng 黃汝成 (1869 ed.), preface. Therefore, it may not be farfetched for Chiang Wei-ch'iao 蔣維喬 to claim that Ku was in the Chu Hsi line. See *Chung-kuo chin san-pai nien che-hsüeh shih* 中國近三百年哲學史 (History of Chinese philosophy in the last three hundred years; reprint; Taipei: Chung-hua Book Co., 1972), 5–9. Hsieh Kuo-chen has made the same claim; see his *Ku T'ing-lin hsüeh-p'u*, 35.

經世濟民 (governing the world and helping the people), was no more than a continuation of the political philosophy of Chu Hsi. Indeed, the nineteenth-century Ch'ing scholar T'ang Chien 唐鑑 (1778–1861) may have placed too much emphasis on Ku's "internality" (*nei* 內) when he argued in his monumental biographies of Ch'ing scholars that the real strength of Ku's "comprehensive and penetrating" (*t'ung* 通) insights lay in his power of conceptual thinking and that as a rule Ku's refined observations weighed in favour of Chu Hsi.[27] But it is undeniable that Ku's criticism of the School of Mind was not at all intended to discredit Sung Learning.

Even though it is debatable whether Ku Yen-wu can be properly characterised as a Ch'eng-Chu follower, an outstanding early Ch'ing scholar, Lu Shih-i 陸世儀 (1611–72), has made it clear that his intellectual self-identification was in perfect accord with the Sung masters.[28] Refusing to serve the Manchu government despite repeated invitations from the court, Lu gained a wide reputation both as a Ming loyalist and as a Confucian master by devoting himself exclusively to teaching and writing. Among his voluminous works, the *Record of Critical Thinking* (*Ssu-pien lu* 思辨錄) alone represents more than twenty years of scholarly effort.[29] His two instructional foci were "dwelling in seriousness" (*chü-ching* 居敬) and "searching exhaustively for the principle" (*ch'iung-li* 窮理), which he asserted were in the spirit of the Ch'eng-Chu pedagogy of integrating the internal and the external. To Lu, "dwelling in seriousness" cultivated a sense of internal self-mastery that resembled the Ch'eng-Chu method of moral nourishment, and "searching exhaustively for the principle" assured a process of personal knowledge that resembled the Ch'eng-Chu method of intellectual development.[30]

Lu's accomplishments as teacher and writer can, of course, be understood in terms of pure scholarship. His refusal to serve the new regime can perhaps also be interpreted as a scholarly preference. In fact, the editors of the *Ssu-k'u ch'üan-shu t'i-yao* 四庫全書提要 were particularly impressed by his solid scholarship, as opposed to the "speculative" thought of many late Ming

---

[27] T'ang Chien, *Ch'ing-Ju hsüeh-an* 清儒學案 (Intellectual biographies of Ch'ing scholars), also known as *Hsüeh-an hsiao-chih* 學案小識 (Brief Notes on intellectual biographies), 6 vols. (epilogue, 1845), 3:3a–b.

[28] For an exposition of Lu Shih-i's philosophical orientation, see his *Hsing-shan t'u-shuo* 性善圖說 (A diagrammatical exposition of the goodness of human nature), in *Lu Fu-t'ing hsien-sheng i-shu* 陸桴亭先生遺書 (Surviving works of Lu Shih-i), 20 vols. (preface, 1899), vol. 15, 1a–11a.

[29] According to Lu's *Nien-p'u* 年譜, he began the task in 1637 and the book was printed in 1661. See *Lu Fu-t'ing hsien-sheng i-shu*, under 27 *sui*, vol. 1, 6b, and under 51 *sui*, 38b–41b.

[30] For a vivid account of his appropriation of the Ch'eng-Chu ideas for spiritual self-development, see his *Chih-hsüeh lu* 志學錄 (A record of the will to learn), in *I-shu*, vols. 13–14.

thinkers.[31] But Lu himself confessed that one of his deep regrets in life was to have missed the lectures of Liu Tsung-chou 劉宗周 (1578-1645), the esteemed "subjective idealist" whose loyalism inspired a whole generation of young scholars in early Ch'ing.[32] It is difficult to maintain that Lu's scholarship, no matter how narrowly defined, was not in a substantial way shaped by his political vision of the world around him. His sense of mission was not simply a concern for a specific line of scholarly inquiry but a reflection of his total commitment to the Sagely Way.

The preservation of the Sagely Way, as differentiated from the loyalty to the Ming dynasty, underlay Ku Yen-wu's statement that each person must assume a moral responsibility when "all under heaven" is at stake. It is not farfetched to assert that, as contrasted with the state, "all under heaven" referred to the cultural tradition informed by the Sagely Way as its ideal manifestation.[33] Actually, in response to his mother's loyalism, Ku never served in the Ch'ing government either.[34] And in Ku's teaching itself a sense of shame, a profound moral compunction for the well-being of the world at large, is inseparable from scholarship.[35] This is the main reason, I suppose, that his empiricist orientation did not alienate him from the Mencian ontology: "All myriad things are already complete in me.

---

[31] For a succinct account of his approach to Neo-Confucian thought, see his letter entitled "Ta Wang Chou-chen t'ien-ming hsin-hsing chih-ch'i ch'ing-ts'ai wen" 答王周臣天命心性志氣情才問 (Response to Wang Chou-chen's questions on the mandate of heaven, mind, human nature, will, vital force, feeling, and ability), in *Lun-hsüeh ch'ou-ta* 論學酬答 (Responses to questions on learning), found in *I-shu* 遺書, vol. 11, 2:2a–6a.

[32] However, according to the *Nien-p'u*, he did benefit from a brief intellectual encounter with Liu Tsung-chou's student Shih Tzu-hsü 史子虛, see *I-shu*, under 35 *sui*, 16b–18b. The characterisation of Liu Tsung-chou as a "subjective idealist" is highly problematical. For example, see *Chung-kuo che-hsüeh shih chiang-shou t'i-kang* 中國哲學史講授提綱 (Lecture outlines on the history of Chinese philosophy), ed. the Department of Philosophy at Peking University (reprint; Hong Kong: Ch'ung-wen 崇文 Book Co., 1975), 91.

[33] See *Jih-chih lu*, *chüan* 13, quoted in Ch'ien Mu 錢穆, *Chung-kuo chin san-pai nien hsüeh-shu shih* 中國近三百年學術史 (History of Chinese scholarly developments in the last three hundred years), 2 vols. (reprint; Taipei: Commercial Press, 1972), vol. 1, 129–30.

[34] See Chang Mu 張穆, *Ku T'ing-lin nien-p'u* 顧亭林年譜 (Chronological biography of Ku Yen-wu; preface, 1843), under 33 *sui*– 16B–17a.

[35] As Hsieh Kuo-chen notes, the statement on *po-hsüeh yü-wen* 博學於文 (extensive learning in literature) and that on *hsing-chi yu-ch'ih* 行己有恥 (conducting oneself with a sense of shame) are found in *Hsiao-hsüeh chih-nan* 小學指南 (Guide to fundamental learning), see Hsieh, *Ku T'ing-lin hsüeh-p'u*, 49. The same statement is also found in Ku's "Yü yu-jen lun-hsüeh shu 與友人論學書" (Collected literary works of Ku Yen-wu), which is included in *T'ing-lin i-shu* 亭林遺書 (Surviving works of Ku Yen-wu), 40 vols. (1888 ed.), vol. 33, 3:1a–2b. So far as the *Jih-chih lu* can be taken as a working out of Chu Hsi's idea of *ke-wu* 格物, Ku's intellectual as well as spiritual self-identification was very much characterised by the two statements.

There is no greater joy than that upon self-examination I find myself to be sincere."[36]

Far from being a romantic assertion about the unity of all things, this passage, according to Ku's interpretation, expresses a root idea in Confucian thought, namely that learning as an ultimate way of self-development necessarily involves a restructuring of political and social realities. Its underlying assumption is as follows: the quest for self-knowledge as a way of learning to be human cannot be a lonely search for private truths. Rather, it is a deepened appreciation of common humanity. Since, unlike mere intellectual reflection on abstract concepts, knowledge of this kind must manifest itself in concrete affairs, its usefulness is demonstrable either in the rectification of politics or in the transformation of society. The sense of serving the community is such an integral part of one's personal task for learning that knowledge without a practical value for politics or society is considered selfish and therefore ought to be relegated to the background. Paradoxically Ku's critique of Li-hsüeh 理學 (School of Principle) reinforced his dedication to Classical Learning (Ching-hsüeh 經學), which was reminiscent of the Ch'eng-Chu tradition, and his attack on Hsin-hsüeh 心學 (School of Mind) further committed him to the moral teaching of Mencius, which was not at all incompatible with the Lu-Wang 陸王 tradition which followed the teachings of Lu Hsiang-shan 陸象山 and Wang Yang-ming 王陽明.

Another significant interpreter of the Sagely Way in early Ch'ing was Lu Lung-ch'i 陸隴其 (1630–92).[37] However, loyalism does not seem to have featured prominently in his life. On the contrary, having obtained a *chin-shih* 進士 degree in the ninth year of the K'ang-hsi 康熙 reign (1670) when he was forty years old, he not only served in local government but also distinguished himself as one of the best magistrates in the country. His outstanding service as an official even won him an honourable imperial citation.[38] In scholarship, Lu Lung-ch'i defined his approach purely in Ch'eng-Chu terms. His teaching and research weighed heavily against the thought of Wang Yang-ming, which he characterised as Ch'an 禪 Buddhist.[39] Although his general intellectual orientation was congruous with the teaching of Lu

---

[36] It is not difficult to see that Ku took this Mencian idea to mean that the responsibility of a scholar is deeply rooted in an ontological vision of morality. See "Yü yu-jen lun-hsüeh shu" 3:2a–b.

[37] See *San-yü t'ang ch'üan-chi* 三魚堂全集 (Complete works of the Hall of the Three Fish), 12 vols. (1868 ed.).

[38] See his *Nien-p'u* (Chronological biography), in *San-yü t'ang ch'üan-chi*, under 42 *sui*, 8b; under 61 *sui*, 24a–29a. Also see 31b–32a for K'ang-hsi's lamentation over Lu's death.

[39] See *Hsüeh-shu pien* 學術辨 (A critical reflection on scholarship), in *San-yü t'ang ch'üan-chi* 2:1a–7a.

Shih-i, in his focused attack on the School of Mind he went farther than most of his contemporaries.

He criticised the Tung-lin 東林 intellectuals Ku Hsien-ch'eng 顧憲成 (1550–1612) and Kao P'an-lung 高攀龍 (1562–1626), for he believed that their critique of Wang Yang-ming did not go far enough. He also felt that by advocating the importance of "quiet-sitting" (*ching-tso* 靜坐), Ku and Kao might themselves have fallen into the trap of passive subjectivism. What he found most appealing in Chu Hsi then was the insistence that self-cultivation necessitates the acquisition of "real" knowledge by an appropriation of practical truths from the classics. Since the principle inherent in human nature is not directly accessible to the mind, Lung-ch'i contended, a quest for empirical knowledge is essential to understanding one's true nature, and by implication, to realise oneself.[40] Understandably his scholarly efforts were focused on concrete human affairs with a particular emphasis on ritual practices.[41]

The emphasis on ritual practices as an authentic way of learning to be human reminds us of Yen Yüan 顏元 (1635–1704):[42] But apparently the two masters never met; nor was there any indication of mutual influence. The Confucian teacher Lu Lung-ch'i did most probably learn about was Chang Lü-hsiang 張履祥 (1611–74), born in the same year as Lu Shih-i. While Shih-i deeply regretted having missed a chance to attend Liu Tsung-chou's lectures, Chang managed to become one of Liu's immediate disciples.[43] However, his encounter with Liu's *Jen-p'u* 人譜 (*Schematic of Man*) convinced him that by stressing the "ontology of solitariness" (*tu-t'i* 獨體) Liu was still under the influence of Yang-ming. Although he never openly commented upon his teacher's "subjectivistic" tendency, he was provoked by Yang-ming's *Ch'uan-hsi lu* 傳習錄 (*Instructions for practical living*) to write a systematic refutation of it.[44] With a profound sense of moral responsibility, he assigned himself the difficult task of reviving the orthodox Chu Hsi interpretation

[40] Ibid. Also see "Yang-ming k'ao hsü 陽明考序" (Preface to *A Critical Examination of Yang-ming*), in ibid. 8:14a–15a.

[41] See, for example, his "Ssu-li chi-i hsü 四禮輯宜序" (Preface to *A Proper Anthology of the Four Rites*), in ibid. 8:9a–10a. However, this should not be taken as an isolated document. In fact by focusing on the importance of *hsiao-hsüeh*, ritual practices that the beginners must learn, such as the care of household affairs, his approach was distinctively Ch'eng-Chu in character. See his "Ta-hsüeh ta-wen 大學答問" (Answers to questions on the *Great Learning*), in ibid. 1:14a–19a.

[42] See Tu Wei-ming 杜維明, "Yen Yüan: From Inner Experience to Lived Concreteness", in *The Unfolding of Neo-Confucianism*, ed. Wm. T. de Bary (New York: Columbia University Press, 1975), 517–20.

[43] See his *Nien-p'u* under 34 *sui*, in *Yang-yüan hsien-sheng ch'üan-chi* 楊園先生全集 (Complete works of Chang Lü-hsiang), 54 *ch'üan* (1872 woodblocked.), 10b.

[44] Ibid., under 62 *sui*, 33b–34a.

of the Confucian tradition.[45] To him, in the Ming dynasty (1369–1644) only Hsüeh Hsüan 薛瑄 (1389–1464) and Hu Chü-jen 胡居仁 (1434–84), the two Ch'eng-Chu masters, were true exponents of the Sagely Way.[46] To assure the continuity of this authentic line of scholarly transmission he spent decades studying and explaining Chu Hsi's writings as a daily ritual.[47] Chang's critique of Yang-ming and his fidelity to Chu Hsi were part of a deeply personal search for an authentic way of learning. As a response to his mother's instruction that he emulate the self-transformations of the two other "fatherless sons",[48] Confucius and Mencius, Chang took learning not merely as scholarship but as the necessary path toward the cultivation of a perfected personality.

When the aforementioned T'ang Chien included in his intellectual biographies of Ch'ing scholars Chang Lü-hsiang and the two Lu masters together with the Minister of Rites, Chang Po-hsing 張伯行 (1651–1725) as the Four Transmitters of the Tao in early Ch'ing thought, the Sagely Way took on a strong ideological significance.[49] Intent on defining the nature and shape of Ch'ing Learning as the transmission of Ch'eng-Chu philosophy, T'ang Chien divided the main body of his work into three interrelated categories. In addition to the four "Transmitters of the Tao", he identified nineteen scholars, including Ku Yen-wu, as "Associates of the Tao" and forty-four scholars as "Guardians of the Tao". As a result, more than one hundred eminent Ch'ing scholars, including Huang Tsung-hsi and virtually all of the prominent members of the Ch'ien-Chia school — for example, Ch'ien Ta-hsin and Tai Chen — are classified under the category of "Classical Learning", somewhat peripheral to the orthodox line of scholarship.[50] Just as Chiang Fan sought to elevate the prestige of Han Learning, T'ang proposed to view the entire development of Ch'ing scholarship to date from the perspective of Sung Learning.

It seems clear that in both Chiang Fan's Han Learning and T'ang Chien's Sung Learning, Ch'ing scholarship was perceived as fundamentally different from Ming thought. The authors imply that Huang Tsung-hsi, who was

---

[45] See his commitment to *Chu Tzu yü-lei* 朱子語類 (Classified sayings of Master Chu), in ibid. under 63 *sui*, 37a.

[46] Ibid., under 62 *sui*, 36b.

[47] As evidence for this claim, see ibid., under 45 *sui*, 19a; under 61 *sui*, 33b; under 62 *sui*, 36b.

[48] Ibid., under 9 *sui*, 2b.

[49] T'ang, *Ch'ing-ju hsüeh-an* 1:1–2:11a, see esp. 2:10a–11a.

[50] Ibid., *ch'üan* 12–13.

in fact instrumental in providing an architectonic structure for Ming intellectual history as a whole, had relatively little impact on the subsequent developments of Ch'ing Learning. Obviously, the judgment is one-sided, if not totally misleading. In fact, Huang's direct and indirect influence on Ch'ing Learning was so great that without an understanding of his leadership, neither Ch'ing historiography nor Ch'ing political thought can be adequately appreciated.

Huang's role in the revival of the so-called Chin-wen 今文 (New Text) tradition was not fully recognised until the late nineteenth century. But, unlike Wang Fu-chih 王夫之 (1619–82) or for that matter Yen Yüan, who was discovered by scholars more than a century afterward, Huang was not only one of the most respected Confucian masters of his generation but also remained a vital intellectual force throughout the Ch'ing dynasty. His disciple Wan Ssu-t'ung 萬斯同 (1638–1702), for example, carried much intellectual weight among the Ch'ien-Chia scholars and Wan's historical writings foreshadowed the synthetic works of Chang Hsüeh-ch'eng 章學誠 (1783–1801).[51] In fact, Ch'ien Mu 錢穆 begins his masterful survey of the last three centuries of Chinese intellectual thought with Huang Tsung-hsi.[52]

While Chiang Fan's Han Learning may have slighted Huang and Ku, which drew a sharp reaction from P'i Hsi-jui, T'ang's Sung Learning was primarily aimed at another early Ch'ing Confucian master, Sun Ch'i-feng 孫奇逢 (1584–1675).[53] Although Sun was approaching seventy when the Ming dynasty collapsed, he continued to enjoy good health and a growing reputation until he died at ninety-one. He allegedly said, "The effort of self-cultivation at seventy was more refined than that at sixty, at eighty more refined than at seventy, and at ninety more so than at eighty."[54] His unceasing process of learning attests to the efficacy of the transformative thinking of the School of Mind. Although in his writings Sun attempted to synthesise the teachings of Chu and Lu, his real strength seems to lie in the "transmission of the mind" (*ch'uan-hsin* 傳心) rather than in scholarship.[55] When he singled out Hsüeh Hsüan, Wang Yang-ming, Lo Hung-hsien 羅洪先

---

[51] Hou, *Chung-kuo tsao-ch'i ch'i-meng ssu-hsiang*, 410.

[52] Ch'ien Mu, *Chung-kuo chin san-pai nien hsüeh-shu shih*, vol. 1, 22–87.

[53] T'ang, *Ch'ing-Ju hsüeh-an* 清儒學案, *ch'üan-shou* 卷首, 3.

[54] See Sun's *Pen-ch'üan* 本傳 (biography), in *Hsia-feng hsien-sheng chi* 夏峯先生集 (The collected works of Master Hsia-feng) 6 vols. (TSCC ed.; Ch'ang-sha: Commercial Press, 1919), vol. 1, p. 5. Also see Huang Tsung-hsi, *Ming-ju hsüeh-an* 明儒學案 (Intellectual records of Ming scholars), 4 vols. (reprint; Taipei: Chung-hua Book Co., 1970), 57: 7b–9a.

[55] See his *Yü-lu* 語錄 (Recorded conversations), in *Hsia-feng hsien-sheng chi*, vol. 6, 13:429–490.

(1504–64), and Ku Hsien-ch'eng as the four authentic interpreters of the Sagely Way in the Ming, he was taking an unequivocal position on the matter of intellectual continuity.[56] To him, for learning to be an ultimate personal concern, the spirit of both the Ming thinkers and the Sung masters[57] must be preserved. This kind of dedication to Ming thought prompted T'ang Chien to raise the banners of Lu and Chang to undermine Sun's teaching of the mind.[58]

Just as Huang Tsung-hsi and Sun Ch'i-feng symbolise the continuous vitality of Ming Learning in the south and in the north, Li Yung 李顒 (1627–1705) has been characterised as the Confucian master who transmitted the Sagely Way in the west.[59] Li inspired Ku Yen-wu with his independence of mind and his diligent pursuit of classical learning.[60] He first lectured in the spirit of Tung-lin scholars in eastern Chekiang. As his fame spread and as local authorities repeatedly recommended him for high official positions in the new regime, Li imposed upon himself a strict social moratorium and engaged exclusively in a quest for personal knowledge.[61] His *Record of Self-Examination* (*Fan-shen lu* 反身錄), a sustained meditative reflection on the deep meaning of internal authentication of the moral self, speaks of the essence of learning as nothing other than the purification of the mind.[62]

Despite Li's refusal to serve the Ch'ing dynasty which he undermined at times by suggesting suicide as a way of preserving his integrity, the K'ang-hsi emperor honoured him with the imperial citation "Kuan-chung ta-Ju" 關中

---

[56] See "Tu Shih-i Tzu yü-lu shu-hou" 讀十一子語錄書後(Comments after reading the recorded sayings of the Eleven Masters), in ibid., vol. 4, 9:280–84.

[57] Ibid. The Sung masters include Chou Tun-i 周敦頤, Ch'eng Hao 程顥, Ch'eng I 程頤, Chang Tsai 張載, Shao Yung 邵雍, Chu Hsi 朱熹, and Lu Hsiang-shan 陸象山. These seven masters plus the four Ming masters constitute what Sun believed to have been the authentic line of Confucian transmission.

[58] T'ang, *Ch'ing-ju hsüeh-an, ch'üan-shou*, 1a–3a.

[59] For an interpretive account on Li Yung 李顒, see Hou, *Chung-kuo tsao-ch'i ch'i-meng ssu-hsiang*, 289–300. For his works, see *Erh-ch'ü chi* 二曲集 (Collection of Li Yung's works), 2 vols. (1694 ed.). Also see *Erh-ch'ü chi*, 12 vols. (1883 ed.).

[60] See Ku Yen-wu's *Nein-p'u* 年譜, under 51 *sui*, 38b.

[61] See *Li-nien chi-lüeh* 歷年紀略 (Brief notes on past events), compiled by Hui Ch'ung-ssu 惠霖嗣 and Ma Yü-shih 馬棫士, in *Erh-ch'ü chi* (1883), 45:36a–39a, 41a–b, 42b, 47b–48a, 56a–b. It seems that the only notable exception to his rule of almost complete avoidance of contact with visitors was his warm reception of and continuous correspondence with Ku Yen-wu; see ibid., 45:45a, 53b.

[62] This particular concern is evident in the titles of several of his works: *Hui-ko tzu-hsin* 悔過自新 (Repentance and self-renewal), in *Erh-ch'ü chi* (1694), *ch'üan* 1; *Hsüeh-sui* 學髓 (Marrow of learning), in ibid., *ch'üan* 2; and *Ch'üan-hsin* 傳心 (Transmission of the mind), in *Erh-ch'ü* (1883), *ch'üan* 6.

大儒 (Great Confucian scholar within the passes).[63] Hou Wai-lu, in his highly selective study of the history of Chinese thought, praises Li for his patriotism, real learning, and democratic tendencies, even though basically Hou subscribed to Chiang Fan's interpretive position on Han Learning.[64] The mystery of Li's prestige, even his rise from extreme poverty, which prevented him from entering any village school, to a position as one of the most esteemed Confucian masters of the K'ang-hsi reign (1662–1722), can perhaps never be fully explored. It is evident, however, that with Huang and Sun, he continued a mode of learning distinctively Ming in character but of vital importance for early Ch'ing thought.

Far from repudiating Sung or Ming Learning in a deliberate attempt to return to Han Learning, the inception of Ch'ing Learning brought together several disparate scholarly developments. I do not intend to suggest that early Ch'ing scholars were consciously trying to achieve this synthesis. Nor do I mean that there was real communication among representatives of different schools of learning. However, the mere presence – in fact, co-existence – of these conflicting trends of thought impels us to go beyond the surface consensus in order to examine the forces that were instrumental in shaping Ch'ing Learning into the particular form it took. There is no reason to doubt that Sun Ch'i-feng, Lu Shih-i, Lu Lung-ch'i, and Huang Tsung-hsi, each in his own way, contributed much to the dynamism of early Ch'ing thought and that Yen Jo-chü, despite Chiang Fan and Juan Yüan's enthusiasm,[65] was but one among them. Furthermore, it should be added, Yen Yüan, who died in the same year as Yen Jo-chü, could have been a formidable critic of the kind of scholarship Jo-chü was thought to have advocated. Even Ku Yen-wu, I suppose, could not have felt comfortable in a world permeated by work of the Ch'ien-Chia style.

Ch'ien-Chia Scholarship

By the middle of the eighteenth century the form of Ch'ing scholarship called Han Learning was much closer to the writings of Yen Jo-chü than,

---

[63] See Chiang Wei-ch'iao, 37. It should be noted that according to *Ch'ien-ch'üeh lu* 潛確錄 (Record of the concealed reality), composed by Hui Ch'ung-ssu, the "four-character" imperial citation, or at least one of them, was "ts'ao-chih kao-chieh" 操志高潔 (conducting his will loftily and purely). See *Erh-ch'ü chi* (1883), 46:7b.

[64] Hou, *Chung-kuo tsao-ch'i ch'i-meng ssu-hsiang*, 299–300. For Hou's endorsement of Chiang Fan's interpretive position on Han Learning, see p. 404.

[65] By now it should become clear that the idea of Han Learning, far from being an adequate description of early Ch'ing thought, is a highly restricted notion. Yet Chiang Fan's version of it has remained a standard on the subject. See Chou, *Han-hsüeh shih-ch'eng chi* 50.

say, to those of Sun and the two Lu masters. To be sure, Han Learning, especially when defined in terms of philological studies, is a misnomer. The range of scholarship exemplified by the Ch'ien-Chia savants is much wider than philology. But even if we accept Kung Tzu-chen's designation of "Classical Learning", what the Ch'ien-Chia "classicists" pursued was significantly different from the classical learning in either the Han or the Sung. For one thing, their fascination with pure scholarship as a communal act was probably an unprecedented phenomenon in Chinese intellectual history. Their assertion that the written word is an essential component of ultimate truth and that the text is a necessary carrier of the Sagely Way was also a freshly argued position in Confucian thought. Their concern for empirical verification, their quest for objective facts, and their demand for erudition also became distinctive features of this new mode of scholarship.

Whether political pressure unique to Ch'ing society or an intellectual thrust common to Neo-Confucian thought was responsible for the rise of Ch'ing Learning, one cannot avoid the question, What did the Ch'ing scholars themselves think they were doing? In addition to tackling the difficult problem of determining the intellectual self-identifications of some of the more representative Ch'ien-Chia masters, we must inquire into the rhetorical situation in which Ch'ing scholarship assumed a shape of meaning neither anticipated by seventeenth-century precursors nor necessarily understood by nineteenth-century interpreters.

A defining characteristic of the Ch'ien-Chia version of Ch'ing Learning was "erudition", or — according to Chang Hsüeh-ch'eng's term — *po-ya* 博雅.[66] The Ch'ing erudite was not only a classicist and a historian but often also an expert in one or several branches of theoretical and applied sciences.[67] Thus, the large fund of specialised knowledge he commanded was obtained by a multiplicity of disciplines, although book learning certainly played the major role. Understandably the Ch'ing scholars attached much value to the acquisition of information. An obvious example was the compilation of the *Ssu-k'u chüan-shu* 四庫全書 (the complete works of the four treasures) still the most comprehensive attempt to bring the entire literary heritage of China into a holistic structure. The apparent political benefit of editing out anti-Manchu references in late Ming literature must not blind us to the tremendous intellectual scope of this endeavour, involving numerous dedicated

---

[66] For the distinction between *po-ya* and *chuan-chia* 專家 (focused scholarship), see Chang Hsüeh-ch'eng's second essay, "Po-yüeh 博約" (Erudition and essentialism), in *Wen-shih t'ung-i* 文史通義 (Comprehensive meaning of literature and history; reprint, Hong Kong: T'ai-p'ing Book Co., 1964), 49–50.

[67] See John Henderson, "The Ordering of the Heaven and the Earth in Early Ch'ing Thought", (Ph. D. diss., University of California, Berkeley, 1977), 132–58.

and competent scholars. The great imperial manuscript library, comprising thirty-six thousand chüan 卷 and a catalogue with succinct comments on more than ten thousand titles, is said to have involved as many as fifteen thousand copyists over a period of nearly twenty years.[68]

This enterprise, under the sponsorship of the Ch'ien-lung 乾隆 court, must have dominated the intellectual scene from 1773 when a group of leading scholars, including Tai Chen, was appointed by the emperor to undertake it.[69] Lest this massive collaborative effort be viewed as an isolated phenomenon, it should be pointed out that several truly impressive works of a similar nature although a much smaller scale were conducted by private scholars. The examples of Ch'in Hui-t'ien's 秦蕙田 (1702–64) *Wu-li t'ung-k'ao* 五禮通考[70] and Tuan Yü-ts'ai's *Shuo-wen chien-tzu chu* 説文解字注[71] should give us a glimpse of what must have been a widely accepted mode of scholarship.

"Erudition" was a shared concern of eighteenth-century scholars; it is particularly illuminating in the case of Li Fu 李紱 (1673–1750). Identified by Ch'ien Mu as a critic of bookish knowledge, Li's commitment to the Lu-Wang tradition does not seem to have seriously affected his own extensive reading. According to his personal reflection, in a period of seven months after he had entered the Hanlin Academy as a *chin-shih* in 1709, he managed to read through twice *San-kuo chih* 三國志, *Chin-shu* 晋書, *Nan-Pei shih* 南北史, and the collected poems of Li Po 李白, Tu Fu 杜甫, Li I-shan 李義山, Wen T'ing-yün 溫庭筠, Su Tung-p'o 蘇東坡, and Li Yü 李煜; he also read once through *Erh-ya* 爾雅, *Hsiao-ching* 孝經, *I-li* 儀禮, *Lun-yü* 論語, and *Meng Tzu* 孟子. In addition, he perused *Shih-chi* 史記, *Han-shu* 漢書, *Hou Han-shu* 後漢書, *Sui-shu* 隋書, *T'ang-shu* 唐書, *Wu-tai shih* 五代史, and portions of several other dynastic histories in the same stretch of time.[72] If this insatiable demand for literary information was found in a student of the School of Mind, sound scholarship, partly defined in terms of knowledge-ability, must have been a supreme value for the educated person in general.

The question remains, however, why classical learning, which had been

---

[68] These are of course rough figures. For a convenient reference, see William Hung, "Preface to an Index to Ssu-k'u ch'üan-shu tsung-mu 四庫全書總目 and Wei-shou shu-mu" 未收書目, *Harvard Journal of Asiatic Studies* (1939): 47–58.

[69] See Tai Chen's *Nien-p'u*, in *Tai Chen wen-chi*, under 38 *sui* and 42 *sui*, pp. 233, 236.

[70] Ch'in Hui-t'ien, *Wu li t'ung-k'ao* (A comprehensive examination of the Five Rites), 100 vols. (1880 ed.).

[71] Although Tuan Yü-ts'ai's *Shuo-wen chieh-tzu chu* consists of only 38 *ch'üan*, it is to date one of the most impressive accomplishments in the etymological and philological studies of Chinese characters.

[72] See the reference in Ch'ien, *Chung-kuo chin san-pai nien hsüeh-shu shih*, 259.

pursued by students for centuries as the necessary means of entering officialdom and practiced by committed Confucians as a form of moral self-
cultivation, was now taken as a subject of scholarly inquiry for its own
sake. Why did "erudition", which had been recognised as valuable in itself
now become so pervasive an ideal among the educated that even the ability
to doubt its validity was rarely exercised. A fundamental change in the
rhetorical situation seems to have occurred. But the reasons for ushering in
a new mode of scholarship cannot be easily identified. The case of Li Kung
李塨 (1659–1733) may provide part of the answer.

Having studied under Yen Yüan for almost twenty years, Li first envi-
sioned his vocation as becoming a practitioner of "real learning" (*shih-hsüeh*
實學). A defining characteristic of this particular approach to learning is its
commitment to "statecraft" (*ching-shih* 經世). A corollary is a commitment
to see knowledge in terms of its practicality. Book learning without a direct
bearing either on the improvement of one's own personality or on social
utility is considered a dispensable luxury. By implication, concrete experiences in dealing with governmental and economic problems are cherished as
worth having, rather than recondite knowledge acquired chiefly from books.
Any attempt to cultivate one's role as a scholar or a writer independent of
the desire to serve the community is neither encouraged nor tolerated.[73]

Li Kung seems to know well the fundamental difference between Yen
Yüan's perception of learning and the scholarship that was conducted in the
major centres of intellectual activity. His trips to the south beginning in
1695 can thus be interpreted as deliberate efforts to confront the erudites as
a way of spreading the pragmatic teachings of his master. Yen Yüan was,
however, aware of the seductiveness of the "southern" scholars and the vul-
nerability of his disciple to the literary influences there. Yen's futile attempts
to rescue his student from the narrow vision of "the student of books"
(*shu-sheng* 書生) and the useless exercise of "the man of letters" (*wen-jen* 文人)
have been noticed by Ch'ien Mu and Hou Wai-lu, among other historians.
Both of them take Li's southern sojourns as serious blows to the development of the Yen-Li 顏李 School of Real Learning.[74] As Ch'ien and Hou
observe, although Li did successfully deliver Yen's message to interested
students in the south and thus substantially enhanced the reputation of

---

[73] For Li's first association with Yen, see *Li Shu-ku hsien-sheng nien-p'u* 李恕谷先生年譜 (The chronological biography of Li Kung), in *Yen-Li ts'ung-shu* 顏李叢書 (Works of Yen Yüan and Li Kung),
32 vols. (Peking: Ssu-ts'un Hsüeh-hui 四存學會, 1923), under 22 *sui*, 1:6a–10a. See also Chin Hsü-ju
金絮如, *Yen Yüan yü Li Kung* 顏元與李塨 (Yen Yüan and Li Kung; Shanghai: Commercial Press,
1934), 7–11.

[74] Ibid., from 37 *sui* to 46 *sui*, 2:9a–3:31a. See Ch'ien, *Chung-kuo chin san-pai nien hsüeh-shu shih*, 206–8
and Hou, *Chung-kuo tsao-ch'i ch'i-meng ssu-hsiang*, 382–90.

his teacher as a theorist of statecraft, he himself, as a result of the trips, significantly departed from his teacher in both methodology of study and epistemology.[75] Li's sense of guilt toward Yen, recorded in his chronological biography and expressed in his own writings, made the trips dramatic in terms of both his life history and the magnetic power of "erudition".

It is commonly assumed that Mao Ch'i-ling 毛奇齡 (1623–1716), the prolific author who was notorious for his questionable moral integrity, was mainly responsible for Li's involvement in a mode of scholarship fundamentally different from "real learning". Li's decision to study the classics, especially the *Book of Change*, under Mao in 1698 is considered the crucial event in this connection.[76] It seems, however, that Li's fascination with the kind of learning characterised by Mao's work was symptomatic of a much more complex process. Mao may have been the principle tempter, but Li had been already exposed to what may be called the "philological studies of the south" through his friend Wang Fu-li 王復禮 during his first journey to the south in 1695. According to Li's chronological biography, his encounter with Yen Jo-chü, Hu Wei, and Wan Ssu-t'ung in Peking in 1700, two years after his meeting with Mao, was particularly significant for his intellectual development.[77] But since Jo-chü died in 1704 and Wan in 1702, Li could not have studied with them for very long. Nor does he seem to have maintained a close relationship with Mao for an extended period of time. Perhaps it was not the influences of single individuals but the atmosphere of scholarly centres such as Yang-chou 揚州 and Ch'ang-chou 常州 in the south and Peking in the north that can really account for Li's "conversion".

Nevertheless, it is quite misleading to take the idea of conversion literally. Li's personal loyalty to Yen Yüan remained strong throughout his life, lasting for almost two decades after Yen's death in 1704. Furthermore, it was because of Li that the single-minded scholar Wang Yüan 王源 visited Yen and pledged his total dedication to Yen's teaching when he himself was approaching sixty years of age.[78] And it was because of Wang's introduction that Li befriended the T'ung-ch'eng scholar Fang Pao 方苞 (1668–1749).[79] The controversy of Fang's interpretation of Li's departure from Yen in an

---

[75] Ch'ien, *Chung-kuo chin san-pai nien hsüeh-shu shih*, 203; Hou, *Chung-kuo tsao-ch'i ch'i-meng ssu-hsiang*, 386–90.

[76] Ch'ien, *Chung-kuo chin san-pai nien hsüeh-shu shih*, 206–9.

[77] *Li Shu-ku nien-p'u*, under 42 *sui*, 3:8a–14a.

[78] Ibid. 3:2b.

[79] Ibid., under 45 *sui*, 3:21a.

unsolicited epitaph should not concern us here.[80] Yet the very fact that a
committed Sung scholar could claim the example of Li as support for his
philosophical position is worth noticing. It should also be noticed that after
Li's first trip to the south, his exposure to Lu Shih-i's *Ssu-pien lu* prompted
him in 1698 to compose a treatise on the *Great Learning*.[81] The treatise
fully demonstrates that Li subscribed to a version of the Chu Hsi view that
knowledge and action are in principle separable and that the acquisition of
knowledge should precede its transformation into action.[82]

Neither the cause nor the effect of Li Kung's newly assumed cast of mind
allows an easy explanation. But the form in which his scholarship was
constructed clearly symbolises the social prestige of erudition. The ability
to conduct purely scholarly inquiry, specifically the capacity to acquire
professional skills in philological studies and textual analyses, became an
unquestioned standard of excellence in intellectual circles. No matter what
other competences one happened to possess, this was the required "rite of
passage" in the Ch'ien-Chia scholarly world. Was it, then, social prestige that
motivated Li Kung to change his mind?

It is beyond question that erudition as a mode of scholarship was a
social as well as an intellectual ethos. The case of Tai Chen is instructive.
Tai's entrance into the Peking coteries of learning was mainly the result of
his sound knowledge of the classics. But without the proper introduction
of well-established authorities such as Ch'ien Ta-hsin, Tai could not have
gained an easy access to "establish friendship" with Wang An-kuo 王安國
(1694–1757), Chi Yün 紀昀 (1724–1805), and Wang Ming-sheng 王鳴盛.[83]
His ability to develop an impressive network of social relations was certainly
a major reason for his success in the high-powered group clustered around
Wang and a few other senior scholars. In the light of examples of this kind,
it is possible that the combined force of personal push and communal pull
accounted for much of Li Kung's significantly altered scholarly orientation.
Li's dilemma is quite understandable: his credibility as a serious scholar was
necessary for transmitting the way of his teacher to the centres of learning;
yet the only way for him to earn that credibility was to take up a mode of

---

[80] Hou, *Chung-kuo tsao-ch'i ch'i-meng ssu-hsiang*, 383–84.

[81] See Li's acknowledgment in his *Ta-hsüeh pien-yeh* 大學辨業 (A critical exercise on the *Great Learning*), in *Yen-Li ts'ung-shu*, vol. 25, *t'i-tz'u*, 3a.

[82] Ibid. 3:2a–b.

[83] See Tai's *Nien-p'u* in *Tai Chen wen-chi*, under 33 *sui*, p. 221. The *Nien-p'u* notes in fact that the other outstanding members of the class of 1854 of *chin-shih* 進士, such as Chi Yün, Wang Ming-sheng, Wang Ch'ang 王昶 and Chu Yün 朱昀, knew about Tai at the same time as Ch'ien did.

scholarship defined in terms fundamentally different from what he had been taught to appreciate as the practical and the real way of learning.

Li Kung's ambivalence toward what his teacher, Yen Yüan, denounced as the learning of the "students of books" and of the "men of letters" was probably not an isolated phenomenon. The very fact that the Yang-chou scholars preferred to characterise their learning as *Ku-hsüeh* 古學 (Ancient Learning) and that the students of Ch'ien Ta-hsin often described his teaching as *P'u-hsüeh* 樸學 (Plain Learning) indicates that the Ch'ien-Chia masters themselves by no means saw erudition merely as a form of pedantry. In this sense, I suppose, Chang Hsüeh-ch'eng's insistence on "essence" (*yüeh* 約) and "singularity" (*chuan* 專) was really meant to be a critique of Han Learning narrowly defined as *K'ao-cheng* 考證 (philology).[84] An important consensus among Confucian scholars of all persuasions was the uselessness of "empty words" (*k'ung-yen* 空言). For the study of the classics to be more than an exercise in words, it would have to be linked up with a structure of meaning greater than philology. Li Kung's feeling of guilt when he confessed in old age that only after he had failed to establish either his virtue or his meritorious service did he take up the task of writing in order to establish the efficacy of his words was more than simply a routine evocation of the famous "three immortalities". With a sense of tragedy, Li recalled how his poor health and frustrated ambitions compelled him to work on classical texts as a commentator and, by implication, to become a compromiser.[85]

One wonders if Li's sentiments were not also shared by many of his contemporaries, including both those who gained a wide reputation as private tutors and those who received imperial recognition as government officials. Intellectual giants such as Tai Chen and Ch'ien Ta-hsin probably never seriously doubted the supreme value of their scholarly works. As definers of a new tradition, they considered scholarship a "calling" and an "ultimate concern". Even among the less-known Ch'ien-Chia masters such as Wang Ch'ang 王昶 (1724–1806), Chu Yün 朱筠 (1729–81), and Lu Wen-ch'ao 盧文弨 (1717–95), there is no evidence to show that they were not wholeheartedly committed to their studies. The problem was not a lack of dedication as researchers and teachers. The available documents clearly show that there was a great deal of that in virtually all of the eminent masters.

However, it is an entirely different matter to determine the perceived value of their intellectual pursuits. The idea of "pure" scholarship, as the

---

[84] For example, see Chang Hsüeh-ch'eng's critical reflection on Tai Chen, "Shu Chu-Lu pien huo 書朱陸篇後" ("Further thought on the essay on Chu Hsi and Lu Hsiang-shan"), in *Wen-shih t'ung-i*, 57–59.

[85] See Li Kung, "*Shih Ching chuan-chu* t'i-tz'u 詩經傳注題辭" (Prefatory note on the *Commentary on the Book of Poetry*), in *Yen-Li ts'ung-shu*, vol. 31, 11:7b.

academicians – for example, the chief compiler of the *Ssu-ku ch'üan-shu* Chi Yün – would have it, might have been widely accepted by the Ch'ien-Chia masters. But the scholarly concerns of Li Kuang-ti 李光地 (1642–1718), certainly one of the most influential court scholar-officials during the K'ang-hsi reign, had by then already fallen into dispute.[86] This partly explains the decline of Sung Learning: Li's effort to promote Chu Hsi's teaching under imperial sponsorship actually prompted a powerful yet subtle reaction against the official line of interpreting the classics, or "official learning" (*kuan-hsüeh* 官學).[87] It is thus important to note that the concept of learning was as much a political notion as an intellectual ideal. And Li Kung's uneasiness in his scholarly endeavours, viewed from this perspective, may have been reflected in a number of sensitive minds in the Ch'ien-Chia reign.

One of the most intriguing problems in the study of early Ch'ing thought in general and the Ch'ien-Chia tradition in particular is the issue of "literary inquisition".[88] The attempt to establish the claim that the practice of *wen-tzu yü* 文字獄 ("literary cases") featured prominently in early Ch'ing politics is, however, not a fruitful way of approaching it. The issue involved is not one of determining how the system of ideological control actually worked in terms of the precise number of people directly affected. Rather, it has to do with the "felt reality" of a highly oppressive atmosphere created by a conscious imperial policy of bringing the articulate minority in line with "official" and thus "orthodox" learning. The difficulty of understanding this complex phenomenon partly lies in a subtle and fundamental metamorphosis in the self-image as well as the prescribed role of the Confucian scholar in the Ch'ien-Chia era. This metamorphosis resulted in no small measure from a deliberate imposition of political standards on scholarship and ingenious appropriation of intellectual ideas for the purpose of ideological control.

Ideally the Confucian scholar, as a full participating member of society, assumes the responsibility of not only cultivating his personal self but also regulating the human community as a whole. Although in practice he may serve as a minor official in a local government, his spiritual self-identification is predicated on a comprehensive vision of self, society, world, and cosmos. The true scholar is thus a keeper of the Way as well as the master of his own house. His consciousness of duty and his loyalty come from a morality defined in broad humanist terms rather than from a commitment to an

---

[86] Hou, *Chung-kuo tsao-ch'i ch'i-meng ssu-hsiang*, 411–12.

[87] Ibid., 412.

[88] A way of examining this complex issue is to ascertain the nature of the books not included in the *Ssu-k'u*. Although the methodological problems are by no means simple, the possibility is perhaps worth exploring. See William Hung's article mentioned in n. 68.